2

"I Will Never Forget"

ALSO BY BRENT KELLEY
AND FROM MCFARLAND

*The San Francisco Seals, 1946–1957:
Interviews with 25 Former Baseballers* (2002)

*The Pastime in Turbulence: Interviews
with Baseball Players of the 1940s* (2001)

*The Negro Leagues Revisited: Conversations
with 66 More Baseball Heroes* (2000)

*They Too Wore Pinstripes:
Interviews with 20 Glory-Days
New York Yankees* (1998)

*Voices from the Negro Leagues:
Conversations with 52 Baseball Standouts
of the Period 1924–1960* (1998)

*The Early All-Stars: Conversations with
Standout Baseball Players of the 1930s and 1940s* (1997)

*In the Shadow of the Babe: Interviews
with Baseball Players Who Played With
or Against Babe Ruth* (1995)

*Baseball Stars of the 1950s: Interviews with
All-Stars of the Game's Golden Era* (1993)

*The Case For: Those Overlooked by
the Baseball Hall of Fame* (1992)

"I Will Never Forget"

Interviews with 39 Former Negro League Players

BRENT KELLEY

This is the third in a series of Negro Leagues
interview books by the author:
the first, *Voices from the Negro Leagues* (1998);
the second, *The Negro Leagues Revisited* (2000)

McFarland & Company, Inc., Publishers
Jefferson, North Carolina, and London

For Tom and Betty Turner

ISBN 0-7864-1481-2 (illustrated case binding : 50# alkaline paper)

LIBRARY OF CONGRESS CATALOGUING DATA ARE AVAILABLE

British Library cataloguing data are available

Cover photograph: Eugene Scruggs (left) and Carl Holden (*Huntsville Times*)

Manufactured in the United States of America

*McFarland & Company, Inc., Publishers
Box 611, Jefferson, North Carolina 28640
www.mcfarlandpub.com*

Contents

Preface

With care and proper management, most natural resources can be saved, or at least prolonged. One resource, however, is fast fading away forever.

Participants in the Negro baseball leagues are a dying breed. When the ones we have now are gone, there will be no more, no matter how much we care or how well we manage what we have left.

In 1995 in Kansas City, there was a 75th anniversary reunion of the Negro leagues. About 300 former players were present.

There will probably be no 100th anniversary reunion. There will be no one left to attend.

I hope to preserve something of what these men and women gave to baseball and to America. Here, in their own words, they tell how it was and talk of the great players and great teams that are no more.

A note about the statistics: complete stats are not available in most cases. Those presented here are based on what is available in print and in the memories of the players.

Bill Bethea

Greensboro Redbirds 1950–1952

BORN AUGUST 21, 1929, GREENSBORO, GUILFORD COUNTY, NC
HT. 6'5" WT. 185 BATTED AND THREW LEFT

Bill Bethea was a lefthanded pitcher who set strikeout records everywhere he went. We don't know how fast he could throw a baseball, but between his speed and his curveball a lot of batters went back to the dugout muttering. Maybe he could reach 100 mph. Upper 90s anyhow. His strikeouts have put him in the South Atlantic League Hall of Fame.

As a member of the Greensboro Redbirds, a black team that played against most of the teams in the Negro leagues, he was so impressive that Gil English, scouting for the Boston Braves, signed him to a minor league contract. He pitched professionally for five years, 1953-55 and 1960-61. In between, he returned to school, eventually earning his BS in recreation from Shaw University. On leaving baseball he worked for the Greensboro, North Carolina, Parks and Recreation Department for 24 years.

BETHEA: I started with a little country team called the Black Yankees and the first time I played I guess I was about 18 years of age.

I had skills from softball, but I had never played baseball. Believe it or not, I was kind of frightened of it because the pitcher would throw so close to the hitters, it looked like. [Laughs] I didn't want to stand up to the plate. I learned more about it once I got into it.

There was a game and they had eight players and they needed one more. They kept asking and I told 'em I didn't know anything about baseball.

They said, "Okay, but you can play outfield for us," so I did. I played outfield in softball as well as pitching, so I played in the outfield.

A few balls were hit to me playing center field, and I had a real strong arm, and when I threw a ball back in to the infield and my ball would tail in and tail out. It had

a move to it. So they decided they wanted me to pitch. I said, "I don't know anything about pitching." So I had to develop my curveball myself; I called it a sinker. I developed it myself, putting one hand across the seams of the ball, and it had a very, very deep bend to it. It was a pretty good curveball.

I continued to play for them for that season; then we were scheduled for a game with the Greensboro Redbirds. They were formerly the Goshen Redwings. They really played in the old Negro leagues by barnstorming quite a bit. They still had players from that team with the Greensboro Redbirds. As a matter of fact, my uncle was one of them. He never knew that I played ball; his name was Hezekiah Day. Herman Taylor was the manager. He was a good ballplayer.

We had scheduled a game with them at Memorial Stadium here in Greensboro. Something happened and we did not get a

1954 Greensboro Red Birds. Back row (l to r): Sidney Blacknell, Bill Bethea, Cal Flemming, Herman Taylor, Quincy Knuckles, David Sims, Herman Edwards. Front row (l to r): Billy S., J. Morgan, Rip Mangum, Charles Herbin, J. C. Rice, Benny Holmes. (Photograph courtesy of Bill Bethea.)

chance to use the stadium, so we didn't play the game. But my uncle saw me and asked me why was I there. He saw me in uniform and I was thinking he knew, but he never knew that I played ball. So everybody said, "You'll see why." They were all excited about it.

Anyway, right as we were getting ready to leave, he said, "We're gonna play tomorrow. We're going to Virginia. Come and go with us."

So I said, "Okay," and I did and I pitched.

Let me go back. With the Black Yankees team we went somewhere and I had 21 strikeouts. That kind of told them things and they were beginning to get more excited about me. I was getting 16, 17, 18 strikeouts a game.

I went with my uncle's team and I pitched. This was a quality team that I pitched against, and I did exceptionally well. I had about 13 or 14 strikeouts with them, so I stayed with them. I liked it be-

cause they dressed like major leaguers and they handled themselves that way. They were a very good-looking team. The other group was upset with me for staying with them, but they understood it later on after I was signed to play professional ball.

I stayed with them and I played with them, and I began to learn things more and more. Basically, I had no idea that scouts were following me. I think I played with them about two or three years; then Gil English signed me for the [Boston] Braves' organization.

I was with Wellsville [PONY League] with the Braves, then I went to Clinton, Iowa [Mississippi-Ohio Valley League], with the Pittsburgh Pirates' organization. Then I got with the Lexington [North Carolina] Indians.

Talk about traveling with the Redbirds.

We could not go into restaurants. They were predominately white restaurants. And we could not go to the hotels and motels.

We had to sleep in the bus a lot. It was a team-owned bus.

And we ate out of the bus. We would go to the supermarket and get Viennas and baloney and stuff of this nature. That's how we would eat unless we went to a town that had some people who would feed us, black families — there were some of those who had invited us to come down. They did make arrangements to help us out on occasion.

Did you ever travel into the North?

We went to Washington, D. C., and we played in Jersey, also. It was different there, especially in Jersey. They had places that could accommodate us and would. There was no problem there.

The Mississippi–Ohio Valley League was a very progressive league for that time. How many blacks were on the Clinton team?

There were three blacks. One of the boys went with the Dodgers. Lou Johnson.

There was a pitcher named Bob Long. Bobby Long. They booed him and did the finger thing. He had a very nasty disposition.

Dave Jimenez won 20 games. He was rangy, slim like myself, but a *very* good pitcher. From Puerto Rico, I believe, or Cuba.

Lou Johnson went to Canada, too. He and I went to St. Jean's, Canada. A white family accommodated us there. They allowed us to stay at their home. That was another place that we didn't have a problem.

Canada was almost a different world. I've talked with many players who went to both Canada and Mexico to play and they said it wasn't the same as in the States.

It was different. It was kind of amazing. Here these people treated us so wonderful. It's hard to figure out why other people couldn't be like they were.

I had to do one thing when I first played in Lexington. We nearly had a little riot there.

They were calling me names and things my first time to pitch there, so when I went out I just pulled my shirt up to make sure that I had "Lexington Indians" on my shirt. I said, "I'm supposed to be with you all. This is the home team and I'm with the home team." [Laughs] But the police came and they got it quieted down.

I had made up my mind I was gonna win 'em over. I'm not gonna come out and be vicious and nasty. That wouldn't solve anything. So when I warmed up there were black kids and white kids who would come out to watch me warm up. I would give each of 'em a ball and they would ask me for bats. If someone broke a bat, they wanted a bat, so I taped it up and gave it to 'em.

That first time that I pitched there in Lexington, by the seventh inning I think I had struck out 15 and I heard one person in the stands — a white gentleman — say, "Come on, Bill," like that. Things had quieted down since the police had to talk to 'em. After that I didn't have a problem.

My strikeout ratio was about 15 strikeouts per game. I had made my mind up and I know God heard my call because after that they would come around and congratulate me. It also opened up places for us that did not allow blacks to go into. If our pitchers pitched a shutout we were allowed to go in and have lunch there for free. It opened some doors.

We handled it and we showed 'em: "Just like you, I'm a human being, and that's all I'm asking you to recognize."

What were you paid in the minors?

I guess about $850 a month, I think it was. I got a little bonus for signing; I got a thousand dollars.

What did you do when you left baseball?

I worked with the City of Greensboro Parks and Recreation Department. I was there 24 years — ten part-time years before becoming full time, then I was there for 14 full-time years.

I was inducted into the South Atlantic League Hall of Fame on June 17, 1996, in Asheville, North Carolina. Hoyt Wilhelm and myself and some others were inducted. The plaque reads, "Bill Bethea holds South Atlantic League record for lowest ERA for season, 1.35 in 1960. Most strikeouts in an extra-inning game, 25." I think I pitched until about the 13th inning. I didn't get the win. [Laughs] "Most strikeouts for two consecutive games, 41. Played in minor leagues for six years for Toronto Blue Jays organization."

I had a recognition also from the Gifford County Commission "hereby extending congratulations and recognition to Bill Bethea for his induction into the South Atlantic League Hall of Fame for outstanding athletic accomplishments and contributions to the game of baseball." I received that here in my hometown.

Do you have any regrets from your baseball days?

Oh, no. It was very rewarding. Like I said, when I came along I was kind of used to some things because here it wasn't completely integrated then. At the theater we had to go to the side and go up and sit in the balcony, and we would not be served lunch in restaurants. We would have to go to the side where they had a window. I was used to some of that anyway. It wasn't something that I really wanted. I just kept trying to figure out why. That was my biggest concern.

A lot of good players felt that I could have gone to the majors. That was inspiring to me and kept me focused and wanting to do so. Then, after I found that I wasn't gonna be able to do it — I went as high as Triple-A with the Toronto Maple Leafs — I thanked God for letting me go as far as I did. I tried, and that's no guarantee that you're gonna make it.

Would you do it again?

I feel I would. From what I learned I really think that I would, because it was a golden opportunity and something to cherish for a lifetime.

PITCHING RECORD

Year	Team, Lg	G	IP	W	L	Pct	H	SO	BB	ERA
1950	Grnsbro, ind									
1951										
1952										
1953	Wellsville, PONY			3	6	.333				7.44
1954	Clinton, MOV			9	6	.600				4.28
1955				12	8	.600				3.18
	St.Jean's, Prov			0	0					
1956-59	Did not play									
1960	Lexington, WCaro			11	3	.786				1.35
1961	Raleigh, Carolina			0	5	.000				7.75
	Lexington, WCaro			5	4	.556				3.49

Scoop Brown
Lexington Hustlers 1945–1949

BORN MARCH 16, 1922, FAYETTE COUNTY, KY
DIED 2002, LEXINGTON, KY
HT. 6' WT. 175 BATTED AND THREW RIGHT

Scoop Brown was born and raised in Lexington, Kentucky. He had a chance to leave — the Birmingham Black Barons wanted to take him with them — but he wouldn't go. And Lexington probably wouldn't be the same if he had gone; he was a famous man in the city.

In trying to find him, I asked one of his former teammates who lives in another town if he knew how to find Scoop. "Ask anyone in Lexington," he told me. "Everybody knows Scoop Brown. Anybody can tell you." He was just about right. Scoop's first name is really John, but there are a lot of John Browns around. There is only one Scoop.

Scoop Brown was a very good baseball player and he will be remembered for that, but his main legacy comes from his career as a sports official. He was a trailblazer for his race as a basketball and football official.

He slowed down. He talked to schoolchildren and appeared at history conferences. Wherever he went, his audience listened.

How did you acquire the nickname "Scoop"?

BROWN: I got that nickname "Scoop" from Paul Sullivan. He used to broadcast our games. He was a friend of mine. One time we were playin' and they were makin' a lotta low throws. Everything they threw low I would pick them up and they started callin' me "Scoop." They used to say, "How low can you go?" They can't go too low; they can throw high but you can't go too low. That's why I got that name.

How and when did the Hustlers originate?

I think they started that team in 1944. They solicited people to buy stock in the organization and it became a reality about 1946 when they raised enough money to build a ballpark on Newtown Pike, which they called Blue Grass Field. It was a conglomerate of about 12 or 13 black guys who united together and put up the funds to form an association to build a ballpark and to organize a black baseball team. At the time it was all black but after 1946, 1947, the integration of other groups led it to become integrated. In fact, it became the first integrated baseball team south of the Mason-Dixon Line. It was the *only* team in the South with a mixed roster — whites and blacks. 1947.

When did the Hustlers stop playing?

I think Hustlers baseball went out around 1949. For some reason the attendance fell off and they disbanded and the people who were members of the organization for some reason separated. It was finally sold, the ballpark. Dr. Lee, who had the majority of the shares of stock, sold it. It's now an industrial area.

Most of the players were professional guys. Some of 'em went all over Kentucky. Some guys were teachers, some were lawyers, and some were general workers and what have you.

John "Scoop" Brown

One in particular, who I started, I took him off of softball — fast pitch softball — and started him playing baseball. Lou Johnson. I took Lou Johnson out to the ballpark and started him playing hard ball and from that he went to Class D ball with Pittsburgh and from Pittsburgh he went up with the Cubs. From the Cubs he went with the Dodgers and he got to play in the World Series.

Dave Whitney and a young man by the name of Leon Higgins and a youth by the name of Buck Clay — I picked those teens off of a fast pitch softball team. I could see the ability in them. In fact, Leon Higgins went up into Class D ball and hurt his arm. Buck Clay, who was a pitcher, went with the Memphis Red Sox but he was in love with his hometown girlfriend and came back home.

Dave Whitney, he went with the Kansas City Monarchs for a while. He was playin' with Ernie Banks and Gene Baker and they didn't wanna give him the financial contract that they offered Ernie Banks and Gene and so, instead of stayin' in pro ball, Whitney started coachin' [basketball] at Texas Southern University. I think he stayed out at Texas Southern 'bout three years and after that he went to Alcorn, where he stayed for a while, appearing in several NCAA tournaments. He retired and they brought him back a few years ago and he was champion of the Southwestern Conference.

He's a beautiful person. I worked in recreation and Whitney lived in Midway [Kentucky] and he came up here to play in our 13 to 15 year old basketball league and I let him in. I could see then that that boy had a whole lot of athletic ability for a little guy. He was about the strongest little guy I think I've ever had a chance to work with. [Laughs] He went on to Kentucky State [University] where he starred in football, basketball, track, baseball, and everything. He was an all-around athlete. I saw him at the Dunbar [High School] reunion in 2000.

How did you start playing baseball?

I used to be a pretty good fast pitch softball player and we li'l ol' boys would go down to the ballpark. There used to be a ballpark down on Fourth Street. They used to have a team they called the Lexington Hardhitters. That was the first all black organization to have a ballpark in the city of

Lexington. The Lexington Hardhitters' park was down on Fourth Street down there where that tobacco barn is, right up the street from where Eastern State Hospital is. It was called the Lexington Hardhitters Ballpark.

The gentleman that run that park was a man by the name of Minor. Mr. Minor. He was the sole owner. George O'Rear and Jim O'Rear was partners with him in the team and they had a heck of a ballclub. I used to go to see 'em play and so I started playin' hardball myself.

We'd go out there and when the foul balls come over the fence we'd get 'em and run. [Laughs] We'd take 'em and play with 'em in our neighborhood. And from then on I started playin' baseball. I was 13 or 14. I wasn't nothin' but a li'l ol' brat.

We'd go over to the stockyard and play. Then they used to have neighborhood teams. You go in the East end or West end and play different teams. Li'l ol' pickup hardball ballgames, you know; no umpire, it was sort of a honor system. You'd play sun-up to sundown. When the sun went down you stopped playin'.

I went over to Dunbar High School after I got through at junior high school at Russell School. I played football at Dunbar, I played basketball at Dunbar. I was a pretty good punter on the football team. In fact, I have the longest punt registered in the Kentucky Negro Athletic League. We were playin' Central and I kicked one about 80 yards in the air. That still stands.

Later on in basketball I was selected as the first black All-American in 1937-38. I made the Kentucky All-Star team. They picked the 15 best black basketball players in the state of Kentucky and we went to play the best basketball players in Chicago. We were lucky enough to beat 'em. They had a guy named Hank Dizzone and a boy that played with the Celtics — Sweetwater Clifton. I played against Sweetwater Clifton. We beat them in the All-Star game in the armory in

Chicago. That was the largest crowd I ever played before — about 18,000 people and we defeated the aforementioned stars.

After that I left Dunbar and went to school down in Atlanta at Clark. I was on the first team, but I was in love with a childhood girlfriend and I didn't stay. [Laughs] I came back home. Right today I'm sorry about that because — not braggin'— I was college material book-wise and athletic-wise.

The girls at Clark used to tell me, "Don't leave for Kentucky. There's plenty of girls down here. We'll get you a girl." [Laughs] But I couldn't see it then.

I spoke to a class over at Lexington School the other day and I was tellin' 'em about some of the things that had occurred to me as a person. I was tellin' 'em about that and I was tellin' them a lot of the time you gotta stick things out when you don't think you're able to stick it out. Don't give up hope and don't give up your dreams.

I ended up playin' baseball in 1952. In 1950 and '51, I played with a team they called the Parkette Market. That was after the Hustlers disbanded. We were the tri-state champions. We went out to Wichita, Kansas, to that ABC baseball tournament. Thirty-eight teams and we finished sixteenth. In 1952 I went out there with Frisch's Big Boy.

Some of the players that played on that team — the Parkette Market — was a boy that pitched for the New York Giants. Dick LeMay. We had Bill White, who later went over to the Cardinals and was the president of the National League. And then we had Eddie Hobaugh, who went with the Chicago White Sox. And my last year with Frisch's Big Boy we had a guy who eventually became the manager of the Chicago Cubs — Bob Kennedy. He played third base for us out there in that tournament. That was my last year in baseball, 1952.

The Hustlers were more of a local team that brought in teams to play us. Durin' that time teams didn't have no facilities like we had. See, teams like the Homestead Grays, Memphis Red Sox, the Cleveland Buckeyes, the St. Louis Stars, Detroit Stars, the Indianapolis ABCs, the Dayton Monarchs, the West Virginia Flyers — we played all those teams. House of David, which was a religious group that traveled around the world — we played them.

My greatest experience was when we played the Birmingham [Black] Barons. I was makin' light of a boy that played center field — how good he was. The catcher for Birmingham was a guy named Pepper Bassett, one of the best catchers around. He said, "Kentucky, you haven't seen anything. You wait 'til Junior comes up the next time we play y'all."

At the time I was 25 and I saw in the paper where Junior was 14 or 15 years of age. So what happened, the next time we played them Junior was present. So we were playin' and the game was goin' on and we got a man on third base — one of our fastest runners. I never will forget it. Beaver Dam Mason, who was one of our better hitters, hit a line drive to right field, about 335 or -40 feet from home plate. This guy in right field went back against the wall, jumped and caught the ball, turned and the man at third base started toward home. He turned and threw to home plate and threw him out about two or three steps. That was Junior. Willie Mays. I never will forget that.

Here's another incident. We was playin' the Indianapolis Clowns when Hank Aaron played with 'em. He played shortstop. This game started at 7:30. At 11:30 — time to turn the lights out — it was still the first innin'. The first time Hank Aaron came up he hit one 350 feet over the left field wall. The next time he came up he hit one 380 feet over the left-center field wall. Next time he came up he hit one to right field 'bout 380 feet. The last time, over there where they got New Circle Road now, he hit that ball and they haven't ever found it. Four home

runs. It was 11:30 and it was still the first innin' and we still didn't get up.

And I saw this guy Josh Gibson, who played for the Homestead Grays. They beat us, 1-to-nothin', out there. We played 'em a 13-innin' game and they beat us, 1-to-nothin'. Josh Gibson hit a line drive. The center field at Hustler's Park was 406 feet from home plate. Josh Gibson hit a line drive so *hard* the ball hit the center field fence and bounced back to second base. That's true.

We had Bill "Dooley" Berry and there was a guy that played with the Boston Braves, Sam Jethroe. At first he played with the Cleveland Buckeyes and Bill Berry went up to take his place for a while, with the Cleveland Buckeyes. He stayed up there for about two weeks and came back home.

Mr. John H. Jackson — the late John H. Jackson — paid or some way made a contract with Satchel Paige. He came down here and pitched for our team against the New York Black Yankees. That was in '48 or '47, and, boy, I've never seen Satchel that angry. They hit him real hard. He was real angry but he was the type of guy you never could understand. He didn't talk much, but he was a very likable, tall — real tall — slender guy. But in that game the New York Black Yankees hit him real hard. I never did bat against Satchel but I had the opportunity to play with him.

Who was the best pitcher you saw?

There was a boy named Chief Bender. Chief Bender went with the Cincinnati Reds. He was one of the hardest throwers I've seen. I batted against him one time and he threw a curveball and tears came in my eyes. He was about the hardest thrower I've seen. He was about six-foot-six; he threw about 95, 98. He was about the best I've seen.

[Not to be confused with the Hall of Fame A's pitcher of the same name, this Chief Bender (first name: Sheldon) never made it to the major leagues as a player but was the long-time Reds farm director.]

I'll tell you another guy you probably remember: Piper Davis. And there was a guy that was still with the Cubs, Buck O'Neil, as a team scout. He was a great friend of Mr. Glass — Butch Glass — and he played with the Memphis Red Sox. There used to be some ex–major league ballplayers come over to the Hustlers.

Who was the best hitter you saw?

Oh, the best hitter I ever saw was Hank Aaron. And Goose Tatum. Oh, I forgot to tell you 'bout Goose Tatum. I played against Goose Tatum with the Clowns.

I was tellin' the kids over there about Goose Tatum. [Laughs] He made a bet with a guy in the stands. He bet him anything he wanted to bet he'd get to third base. Goose made all these gyrations — shake his body and shake his bat — so he came up this time and he hit a hot smash between the first baseman and the second baseman and 'stead of goin' to first base, he flew down to third base and slid into third base. He said, "I *told* you I was gonna get to third base!" [Laughs] And the crowd went wild.

When the Clowns would come to town — we'd play them two or three times a year — they'd have the city bus run out there and the crowd would start comin' in the park about 5:30. They'd be all the way around the park; they'd have 10- or 12,000, 14,000 people at the ballgame. They had a guy they called Nature Boy, a little short guy. It was really a fun game.

And then the amazing thing about it, if you looked at the fans in the stands, it was a mixture of people of all races. And there never was no problem. The teacher over at Lexington School, she was amazed. "Did they get along all right?" Yeah, wasn't no problem. Those people was enyoyin' the ballgames. That was back in the '40s.

Later on in Lexington they had what they called the Lexington Ballpark on High Street. When we went to go to the ballgame they had a section for us down the right field line, "For Colored Only." But the difference at the Hustlers' ballpark, the restrooms, the seating in the stands — it was all democratic. There wasn't no segregated area.

How much were you paid by the Hustlers?

When I played for the Hustlers I was kind of a star on the team. Most of the guys made $25; I made $50 a game. That was big money for me. We played five games a week: Mondays, Wednesday, Fridays, Saturdays, and Sundays. We didn't play too many double headers.

We traveled by car. We went to New Richmond, Indiana. That's about as far as we went. Winchester, Bourbon, Pikesville, West Liberty. In fact, I'm goin' to a reunion up to West Liberty in June. I played with Steve Hamilton when we played with the Parkette Market. He went up and pitched for the Yankees.

Do you know any of your statistics?

No, I don't. I can't remember those, but I know I was voted the Most Valuable Player one year and I was the leading hitter one year. I still got the old trophies. I was a line-drive hitter. One year I popped up a lot. They called me "Pop-Up Scoop."

I was a pretty good athlete. I had a chance to go with Junior but I was a mama's boy. I didn't wanna leave home. In 1947, Mr. Hayes, who was the business manager of the Birmingham Black Barons, he wanted to take me with the Barons but I wouldn't leave Lexington.

One thing about tourin' with those black teams: I think they made about 10 or 15 dollars a game and had to sleep on the buses and things. They were segregated, of course; they couldn't go into restaurants and eat. They had some terrible situations. Baloney and cheese and sardines. [Laughs]

You sound as if you really enjoyed playing.

Would you do it again if you were a young man?

Oh, yeah. I sure would. I'd do it all over again. I'd do it much better, though. I'd be more refined. I think I would take it more seriously. It was more or less to me my first love in athletics. I think if I went through it now with what the guys are makin' in baseball and basketball, I think I would really devote myself to it.

What did you do away from baseball?

I was a recreation supervisor. I worked for the City Parks and Recreation off and on for 41 years and I retired in 1983.

Also, I was a basketball and football official and I was starter in track. I had the pleasure of being the first black in quite a few things: first to call high school basketball in the state tournament in Kentucky, the first to belong to the Ohio Valley Conference in basketball, the first to call the NCAA tournament in Statesboro, Georgia,

first to call the Grantland Rice Bowl in Murfreesboro, Tennessee, and the first to call the NAIA tournament in Kansas City, Missouri. I've had a pretty good life.

You might think about what I'm gonna say. I was tellin' the kids, there's 365 days in a year. Say if you're ten years old. I want you to multiply ten by 365 days and see how many days you've lived in your lifetime and how you have valued or how you've used those days. And if you live ten more years how you are going to try to improve on what has happened to you the past ten years. They looked at me and said, "Mr. Scoop, I never thought about it." Heck, I didn't think about it until I was readin' about it.

I'm 79 years old times 365 days. Look how many days I've lived. Were those days important? Did I use 'em wisely? How did I use 'em? How am I gonna use my other days before my time comes? That's somethin' to think about. [Laughs]

No records available

Paul Casanova
Indianapolis Clowns 1960

BORN DECEMBER 21, 1941, COLON, CUBA
HT. 6'4" WT. 180 BATTED AND THREW RIGHT

Age has few advantages that I can think of, but one that does come to mind is the fact that I am old enough to have seen some actual Negro leagues games. When I was a small boy in Atlanta my stepfather took me to see a couple of games. I don't remember much about them, but in looking back I think I must have seen a very young Willie Mays. It was in the late 1940s and one of the teams' players had "BBB" on them. I have come to learn that that means it was the Birmingham Black Barons and that was Willie's team.

Those couple of games created an interest in Negro league baseball in me that has remained. As I grew older, I paid special attention to former Negro leaguers who made it into "organized" professional baseball. I remember seeing Piper Davis, Artie Wilson, and Granville Gladstone in the old Pacific Coast League. Then when major league ball came to the West Coast (my family moved to California in the early 1950s) I was able to see Mays, whom I was now aware of, Hank Aaron, Don Newcombe, and several others.

I returned to Georgia for college and there I saw Paul Casanova, a tall, rangy catcher with a wonderful arm. Since then I've seen Johnny Bench, Charles Johnson and Ivan Rodriguez and they, too, have wonderful arms, but I don't think any of them threw any better than Casanova did.

Paul Casanova loved (and still loves) baseball, but as a small boy in his Cuban home-town he was not very good at it. Hard work and dedication paid off, though. Not only did he eventually reach the major leagues, but he was named *The Sporting News* American League all-star catcher as a Washington Senators rookie in 1966 and was selected for the All-Star game in 1967. He led the AL in double plays three times.

After seven years with Washington he ended his career in Atlanta, where I saw him play. He continued to gun down runners until the end.

How did you enter the Negro leagues?

CASANOVA: When I got there the Negro league was already gone. We just played exhibition games all over. We have two team traveling with us, one they called the Royal and the Clown. Different uniform; the Royal would wear yellow uniform and we would wear the black. Sam Paula used to own the team. Eddie Edmonds was the general manager; he used to travel with us. I think they all pass away by now.

The reason I got in the Negro league is I came from Cuba and I was signed by the Cleveland Indians. Then I got a release my first year. But I was so young they invited me again the following year and then I got another release. Then I went to Chicago Cub when I play with the Clown, after I got a release from Cleveland. The general manager from San Antone, which was Don King, saw me play one day with the Clown and then he recommend me to Chicago, but I had to play the whole year. They was paying my salary, which was 300 dollar. I

Paul Casanova

play with the Clown the whole 1961 season.

There was a scout by the name John Caruso. He pass away; out of Massachusetts. He saw me play and he want to sign me to a contract, but it was no way he could get a contract with me because he thought I was back in Cuba, but I wasn't. I was in New London, Connecticut. I was playing in the city league and he came down to watch one of the games. He saw me playing. He said, "Wow! I been looking for you for eight months. I just need for you to come down to Massachusetts and we have a tryout and I want to see."

Before that, I went on a tryout with the New York Mets and they never look at me. John Caruso know a little bit about me. The only thing, he wanted to see my arm so when he saw me throw, he said, "That's that." So he signed me to the Washington Senators. That's how I got to the major league in three year.

But by playing in the Negro league I accomplished a lot, because by being with Cleveland they never let me play. I only went to bat six time. [Laughs] In the minor league. When I played with the Clown we played against some tough team. I played against Satchel in Kansas City, Missouri. He was playing with the Kansas City Monarch and we play an exhibition game. That day we played three games: one in the morning, one in the afternoon, and one at night. And I caught the three games. And I went 5-for-5, the first time that I ever went 5-for-5 in my life. And I got a basehit against Satchel Paige, so to me that was a big thrill.

I went to spring training and they start advertising by me making it to the major league. When I play with Atlanta, Hank Aaron and I, we become real close because he also play with the Negro league before I did.

The Negro league was gone and all we did was play exhibition game and travel all over the country for three month. We sleep in the bus most of the time. [Laughs] And we get two dollar meal money. [Laughs] A steak would cost five dollar and it was only on payday every two week that we got a steak. [Laughs]

Three hundred dollar a month, but I wasn't paid by the Clown. The Clown pay half of my salary and San Antone — the general manager — would pay a half. At the end of the season he took me to Chicago and I stay there for a month just working out with them and catching batting practice. Then I got signed by Chicago, went to spring training in Mesa, Arizona, and they assigned me to San Antone as a backup catcher and I went to bat one time and they release me again. That was before I signed with Washington.

That was my third release. When John Caruso saw me he give me another shot and that's when I made it to the major league.

Do you know your batting average with the Clowns?

Oh, I wish I can remember. I know I was hitting pretty good because I started with the team that have to lose every night, which was the Royal. One day we was in San Antone and the manager told me — I don't speak English that well at the time; I still don't [Laughs] — the manager told me to throw the ball in center field so that way the Clown can win. There was a scout in the stand and I don't wanna throw the ball away and look bad, so I throw and got the guy out. The manager got all over me. [Laughs]

So the next day from San Antone we went to Austin, Texas, and the other catcher that was playing regular for the Clown, George Sherry, he signed with the Chicago White Sox; they give him a big bonus but the Clown keep some of that money. So they called me up to the Clown, the team that never lose. [Laughs] From there I was hitting eight; I had to sit in the back of the bus because when you're a rookie you had to sit in the back of the bus and then hit your way into another seat in the front row. [Laughs]

I been riding all day and all night long in that back seat so one day I got mad and I told manager there was another seat right next to me. I said, "I need to get some rest. I'm gonna sit here regardless of what happens." Then we got in the argument on the bus and then finally we became best friends on the team. [Laughs]

I was riding in the back of the bus and that's an old bus. Once I start hitting the ball, he was hitting third and I was hitting four. I was hitting pretty good.

We played against different teams. We were in New Jersey against a tough black team. Joe Black was pitching and I hit a home run against Joe Black. I remember Gil McDougald, played with the Yankee; he was a scout for the Met and he saw me but he never say anything to me. I hit a home run in New Jersey, I say, "Oh my God! There's a scout looking." We looked for scouts to see if we can get signed. I was the only one that got signed out of that group.

I saw you play with the Braves. You had a heck of an arm.

Oh, yeah. I was known for throwing guys out. [Laughs] That kept me up there for a long time. Before that I played six year for Washington and I was an all-star one year, in '67. I was voted the best catcher in the league.

When I got in the big league I was hitting pretty good. My first year I hit about .258, but what happen is that I don't know how to call a game. I don't have the natural ability like the other guys, like Bench and those guys that can switch from hitting to catching, so I concentrate more on catching. That was the reason why I stayed there long because I was a good defensive catcher. I can throw guys out; I call a good game.

I caught [Phil] Niekro's no-hitter — knuckleballer — in Atlanta. That was a big thrill to me.

When I was with Washington we play 22 innings and I think I went 1-for-9. I hit into a double play twice. In the twenty-second I got a basehit with the bases loaded to win the game so everybody forget about the other eight time at bat. [Laughs]

I also throw out six guy trying to steal in that game. Then I pick off three guys after they was already on base. I remember Tommy Agee — he just pass away, God bless his soul, my good friend — he was on first base and I pick him off. I don't think that ever happened in the history of baseball, because that was the longest night game that they ever play and from that day on they would never play another long game because they had a curfew now. The game ended about 3:45 in the morning. [Laughs] I caught the whole game.

I think in the inning 16, Tom McCraw — he's the hitting coach for Houston now — he hit a double and I throw to second base and pick him off with nobody out. Then

I think in the 19 inning, Don Buford hit a triple and nobody out and I pick him off on third base. [Laughs] I pick one at first and one at second and one at third and I throw six guys out, so the reason why the game went so long was because of my defense.

How did you get to the States from Cuba?

In 1960, winter ball in Cuba, Tony Taylor recommend me to Almendares team. There was four teams in Cuba that play winter ball. The guy that owned the team — he pass away a long time ago; he got killed in a truck accident — he was a scout for Cleveland.

I was 17 year old and he give me a contract to go to spring training at Daytona Beach in 1960. I make the team as the second string catcher and then they send me down to Minot, North Dakota, as a backup catcher, but I only went to bat six time. The following year I went back to Cuba and '61 was the last year I ever played pro ball in Cuba.

But I never got to play. The last time I play ball in Cuba I was gonna pinch hit in the ninth inning with two out and the guy made an out and I never got to hit. They haven't played ball in Cuba professionally since.

The have so many marvelous ballplayers in Cuba now.

I think it's a political thing. That's the reason they all escape Cuba because they wanna have a better life. Like if I would've went back to Cuba I would've never make it to the major league because I would've been black out. When you have a release over here and you go to Cuba, nobody wants to take a chance on you. At that time Castro don't want anybody to come to United States. 1962 was the last time anybody can leave through Mexico.

So if I would've went back to Cuba I probably would've been Cuban and never got a chance to play here.

You talked about the 22-inning game and

playing against Satchel. What is the game you remember most? Is it one of those or is it another game?

To me, it was the best game I ever played. The 22-inning game. That's gotta be my highlight because throwing out these guys — they used to call 'em the Go-Go Sox in those days. Tommy Agee, Don Buford — they had a lotta speed. They used to fly. They don't have any power at that time; they just get on base and run. And I stopped them that day. [Laughs]

It wasn't easy because you don't steal on the catcher. You steal on the pitcher. What happen is if the pitcher give the catcher a little chance to keep it close to the bag and you have a good arm and you got confidence in your arm I can throw anybody out. But the ball has to be there. It's a timing situation, you know. Everything is boom-boom-boom. But I was lucky enough to learn that quickness, be quick with my feet and have a good strong arm.

The reason why I became a catcher was because I was no good at all. There was a lotta good ballplayers in my hometown so I never got to play. I only play when I had to catch, no mask. I play right field when somebody doesn't show up or something.

I was always picking up balls. If they hit a foul ball I would go and pick it up and bring it in and they'd let me play. They'd let me be in the ballpark. [Laughs] The only way I can look at the game is from home plate on because I was always picking up ball and batboy and carrying bags. I was always around home plate and I admired the catcher, the way he handled the game.

Ever since I was a kid I wanted to play so bad. I escaped school to go and play. One day I remember if they didn't let me play I was gonna make my own team, so I went over and cut a tree and made my own bat, made my own mask out of wire, made my own glove. I had a team. The kids who never get to play, we made a team and then we played. [Laughs] I was about nine year old.

Then my family moved to Havana and then is when I played Little League. 13 year old. I got to play catch. I was real tall and skinny, so there was a semipro team in Havana. There was an old man that used to be an old catcher. He used to bring teams from Cuba to play in the Negro league. There was a lot of guys there; everybody was about 27, 28, 30 year old because they've already been signed and released so they go in the Negro league and play. So when I was 13 year old I happened to fix home plate so he let me catch one inning when they were losing. [Laughs]

I was always fascinated with being a catcher and in those days when I got here I learn a lot from Earl Battey from Minnesota and then John Roseboro. I never got to see Campanella because it was in '58 and I was in Cuba. But then I got to play with Roseboro in Washington. I got to play against Elston Howard when the Yankees come to town. By being black you admired the catcher because in those days they don't let too many black catchers play. The catcher was like a quarterback.

The only reason I get my break because everybody got hurt and they had to play me. [Laughs] I was number five — that's how come I wear number five — in the whole farm system from the top down. They don't have any intention for me to catch but they don't have nobody else and I was coming over out of Double-A ball. I went to Venezuela in '65 and I played against Aparicio, so I was playing against the same guys that were playing over here when I play winter ball.

So when I go away all I had to do was put my tent together because I played against these guys in winter ball. They help me a lot.

Who were some of the real good players you saw?

Oh my God. Don't forget, I played from '65 to '74. Going in '75 I hurt my arm

and I never play again. I was 33 year old. I've seen so many good ballplayers it's amazing.

To me it was a thrill to be playing against Willie Mays, McCovey, Mantle, Kaline, Killebrew, Oliva, Yastrzemski. I mean, I can name you a million players. Clemente, Wille Stargell. There was so many good ballplayers in those days and they all stayed with the same team for so long and you get to admire when you played against them.

One day we play in Washington and Mantle came to the plate and we struck him out four time in a row and I was catching. I think he had a rough night the night before and he can't even pick up the ball. I mean, he was just swinging out there. Joe Coleman was pitching.

Two week later we went to New York and I guess he was rested and he went 5-for-5. [Laughs] That's something that sticks in my mind.

Like my first year in spring training, the minute I saw Mantle it was like seeing Jesus. Oh my God. The kid you admire so much and you're playing against him. So when he gets to home plate and I was catching — my first year, it's an exhibition game — he came over and say hi to me and he said, "Welcome to American League." To me, that was like the biggest thing that ever happened.

We went to New York and we were playing the Yankees and I went downtown and bought a big poster of Mantle and put it in my basement. [Laughs]

Who were some of the players you saw while with the Clowns?

To be honest with you, I played with so many guys that I don't remember half of them. I know Nature Boy William Harrison outta Washington. We had a midget playing with us; his name was Willie Maucum, a little guy. He played shortstop but he don't play regular. He still lives.

None of the guys made it. It was hard

for them to make it in those days because you really had to be an exceptional ballplayer because there was so much competition in those days. It was hard for them to break in. They all had a dream to make it but you had to be really, really, really, really lucky for somebody to sign you in those days. There wasn't a Negro league; it was just exhibition game that we played.

They had a lotta good black ballplayers in Triple-A and all the way down. Remember, in those days it was A, B, C, all the way down. And I can recall about a *thousand* black ballplayers that could've make it into the major league. I mean, they had so much talent but there wasn't no room for them. There was not enough team plus there was a lotta — I don't go down to discrimination but I just go down to the quality of players.

Oh my God, I've seen some guys that could *play!* Oh! But they were either too old or they don't have a bonus. In those days bonus babies dominate the game. You got a guy that got 20,000 dollar, they're gonna look at that guy before they look at you who got 500 dollar.

And they keep a lotta old guy in Triple-A ball in case somebody get hurt up there. I know a couple guys that stay in the minors for 12 year waiting for the other guys to retire or something.

What was the racial situation like when you joined Washington?

When I joined Washington I had to go through the minor league system. At one point I was the only black on the team and I know that for a fact when I went to Burlington, North Carolina, which was A ball, there was only two other black guys: Frank Coggins and Frank Garnett and myself. In Geneva, New York, in '64 we only have George Lewis and myself. In the PONY League in New York we'd stay at the hotel, but in North Carolina we can't stay at the hotel. We have to stay over at black people house.

We also did that with Clown when we go to different towns. But I was used to that. The only difference was that I don't know what race was because in Cuba we don't have that. It was racist but not like here.

I remember in San Antone we went in the road trip and there was only two black guys on the team. It was Don Eaddy and myself; we was roomies. We went in the bus and we went to Austin, Texas. That was the first year they was gonna let the black ballplayers stay in the hotel, so we went in our room. We was taking a shower after driving all the way from San Antone and the telephone ring. A guy said, "I'm sorry, but you can't stay here." [Laughs] We had to pack our bag and the bus took us to a black section of the town and we stayed there.

But if they would've told us before it wasn't no problem because we feel comfortable where we was. But it was a surprise that they gonna let us stay and then they tell us not to stay. But I never talk too much about that. My goal was to try to make it as far as I could.

To me, it was a hard road at the beginning but it all paid off. So whatever I did I'm proud that I never give up. That's how come when I'm teaching kids now I tell 'em, "You can't give up. You gotta work harder and harder and harder. Something will happen on the way."

I was working with the Chicago White Sox as an instructor. I was in Hickory, North Carolina. I worked there for two year, going on three, but when the strike came over they let everybody go. I was working as a first base coach and teaching the catchers. First, I was with the big team as a bullpen catcher, but I can't see the ball too good, so they send me to the minor league that I can teach.

Now at my house I got a batting cage and I teach the catchers and the hitters. Magglio Ordonez from Chicago White Sox. [Laughs] I got him in Hickory, North Carolina, for two years and I went to Venezuela to work with him. I'm not the reason why he make it but I know I put a little bit in there. He hit at my house this winter. He stay here with me this winter. We live about a mile apart and he came every day for a month.

If you were a young man, would you do this again?

Of course. [Laughs] I wouldn't change that for nothing in the world. I think baseball has to be in your blood to put up with all the stuff that I did. But I really don't feel that I put up with a lot because I know there was a *million* ballplayers before me that had a lot of problems before I did. So I'm very satisfied with what happened. I never regret nothing about the way that I was treated. No, no. No regrets at all.

Where can you find a job like playing baseball? What about the slave times when people was slaves? It's just like about the money right now. You think I'm jealous because the guy making money? No. Of course not. It was a different time. With the money we made we did the best we could. I made 37,000 dollar. In those days a Cadillac cost 4,000 dollar. [Laughs] I never drove a Cadillac; I drove a Pontiac.

But I don't have any regret. If the guy making a billion dollar, more power to him. What about Lou Gehrig, what about Babe Ruth, what about Ted Williams, which was my manager in Washington for three years? What about Joe DiMaggio and all those guys that were really super, super stars and they never got to make their money? I played with Hank four years in Atlanta, going on five. It was different.

Hank — I'm in his book, too — when he was breaking the record he was going through some rough time and I was right there for him because I understand, because we both play on the Clown at different time. Hank, he was only making a hundred thousand dollar, 125 when he broke that record, when he surpassed Baby Ruth's home runs.

The reason why he went to Milwaukee was because the Atlanta Braves, they offer him 25,000 dollar to be in the front office and he say, "Heck, no. I'm going to Milwaukee." He went to Milwaukee for 400,000 for two year. When Ted Turner bought the team he came back and he doing okay.

What a super person. What a super player he was. You gotta really know him as a person. I traveled with that guy for five year. Super nice guy. He keep so much inside. I love him to death.

When I got traded from Washington to Atlanta and we went to spring training and Dusty Baker, Ralph Garr, and those guys were there. And Orlando Cepeda, which is still my friend; all those guys. Rico Carty. And when I came in on the team, they make me feel at home even though I come from the American League. By coming over there to Atlanta really relaxed me because I wasn't a starter. I was a second-string catcher and I know my job. Hank became a friend when he found out I play with the Clown. He know what you have to go through to play with the Clown.

BATTING RECORD

Year	Team, Lg	G	AB	R	H	2B	3B	HR	RBI	BA
1960	Ind, NAL									
	Minot, NoL	10	6	4	0	0	0	0	0	.000
1961	Did not play									
1962	San Antonio, TxL	2	1	0	0	0	0	0	0	.000
1963	Geneva, NYP	94	329	40	86	18	4	7	34	.261
1964		120	480	98	156	27	2	19	99	.325

Year	Team, Lg	G	AB	R	H	2B	3B	HR	RBI	BA
1965	Burlington, Caro	142	506	62	145	25	5	8	76	.287
	Wash, AL	5	13	2	4	0	0	0	3	.308
1966	Wash, AL	122	429	45	109	16	5	13	44	.254
	York, EL	5	19	5	4	0	0	0	3	.211
1967	Wash, AL	141	528	47	131	19	1	9	53	,248
1968	Buffalo, IL	24	84	10	23	1	0	2	8	.274
	Wash, AL	96	322	19	63	6	0	4	25	.196
1969	Wash, AL	124	379	26	82	9	2	4	37	.216
1970		104	328	25	75	17	3	6	30	.229
1971		94	311	19	63	9	1	5	26	.203
1972	Atlanta, NL	49	136	8	28	3	0	2	10	.206
1973		82	236	18	51	7	0	7	18	.216
1974		42	104	5	21	0	0	0	8	.202

James Colzie
Indianapolis Clowns 1946-1947

BORN JULY 12, 1920 MONTEZUMA, GA
HT. 6' WT. 160 BATTED AND THREW RIGHT

James Colzie played baseball for a long time — 21 years — and won the amazing total of 265 games. That puts him in pretty elite company. The team with which he is remembered mostly is the Indianapolis Clowns, but he joined it in Cincinnati, before it moved to Indianapolis. Before that he played with the Atlanta Black Crackers.

During the winters he attended college and taught junior high school math and history until he retired. He also worked with Little League teams, umpired and was president on the local chapter of the NAACP.

He and his wife had four boys and two girls, and two of the boys turned out to be professional athletes. Richard played and managed minor league baseball and Neal was a star in the NFL.

Three different references list you as having played different years. What is correct?

COLZIE: I started in 1937 until '57. I played with the Macon Colored Peaches. I was playing with three different teams: Macon Colored Peaches, Atlanta Black Crackers, and the Albany Black Travelers.

I left there and I went to the Clowns the next year. I was with 'em off and on for about ten years. I was in the military from '42 to '45.

I was managing the baseball team [in the service] and they [the Clowns] would come down. I didn't get them when they'd be coming to spring training in Jacksonville; I'd catch them when the season ended. They'd come down barnstorming and Syd [Pollack] would let me know when they were coming down and he would give me games to play.

Your career was a long one.

That's the reason I can hardly raise my arm up. [Laughs]

How did you join Macon?

My home was only 50 miles from there. I'm originally from Montezuma, Georgia; that's my home. We had a little local team down there. I hardly ever played with them. The manager would take me to Macon to play. When I started I was 17.

How did you join the Clowns?

First, they were the Miami Clowns. I didn't play with them. I played with 'em in Cincinnati. Then they moved to Indianapolis. I left home and went to spring training in Jacksonville, Florida, to join them.

When did you attend college?

I come out of high school in '37. I went to Fort Valley State in the winters.

You pitched a lot of games in 21 years. Does one stand out?

I beat Satchel Paige. [Laughs] This was '47 and we had played 'em in St. Louis. At that particular time they only had one black hotel. Or rooming house. That's what we stayed in mostly. Satchel was playing with the Kansas City Monarchs. He pitched that Wednesday night against me and he beat me, 2-to-1.

We were coming out of the stadium — Sportsman's Park — and I said, "Satchel, I'll meet you again one day."

And he asked our manager — he was named Hoss Walker, he was from Birmingham, he played with the Birmingham Black Barons — he said, "Hoss, when is Colzie pitching again?"

He said, "Sunday in Kansas City."

He said, "I'll be there, Colzie."

We hooked up again. It was 107 [degrees] in the dugout. I don't know what it was out on the field. We hooked up and I beat him the same thing, 2-to-1.

He beat me with a hit in the bottom of the eighth inning. I was fooling with him and didn't think he was gonna swing at the pitch. I figured what he might try to do is get the man to third base. He hit the ball between first and second.

So that Sunday we was hooked up again. He fooled around and got one of his fastballs up and I hit it between Buck O'Neil and [Chico] Renfroe at second base. I beat him with a hit.

Do you know any of your seasonal records?

I know my record altogether: 265-135. We played longer then. Now them guys making them millions and millions of dollars they give 'em the ball and say, "Give me five innings." When our manager give us the ball, he'd say, "You're pitching." He didn't tell you to give him five. [Laughs]

What kind of hitter were you?

I was a pretty good hitter. I wasn't no .300 hitter; I maybe hit .220 or something like that.

Your son Richard played professional baseball.

That's right. He managed up in Batavia, New York, for three years. He bounced

around in Double-A and Triple-A ball. He never got up to the majors. He was with Cincinnati. He was fixing to retire and they called him and told him did he want to manage a baseball team and he told 'em yes. So he went up to Batavia, New York.

You wouldn't believe it. Three years ago I was at a parking lot parking cars and someone got out of a car and said, "I'll be right back, Mr. Colzie." That was a young white kid, maybe 25 years old. He said, "Did you have a son playing ball up in Batavia, New York?"

I said, "He managed the team up there."

He said, "My daddy played against him." He went and got his daddy and gave me his name, so I went and called my son and told him.

He said, "I've got to think. I've seen plenty of ballplayers." He thought and then he called me back. "I remember him. He was an outfielder."

My son was a good outfielder. He pitched a while but I didn't want him to pitch. When he got his scholarship he pitched. That was at Miami Dade South. He was the first black baseball player at Miami Dade South; he was the first black baseball player at Florida State. Now he's the manager of a large lumber company.

Your son Neal played football.

He played four years with the Oakland Raiders, one year with the Miami Dolphins, five years with the Tampa Bay Buccaneers. Now he's practically not doing anything. [Laughs]

The oldest son, he played baseball but he didn't get no scholarship. He pitched for the high school and went up to Albany State and didn't make the team. The coach of the team liked him and he took him and he was his righthand man. The other one, the pitcher, they put him in the outfield; he's managing the lumberyard in the northeast section of Miami.

The oldest daughter, she played basketball. Only in high school. All of 'em played sports. The younger girl, she ran track. And the baby boy, he played three sports. He went to basketball. My wife was a basketball player. I was her first coach. That was in Georgia.

You played from the '30s to the '50s. How did the travel change over those 20 years?

'Bout the same. When I was in Atlanta in the service there and I had my baseball team — see, I was managing the baseball team where I was stationed there — we traveled by what we called carryall. And when I was playing for the Clowns we rode the bus. And the Black Crackers — bus. In Albany we traveled in cars; sometimes we'd get a bus, a school bus. I had never flown up until my son went to college.

How did the accommodations change over the years?

It didn't change too much while we were playing. There were certain places we just couldn't stay. What they would do — I was close to the business manager, I helped him with the books, I helped to type up the reports — and say we were going to New York. I'd call such-and-such a place and ask if they got any rooms. They'd say, "How many?"

I'd say, "There's 12 of us. How much are the rooms?"

They'd tell me and I would tell them, I'd say, "We are colored."

"You know there's a convention coming in here. I have to have those rooms. I'm sorry." [Laughs] That was just a lie.

We'd go in different places — restaurants — and we all would sit together. When the waitress come to wait on some of the whites one of the players would call her. She'd say, "One moment," but she would never come back. Then another waitress would come and one of 'em would call her. She'd say, "One moment," and she never came back. When the third one come and she don't come we'd just up and walk out. We didn't raise no sand.

We come along just like Jackie Robinson did. He had special places he ate. We stayed in older hotels. Some of the hotels were pretty nice — Chicago, Detroit. We knew what we had to do. Like Jackie Robinson did — he took so much. That's the way we were. We were talking 'bout younger people nowadays — rough as they are now — like when we come along there would've been a lot of killing because they wouldn't accept it. They'd've raised sand. We never did.

Only one time I can say that we actually had a fight. Our home grounds was in Indianapolis and we were living in a predominate white area where a black man bought a hotel. All our surroundings were white. They were very nice. The hotel was on one side of the street and Hart, Schaffner, and Marx was on the other side. We'd go over there and they would make our suits.

The man that had a little restaurant across in front of the hotel, he asked us when we first moved up there to come in. He said, "Let me know when you're coming in and I'll stay open for you." He was *very* nice.

So we come in that morning around 1:30 — we had played that night in Columbus and when we played in Columbus we'd always come back to Indianapolis — and the manager said, "You all going to eat? We won't leave until tomorrow noon."

We went across the street. He had two doors. That was the main street — Capitol — and the other street was 14th, I believe. We went in the front door and he hollered, "You *n*'s don't come in this way. You come through that side door!"

And my roomie, Preacher Henry, said, "I'll tell you what. Wait 'til we come back."

Just as we got up the steps going back to the hotel the team was coming up. We told 'em, "That man called us the *n*, wants you to come in the side door."

Each one of 'em went back. They got

.38s, .32s, .45s. And we had some Spanish guys. They got the machete knives. We went in that front door. A big guy named Johnny Williams — from Louisiana — said, "What did you call us?"

"Anything you want you can get. Just let me alone."

He sold out the next day.

We played in Gulfport, Mississippi, and they was getting 20 percent of the gate. My roomie, Preacher Henry, said he's got to go to the restroom so he got up, went around. We saw the two white guys standing on the side of the door and we started in and they stepped in front of us. They said, "Where you going?"

We said, "We're going to the restroom."

"Can't you read?"

You know what it read. "White Only." We turned around and went back and told the manager. So he told the chauffeur to move the bus from the front of the stadium 'round to the first base side so we go out there and use the restroom.

I remember 1935. My mother was working for a family. She worked for 'em 'round about 30-some years. I was 15 years old and he was an ophthalmologist and he'd go different places. This particular day he told my mother, "Tomorrow I want J. C. to go with me up to Atlanta. We're leaving early."

So we left around 6:00. We got to Atlanta, parked on the street, and there was a black guy and a white guy sweeping the street off. There was a hotel and a cafeteria right where we parked. He asked the two men, "Do you mind me parking here?"

"No, sir. You can park."

He said, "I want J. C. to stay in the car." So he gave each one of 'em five dollars. "You watch him."

"Yes, sir. We'll watch him."

So he come out about five or ten minutes after twelve and said, "J. C., aren't you kinda hungry?"

I said, "I dunno."

"Well, let me go in here and see can we eat." He walked in and it was full. It was a large cafeteria. He walked over to the desk and said, "I have J. C. here with me. Will you feed him? I'm hungry and he's hungry."

He said, "You've got these tables up under that counter. How 'bout taking one of those tables and put it up and put two chairs there?"

He said, "All right."

So he did. People looked at us but they didn't say anything at all.

We got in the car and we was coming down. We got to a place by the name of Barnesville, Georgia, and he said, "J. C., I've got to use the restroom."

I said, "I have, too."

He stopped at the next service station. He told the man, "Fill it up." At that time you had to pump the gas all the way up to the 12 gallons, then you put your hose in.

He come out and he told me, "Okay, J. C., you go to the restroom."

So this man that was putting the gas in said, "He can't use the restroom!"

He said, "If he can't use the restroom, don't put no gas in."

So he said, "Okay, let him go."

So I went on to the restroom. When I come out the man I was with, he was standing at the door and there was about four or five whites sitting in chairs in front of the service station. I knew why he did it but I was gonna ask him. I said, "Mr. Williams, why did you stand at the door?"

He said, "J. C., you saw those white men sitting in front of that door. And behind that service station was a thicket of woods." He said, "If you'd've went back there alone they'd've come around the back of that service station and killed you like nothing had happened."

We rode about maybe eight or ten miles and he spoke. He said, "J. C., one day the colored man's gonna be equal to the white man."

I was telling my wife a few years ago about him. I said, "I wonder if he lived to see it," because he moved away to South Carolina right outside of Augusta. That was 1935.

I used to see white ladies or white men come to pick up their maid in the morning and they would get out and open the back door. There were four doors and if there wasn't they would pull the seat up so they could sit in the back seat. They didn't do my mother like that. My mother sat in the front seat. My brother and I would sit in the back.

Then when they got out of the car, they had to go around to the back door to go in. My mother, she'd go in the front door right with them. They'd open the door for her and she'd go right in. And he had everything; he had football for us to play with, basketball, baseball, all that for us to play with.

Let's get back to your baseball days. Was there a hitter who gave you a lot of trouble?

I would say one that I can remember, and he gave everybody trouble. That was Josh Gibson. He hit the longest ball ever hit in Yankee Stadium. They say Babe Ruth and Mickey Mantle hit the longest balls, buy Josh Gibson hit the longest one. That's before they brought it in around 15 or 20 feet. He hit it like two tiers up in straightaway center field.

I remember we played 'em in Washington at the Senators' park. Josh come up and he was hitting it outta all places — left-center, right field, straightaway, left field. I said, "Bus" — Buster Haywood — "you know what I'm gonna do? I'm gonna throw Josh a fastball right down the heart of that plate. Let's see if he's gonna swing."

Sure enough, he comes up there in the top of the second inning and I threw it right down the heart of the plate and he looked back at Buster. I was laughing. He said, "He's gonna get someone killed out there."

And I threw him a changeup curveball.

And you could've went to sleep and waked up and he went through his stride and he hit it 525! Straightaway center field. They had a green monster out there just like the one that's in Boston. He hit it over that.

And he didn't hit it with no strength. He hit it with wrist power. It was 525 to the fence and that was 40 or 50 feet up. He was one of the best I think there ever was.

Who was the best pitcher?

I'll pick Satchel Paige. I'm not color-blind now; he was just a great man.

We played in St. Louis and we was all standing in front of the hotel. We'd always tell jokes and things. There was a lady coming along, a lady and a man but I guess the man was about 15, 18 feet behind her. And he [Satchel] just spoke. He said, "How you, Miss Carrie. Would you like to marry?"

She smiled and said, "I dunno. Ask my husband back there."

Satchel ran back into the hotel.

She said, "What's the matter with him?"

Buck O'Neil said, "He ran in the hotel 'cause he didn't know what he was gonna do."

The man was laughing. He said, "We just wanted to get an autograph from Satchel."

Buck said, "That was him just ran back in the hotel." [Laughs]

It took about 15 minutes to get him out. [Laughs] We all laughed about it.

I remember when we was going out on Long Island up in New York to play that night and Satchel was pitching. He was ahead of us and we saw maybe about five or six police cars surrounding a car. One of us on the team said, "That looks like Satchel." And he pulled up on the median and we all got out.

The cops are writing him up. We said, "What's the matter, Satchel?"

And this policeman said, "Are you Satchel Paige?"

He said, "I am."

James Colzie

"Well, I'm sorry."

So Syd asked him, "How much is the ticket?"

He said, "Twenty-five dollars."

He said, "I'll pay it."

Satchel told him, "Give him 50 'cause I'm coming back this way when I'm leaving." [Laughs]

Satchel was a really nice man. He told his chauffeur, "Slow down," and he opened the door. He took out about a hundred of those small boxes of raisins and we enjoyed 'em. He was just that type of a friend.

Would you play baseball again if you were a young man?

Yes, I would. I really would.

PITCHING RECORD

Year	Team, Lg	G	IP	W	L	PCT	H	BB	SO	ERA
1946	Atlanta, ind									
1947	Indianapolis, NAL									

Bunny Davis
Lexington Hustlers 1940s

Born June 9, 1917, Perryville, KY
Died May 10, 2001, Danville, KY
Ht. 6' Wt. 180 Batted and Threw Right

Bunny Davis came to the Hustlers from the Danville Yankees as a shortstop. He could not unseat the incumbent, so he moved to right field for a great career.

Back in the 1940s, the term "five-tool player" was not in use, but Davis, by all accounts, was one. He hit for average (newspaper accounts tell us that), he hit for power (he led his team in home runs), he could run (a race against Cool Papa Bell was suggested), he could throw (the best outfield arm plays in right field), and he could field (he took his infielder's fielding ability out there).

Perhaps he did not play in a recognized league, but he played against the best players that black baseball could offer: Josh, Satchel, Buck Leonard, Cool Papa, Jackie, Newk, and all the stars of the '40s.

He spent his non-baseball time as a youth recreation director in Danville, and for 28 years he served as the chief doorkeeper in the Kentucky House of Representatives.

***

Who owned the Hustlers?

DAVIS: Johnny Jackson. He owned an insurance company. And Oran Haskins.

The park was called Hustlers Park on Newtown Pike. I think there's houses and service stations there now. It was taken down somewhere in the '50s, when the majors begin to recruit the black boys. That was the fall of it.

How did you come to join the Hustlers?

I played baseball for the Danville Yankees. That was an independent baseball team. I had played a game against these guys and I played baseball all over the state of Kentucky. I started with Danville when I was in school in the '30s. Scoop Brown was the [Hustlers] manager at that time. He asked me to play for him.

Where did you bat in the lineup?

I usually batted around third and I bat-ted fourth some time, but mostly I batted second and third.

Do you know your batting averages?

I was a .3-something hitter. I have a photograph here that the Lexington paper took back in the '40s somewhere and it said the Hustlers' leading hitter was Bunny Davis. They showed three or four of us that were the highest hitters on the team.

Where did "Bunny" come from?

I got that from running. I was a running back on the football team. I was pretty fast; I ran a 9.6 and a 9.7 hundred. That was *world* speed back in those days.

They called me "Bunny Rabbit" where I used to duck and dodge. I didn't like that name "Bunny Rabbit." I was mad all the time they's callin' me that. The coach had to call me in and straighten me out. He told me, "That's an honor to you. They're callin' you 'Bunny Rabbit' 'cause that's the way you run on the football field."

So that's all they called me: "Bunny Rabbit, Bunny Rabbit, Bunny Rabbit." So they dropped the "Rabbit" and they started callin' me "Bunny." Now that's all I'm known by.

The doctor had told me to be in his office one time. He said, "I want you to be here at 11:00 because I've got to leave town at 11:15." So I got in his office around ten. He knew me real well and he and I were good friends.

So I kept sitting there and sitting there, waiting and waiting. Every now and then they'd holler, "William Davis." I never did move. So finally I got a little angry. I said, "Now these people are segregated against me. Discriminating against me. I'm going to talk to the boss."

I went and said, "I want to see the doctor." I said, "Doctor, you told me to be here at 11:00. I've been here ever since ten." I said, "I've had people come in and go out of this office, goin' and a-comin' and they've *never* called me."

That lady said, "Well, what's your name?"

I said, "My name is Bunny Davis."

"I don't have that down here. I've got a William Davis and I've been callin' him ever since 10:30. I came out there and you looked at me when I said William Davis but that was all you did: look at me."

I didn't even recognize my own name. [Laughs]

The Homestead Grays and other Negro league teams came through Lexington. How many games did the Hustlers play against those teams?

We played two or three times every year. Kansas City Monarchs, Homestead Grays, Birmingham Black Barons, Indianapolis Clowns. They had a great team back in those days, Indianapolis did. And New York Black Yankees and Memphis Red Sox.

So you saw all the big names in black baseball.

Not only did I see 'em, I played against 'em.

Josh Gibson was the greatest catcher I've ever seen. Like sittin' in a rockin' chair and throw you out at second base. He threw me out at second base from a rockin' chair and I had world-class speed. But he didn't do that no more 'cause that embarrassed me. I knew nobody could throw me out; I didn't think he could throw me out. But he did. When I got on first base it was automatic second 'cause I was gonna take it.

He was a big rascal. He weighed about 230-40 pounds. Hit that baseball! Hit it a mile and quarter. He could really hit. Oh, God. I've seen him hit 'em over the 400 foot mark and the ball was still flyin'. Ain't no tellin' how far he hit that baseball.

And he was a good guy. He mouthed at Satchel. Satchel didn't believe nobody could hit him, Josh Gibson didn't believe nobody could throw it by him.

Did you ever bat against Satchel?

Oh, yes. Satchel was the smartest pitcher you ever laid your eyes on. With nobody on base he'd tease you to death with that baseball. He'd throw a curve and it'd break four foot. It'd start off behind you and by the time you'd bail out it'd cut right over that plate. He could curve that ball!

Back in our days we called that a curveball and the one they threw up there and it dropped to the ground, we called that a drop. And one that broke in on a right-handed batter, we called that an in-shoot. We had some knuckleball pitchers, but not too many.

Who was the best pitcher you faced?

Satchel was the greatest pitcher I ever batted against and Josh Gibson was the greatest catcher I ever saw.

Do you remember Buck Leonard?

Buck Leonard was a *good* baseball player. Buck Leonard was on the same team as Josh Gibson and they used to come up in a big Cadillac. They'd drive around in a big blue Cadillac. He was a fine guy.

When ballplayers come in they liked to clown with the girls, you know. I hadn't been long married; I had to get back home. They'd say, "Man, why don't you stay and go with us?"

I'd say, "I got cows to milk." [Laughs] I didn't have no cows, but I'd tell 'em that to keep 'em off of me. The guys'd go out and stay all night and come back and play baseball the next day.

The *fastest* guy that I've ever seen was Cool Papa Bell. They tried to get him and I to hook up in a race but we never did get around to it. He was a speed man.

Who were some of the other great players you saw?

You name 'em and I played against 'em, but there was Don Newcombe and Jackie.

Jackie was a gentleman but he was a *mean* ballplayer. He didn't take no stuff off of *no*body. Man, when he came into second base you better be watchin' him. He'd cut you *all* to pieces. That's the way he played; he just played hard. He wasn't dirty now. He wasn't dirty; he just played hard. He was all business.

What was the general feeling when news of his signing by the Dodgers was made known?

Well, the black folks were all happy. When he come to Louisville or anywhere around here close, the black folks all went to the games. If he'd pop up they'd cheer like he hit one over the fence. [Laughs] He could really hit the baseball and he could run. He was a runnin' back at UCLA.

Some have said that he and Jim Thorpe were the two greatest athletes that America has ever produced.

I didn't see Jim Thorpe but I know Jackie was a great one.

I'll tell you another boy was a great athlete: that Willie Mays. He could tickle you to death catchin' a baseball. He came up here. They told us about him. He came to our park and he hit that baseball! He hit in the corners, he hit it over the corners, over the tops of the wall. And he could run like a deer. He wasn't as fast as Cool Papa. Cool Papa's the fastest man I saw in the old Negro league.

Did Henry Aaron come through here?

They snapped him up pretty soon but he could hit the ball. Always could hit. He had a whiplash sorta style of batting. Looks like he'd gone to sleep with the bat and when the baseball got up near the plate he woke up. [Laughs] He'd knock the dickens outta that baseball. He'd always act like he was asleep but don't you let that baseball get near that plate. He'd whiplash that bat around.

Does one incident stand out?

I was battin' against Don Newcombe. Newcombe, you know, could throw that ball 'bout a hundred miles an hour. And he was *throwin'* at me. I went out there and I told him, I said, "Now hear. You hit me and you're not gonna get out of Kentucky."

He said, "Who's gonna stop me?"

I said, "I am. Me and this bat." He's much bigger than me, you know.

He could *fire* that baseball. He never did hit me but he *was* throwin' at me. If you got a hit off of him and you came the next time you better be duckin', brother.

I always thought that was the dirtiest baseball in the world, them guys throwin' at you. They'd try to hurt you.

There was some more of those boys. The Kansas City Monarchs, they had two pitchers. They had a righthander and a lefthander. If you hit the righthander they'd bring in the lefthander. You hit the lefthander they'd bring in the righthander.

Was the righthander Hilton Smith?

I believe you're right. Hilton Smith. That sounds familiar to me.

Bunny Davis

Were you a power hitter?

Oh, yes. I was a power hitter. I led the [Danville] Yankees in home runs. A little ol' guy played third base; he was about five-foot-three, little fella. He was a good runnin' back in football, good at basketball; he was just a good athlete. He'd be second to me but if he'd been 20 pounds heavier he woulda beat me hittin' home runs.

Who were some of the others on the Hustlers?

One of the old-time Hustlers was a guy by the name of Dan Tye. He was a home run hitter. He was playin' when I was a boy. The Hustlers go way back.

Butch Glass was the manager when I left. He was a lefthanded pitcher in the old Negro American League. He was a good man. Scoop Brown is younger than me, maybe two or three years. Scoop was the manager when I was there. Great guy, loves to talk. Scoop was a great athlete.

How often did the Hustlers play?

We played every Tuesday, Wednesday, Thursday, Friday, Saturday, and Sunday, some double headers. I think we had a off day on Monday.

I was recreation director here in the city and I'd go over there and I'd be worn out when I'd get back home. I commuted back and forth from Danville. We played afternoon ball; we didn't have too much night ball.

What was the capacity of Hustler's Park?

I always felt like it was about 6-7,000. 'Course, they didn't have that many seats. They had 'em standin' all 'round the sidelines, down the right and left field lines. They were standin' all over the place.

How much were you paid?

I was gettin' 'round 'bout 500 a month. That was pretty good pay. Some of 'em may have gotten more.

The boy that won the most valuable player for the Hustlers two or three times was Chuck Settles. He was from California, I believe. He was a stompin' down good one. Man, I'll tell you! He was a catcher.

You know, you take a good catcher, a good shortstop, and good center fielder — that's the nucleus of a good ballclub. We had all three of 'em. The shortstop was Beaver Mason. Beaver Dam Mason. He was an all-state basketball player. I played against him. He was from Beaver Dam, Kentucky.

The center fielder for us was a guy by the name of Bill Barry. Bill "Dooley" Barry, widely known. He was a big boy. He hit that ball just about like Josh Gibson. He could really tattoo it, too.

I played right field most of the time. When I went up with them I was a shortstop, but it was gonna take a man as good as Pee Wee Reese to shoot Beaver Mason out of there.

And you got a white boy in there:

Bobby Flynn. Bobby was a hell of a ballplayer. His son is Doug Flynn. Doug used to come out and we'd have hitting practice. He'd get out there on second base and shortstop and field them balls. I used to tell him, I said, "Son, if you hit like your daddy you're goin' to the big leagues." And he went to the big leagues. Man, he'd get out there — and he was a little fella — and he'd dig them balls out.

His daddy, Bobby, was a *great* ballplayer. Great ballplayer.

We had another boy named Pete McCowan. He played with the Hustlers but he's never had any publicity. He started out with me when I was with the Yankees and I almost taught him to walk. Great athlete. Football player, baseball player, and basketball player. About six-two or three.

He was a pitcher and a *damn* good one. The [New York] Yankees sent a man in here to scout him durin' the Korean War. He fought in that war. Uncles fightin' uncles, brothers fightin' brothers. They broke in his barracks and he was sleepin' and he just knew he was gonna get killed. They wounded him but the Yankees were after him that year. Now he could throw that ball a hundred miles an hour. He had a curveball outta sight. Nice young man. He also played out in Canada. He came in the '50s after he got out of school. He's a good boy.

Was there much of an opportunity for any of the Hustlers to sign a professional contract?

Oh, yes. They tried to get them but most of them boys were like me. I was scared to death of an airplane. You couldn't throw me on an airplane.

After my playin' was over I was an umpire. I umpired up there in Aurora, Illinois, right near Chicago. They had some of the finest softball teams up there you ever seen in your life and they had me as one of the umpires. I called the championship game at the plate, so that shows you I had to be a pretty good umpire.

The point I'm tryin' to make to you is we're talkin' about travelin'. They sent me airfare. They had three guys from Kentucky for a four or five day tournament. They're playin' all day so they had a whole lotta umpires. So all these guys from Kentucky got plane fare.

They sent me plane fare. I was gonna call 'em and tell 'em I wasn't comin' but somebody said, "Man, drive up there. You can drive up in six-seven hours." So that's what I did.

I drove up there and the first day I got there they was waiting on me. I got there and they said, "Where you been? We're waitin' on you. We been out there waitin' for the plane to come in and you wasn't on none of those planes."

I said, "I drove up here."

"Drove up here! You're scheduled to call the first game at the plate."

I called the ballgame and that's when they made the schedule out. They scheduled me for the last game.

I had *never* seen guys throw a softball like that. Lord have mercy, I'm tellin' you. I had never seen any better pitchers. Them guys was curvin' that ball, droppin' it, throwin' it to you and it'd break up. I was a good hitter and I wanted to bat against some of them guys. I said, "There ain't no use me battin' against 'em. They're gonna make a monkey out of me."

We had a guy named Sturgill. He was an All-American. That guy — Lord! — it was just a Christmas present to get behind that plate and watch him throw that softball. He dipped *real* low when he was pitchin'. He threw his right arm up in the air and he almost hit the ground with that ball when he delivered.

I went to Mayo Clinic on an airplane but I was scared to death. When I got off I kissed the ground. [Laughs] I said, "You'll never catch me on this thing no more." The girl dropped a bag of ice and I liked to jump outta one of them windows. [Laughs]

If you were a young man, would you be a base-
*   ball player again?*

Oh, yes. I made more money in baseball than I did in anything. I was recreation
director and I worked on the playground
from 8:00 in the morning until 'bout four
in the afternoon.

No records available

Ross "Satchel" Davis

Baltimore Elite Giants 1940
New York Black Yankees 1940
Cleveland Buckeyes 1943, 1947
Boston Blues 1946

BORN JULY 28, 1918, GREENVILLE, MS
HT. 6'1" WT. 160 BATTED AND THREW RIGHT

Look at the record of Tim Salmon. Look at Eric Karros. Year-in and year-out these guys produce superior numbers. They are important members of their teams. Yet neither has ever been selected for an All-Star game. They must wonder what a fellow has to do.

Ross Davis can sympathize. He was also never selected to play in an East-West game, the Negro leagues' version of the All-Star game. He had an overpowering fastball and a sharp curve and impressed Satchel Paige so much that Satchel gave him his nickname.

A tall, thin righthander, Davis was highly regarded by his opponents if not by the all-star selectors. Josh Gibson hit the only home run Davis ever gave up and Luke Easter only had one hit off of him. Bob Boyd, who just did not strike out, fanned three times in one game against Davis.

His name might be better known today if his unnecessarily short career had not been plagued with health problems.

How did you get the nickname "Satchel"?

DAVIS: Satchel gave me that name when he came through St. Louis. He called me "Junior" and he used to come through and pick an all-star team to play against the semipro white team across the river in Belleville, Illinois, and his thing was he pitched the first three innings and I would relieve him and then another guy would relieve me.

I was warming up gettin' ready to go in the fourth, and he came down and wanted to know who was this young fella throwin' these salt tablets. They said, "That's Ross Davis." He said, "Well, he throws the ball harder'n me."

Of course, the guys didn't have any idea they were gonna hit Satchel, so they knew that we were comin' behind Satchel. They started grittin' their teeth, taking their vicious practice swings, and Satchel with his big mouth said, "No need for you so-and-so's diggin' in. That's my son out there. He throws the ball harder'n I do." [Laughs]

The newspapers took it up, started to call me "Satchel Paige" Davis and then they reduced it to "Satchel" Davis, and "Young Satchel" and all that stuff.

33

Was that your start in baseball?

No. The other game in St. Louis used to be a game they called corkball. It was one strike you were out, one foul tip you were out. They had a foul line parallel to home plate. You could play with two men or three, but most times it was a pitcher and a catcher. That game was pretty popular and my cousin and I were pretty good at that.

Somebody saw us playing and asked about playin' ball. They didn't even have uniforms or anything. We told 'em, "Yeah, we'll play," 'cause we played all day. So we went down there. They had a pretty good little ol' team down there. Other teams come down there to practice on us and left there limpin'.

My cousin, he caught for me, but he really wasn't strong enough to catch me because I didn't even know I could throw that ball that hard. But after I got started there, we really had a pretty good team.

Then a uniformed team was down there and they saw me and they raided our team. They took three of us with them the next year. The team broke up because the general manager stole all their money. What happened, he hit upon a beautiful idea it seemed to us. Instead of us collectin' our little four or five dollars after each game, he would put it in the bank for us and then at the end of the season we'd have some money. At that time, you know, you played the game 'cause you loved it. So that sounded good. One Sunday we had a game and we all congregated at his house and he had moved. [Laughs]

So then I went with a team called the St. Louis Blue Sox to finish out the season with them.

Back in the Depression times in '36, a friend of mine was workin' at the steel mill. In fact, he played on that first team. He lived up the street from my mother and he tells me, "Look, they're gonna be hiring. They're gonna sponsor a baseball team and if you can make the team you can get a job

at the steel mill." That sounded good, so he said, "I'm on the seven-to-three shift." He gave me carfare to come out there and he was gonna bring me back home. Carfare I think was 15 cents; he gave me 50 cents. [Laughs]

I was walkin' around with 50 cents in my pocket and an old guy saw me standin' on the corner. A pitiful ol' man and he said, "Son, I haven't had anything to eat in three days. You got any money to buy me a hamburger or hotdog or somethin'?"

Someone had told me to never give a guy the money. If he was really hungry, offer to buy him a sandwich or somethin'. So right up the street was a place I'll never forget called the Star Restaurant. For 15 cents you could get a big plate of liver and onions and rice, biscuits, and refills on your coffee, so I said, "Come on over here." I figured if I gave him 15 cents I would still have 35 cents and I could get back home. I figured I could catch Woodrow on the way back and ride back home with him.

But anyway, we go up there and the guy inhaled that first plate. I felt so sorry for him I asked him, "You got enough?" He said, "Well, no, son. Like I told you, I ain't eat in a long time." So I just spent the rest of it on him.

So then, naturally, I couldn't go out to the steel mill. So when Woody came back that evenin' he said, "Man, I had the man all set to give you a job. He hired somebody else." I told him what happened. He said, "You're a fool."

But anyway, I went out later to try out for the team and I made the team and I did get a job. It didn't last long.

At that time there was a league in St. Louis out in Tandy Park, out in front of Sumner High School, a black high school. They had a mini league out there, four teams. So we, the first year, ended up in second place. But in '38 and '39 we won the championship. In '39 was when I really came to myself.

That job at the steel mill didn't last long. I was laid off. I was practicin' every day and by that time I was gettin' a little attention. I was the number one pitcher for the east-west game, they called it. I walked the bases loaded in the first inning. Nobody out. The catcher came out and asked me, "Man, your curveball is breakin' so wide. What you wanna do?"

I said, "You know more about it than I do." He had played fast semipro ball.

He said, "Your fastball is really jumpin'. You wanna throw fastballs?"

I said, "What do you think?"

He said, "Yeah, let's go with the fastball."

So I struck out the side.

A man from Mexico was in the stands, so that winter I got a letter from Mexico. $125 a month, man. Damn! [Laughs] So I went down there, but I was chasin' the broads and drinkin' beer. They sent me a hundred dollars and when I went across the border I had so much money I couldn't put it in all my pockets. I changed it over.

That man didn't want to see me down there playin' with all those Mexican girls, so I came on back. In Monterrey I met a guy from the Baltimore Elites. Wild Bill Wright. He said, "Why are they gettin' rid of you?"

I said, "I don't know." But I did know. Like I said, I was gettin' all the headlines. I was strikin' out everybody.

He said, "I'm gonna call Mr. [Tom] Wilson. He owns the Baltimore Elites. I'm gonna tell him about you."

By the time I got home I got a telegram to come to Nashville and meet the team, the Baltimore Elites, in Nashville. I went down there and made the team.

I was sick, though, and they got rid of me. I pitched a no-hitter against the Newark Eagles. My record was 2-and-nothin' when I left there. I was there about a couple of months at the most.

And then the Black Yankees picked me up and I ended the season with them. But I was sick and I came back home. I stayed in St. Louis the next two years.

I don't think the Elites treated me fairly because I was doing everything for them. Relieving. In the season opener I came in and relieved and shut the team—the Philadelphia Stars—down and then the next day I pitched in the second game of the double header and went the route.

Then Decoration Day in 1940 I pitched a no-hitter against the Newark Eagles. That's when they had Willie Wells and [Lenny] Pearson, Monte Irvin—all those guys. You would've thought that they would have put me under a doctor's care and kept me, but it wasn't like that.

But I came home after the 1940 season and got well, went back to my old team. By that time I did have a steady job workin' at a steel mill. The same place. By that time I was such a good player that layoffs didn't bother me at all. They were gonna keep me regardless.

Sam Jethroe had told Wilber Hayes of the Buckeyes about me. Sam told him, "There's a guy in St. Louis can throw the ball harder than Satchel." They was tryin' to win the championship in the Negro American League, so Wilbur Hayes came all the way out to St. Louis to talk to me, but me with my loyal self I wouldn't leave the team 'cause we had a championship game comin' up in the little league out there. But he gave me a contract right then and there and asked me to sign it for the following year, '43. So I signed it.

I went out there in '43, had a good year and went in the service in November of '43. It was rumored that I was gonna go with Jethroe to the [Boston] Red Sox for a tryout. He went, but I was goin' under the Golden Gate Bridge the day we was supposed to be in Fenway Park.

I stayed over there and went all through the service and then got sick over there. Hepatitis, which I still have. It was so bad the guys were dyin' like flies over there with hepatitis. I was supposed to be a bed patient but whenever I could I'd sneak out and go to the latrine. It was nothin' to see a big bucket of livers cut out where guys had died.

When I got discharged, at my induction center they looked at my record and they wanted to send me to medical school. I had been a medical technician in the service. I picked up a Bronze Star for some reason. I don't know. But anyway, they wanted to send me to school to really be a real medical technician, but I told 'em, "Man, just let me outta here. I've had it with the Army. It messed up two years of my life."

There was an old man down in southeast Illinois — out of Cairo, Illinois — named Allen Johnson. Rich. He owned, I imagine, half of southern Illinois. [Laughs] He come there, I think they said, with 50 cents in his pocket from Memphis. They called him "Memphis." That was his nickname. He got in a crap game and pretty soon he had all that property down there. And he *loved* baseball so he wanted a baseball team. He heard that I was back home.

Man, I was enjoyin' my musterin'-out pay and I'd been sick for six months, so I was havin' a ball. One of the ballplayers in my hangout said, "Say, Allen Johnson wants to talk to you."

I said, "For what?"

"He wants you to play ball."

"I can't play no ball. They told me that when I left my induction. They showed me right here: 'No more baseball for you.'" I said, "I don't care. I'll find somethin' else to do." I told him, "I can't play no ball."

So the next couple of days he walked back in and said, "I'm gonna play with him but he keeps tellin' me he wants to see you."

I said, "Man, I can't play no ball."

He said, "Well, look. He sent me ten dollars to give you." It didn't cost but three dollars to go down there. "Why don't you just ride down there."

So I rode down there with him. Em-mett Wilson was his name. Mr. Johnson had a big ol' barn of a place, supposed to be a nightclub. When we got there he wasn't there. He always smoked big cigars and drank Canadian Club. That was his drink.

We went and sat at the bar. When he came in, he came over and he spoke to us. He told Emmett, "Come on upstairs. I wanna talk with you. I know I'm gonna have trouble with Davis here."

So Emmett came back down. He said, "Man, I don't know how much he's gonna offer you, but he offered me $350 a month."

Mr. Johnson told the barmaid, "Honey, give Davis my bottle and two glasses to bring up here." His office was upstairs. So I go up there.

He pulls out two big shots. He says, "Emmett says you don't wanna play ball."

I said, "No, I didn't say I don't *want* to play, but the Army doctors say I can't play. I was in the hospital for six months with hepatitis and I'll die with hepatitis."

He said, "Davis, do you remember a game you pitched in 1939 when you loaded the bases up and here come Luke Easter and Sam Jethroe and Jesse Askew?"

I said, "Yeah."

"What did you do?"

I said, "I struck 'em out." [Laughs]

"I said then and there if I ever have a team, you would be on it. Now you say you can't play. I'm gettin' a team up and they're trainin' down in Alexandria, Louisiana. I want you and Emmett to get on that train tonight and go down there."

I said, "But I can't play."

He said, "I heard what you said. I want you to go down there and help Tom coach the pitchers."

So I figured I'd go down there. What the hell.

I was showin' a guy how to pitch from the stretch down in the bullpen. I threw the ball to Chester Gray, who was catchin'. He said, "Damn, man, I need to get my sponge. You're throwin' that ball awful hard."

I said, "What? I wasn't tryin' to throw it hard."

That put a little bug under my butt, so the next day when we got through I asked Chester if he could stay behind with me after everybody left. I wanted to see. So I loosened up real good. He said, "You're throwin' bb's." [Laughs]

So then we had a game with the New York Black Yankees that Sunday. I asked Tom Parker, who was the manager, "Who's pitchin' Sunday?"

He said, "You're the pitchin' coach. What do you think?"

I said, "How 'bout me startin'?"

He said, "You mean that?"

So I pitched the first three innin's, struck out seven men.

Mr. Johnson came down with a blank contract. I made more money with him than I made with anybody. I had a pretty good year.

That was when Branch Rickey was tryin' to compete with the Negro American and National leagues; they called it the United States League. We were called the Boston Blues. There was the Boston Blues, the Pittsburgh Crawfords, and Cleveland Clippers and Brooklyn Brown Bombers or somethin' like that. But the only two teams that was any good was our team and Pittsburgh. In fact, we played off for the championship up at Montreal.

They wore me out because I *had* to make an appearance everywhere we went. I never had a sore arm, but my arm was dead as a doornail. I don't know how many innin's I must have pitched that year 'cause I could pitch a nine-inning game tonight and go somewhere else and had to do somethin'. If any pitcher got in trouble they asked me to relieve and all that stuff. I got so I didn't have any feelin' in my arm. [Laughs]

Next day I was almost on the verge of quittin' then 'cause I had taken a job in Cleveland and I looked in the paper and saw that the Buckeyes were openin' up the sea-son in 1947. Me and Sam Jethroe had been pretty close and I went down just to talk to him. He saw me walk in with civilian clothes on. "What the hell you doin' with that shit on, man? You ain't playin'?"

So he went over to Quincy Trouppe and said, "Looka there. You got a pitcher over there."

So Trouppe carried me down to the bullpen and I hadn't had my hand on a ball since September, but he liked what he saw. I left there with 'em when they left.

I had a pretty good year. I lost one ballgame. I did happen to pitch in the Negro World Series against the New York Cubans. '47.

I didn't go back. I got so I was havin' terrible headaches. So I gave it up. I was 28. I've second-guessed myself 'cause the Newark Eagles and the Monarchs begged me. I got telegram after telegram wantin' me to come back with them.

But I was pretty well fed up with baseball. I had some pretty bad experiences.

When I left I worked with General Motors for a while. I drove a bus for Cleveland for a while. Ended up workin' at the post office as a clerk.

Like I say, I had the bad headaches. Developed ulcers. They were tension headaches. Started off with migraines, then I graduated to histamines. What they called cluster headaches. Every spring and fall you could bet I was gonna be sick.

Cool Papa used to tell me I didn't get the ink. Josh Gibson and Cool Papa — you'd hear them talk and you'd swear nobody ever need pick up a ball 'round me. I wasn't that good, but to hear them talk. Josh would tell me all the time, "Why don't you come over to a team that appreciates you? Them guys over there are jealous of you 'cause you got more on the ball. You can pitch drunk better than they can sober."

Did Josh ever take you out?

One time. He was the only one, too. I

never thought about that 'til after I quit playin'. One guy called me one day, said, "Did you ever wonder why nobody ever carried you except Josh?"

I said, "I never thought about it." I played against Buck [Leonard], Monte Irvin, and Pep Young and all them guys. I know I used to break up bats.

This guy had caught me a few times. He said, "Did you ever notice I had tape on my wrists whenever you pitched? Man, your ball was heavy. You had a dead ball." [Laughs] "Catchin' your ball was like catchin' a shot put or somethin'."

I didn't know that. If somebody asked me how to throw a heavy ball I wouldn't even know how to tell 'em. One reason I figured out why most everything I threw moved — see, I didn't have big hands like a lotta guys. I had real strong hands. The ball naturally had more room to move comin' outta my hand than it did outta guys with big hands 'cause some guys could cover a whole baseball. I was just coverin' 'bout half of it. I used to get calluses on my fingertips and that's why my ball really moved all the time.

But I never thought about it. I think it was Josh one time in Pittsburgh, he took his best cut at the ball and the bat just busted. [Laughs] He hit a short fly to the shortstop.

A guy called and said, "This guy is throwin' 95. What do you think you would get?"

I said, "I don't know." [Laughs]

I was never chosen for the East-West game, no matter what I did. That was one thing that started gettin' down on it. The same guys would go all the time. No way Sam Jethroe shouldn't have gone to the East-West game, but, hell, they knew who was gonna play in May.

And me, in '43, I betcha I maybe won 'bout 19 or 20 ballgames altogether and lost maybe one or two. I can remember two I lost. That's 'bout all. But I was just fed up with it really.

I don't wanna be quoted, buy like I told you, everybody knew who was gonna play. You could bet Satchel was gonna be there, and Hilton Smith. Hilton Smith, to me, was one of the best pitchers I ever seen. And Buck, Josh, Monte Irvin. All the guys that had the marquee names, you know.

Okay, Cool Papa, Monte Irvin, Satchel, Hilton Smith, Buck, Buck O'Neil — all those guys already had names. But, see, there were other guys just as good. They could've put a little ink on them and that'd made it that much better.

I pitched a game against Dan Bankhead just before he went to the Dodgers. I beat him, 5-to-1. Struck out Bob Boyd so many times he had the umpire look at the ball. He got me thrown out of the game, too.

I beat 'em, 5-to-1. The newspaper came out that weekend with about six paragraphs about the game and five or 'em was all about Dan Bankhead. I had about three lines: Davis struck out so many men, gave up such-and-such hits.

That was another thing that disgusted me. Bob Boyd came up with two men out in the ninth innin'. Oh, man, I had a curveball that day! And you talk about throwin' a salt tablet! I was throwin' one. [Laughs]

So every time I'd get ready to pitch, Bob would call time. He claimed I was cutting the ball. And the umpire, of course, a Memphis man, made me throw the balls. Quincy Trouppe was my manager and Quincy said, "Every time they throw you a new ball, throw it over here to me." I kept doin' that. Every time I'd get ready to throw, Bob would call time and the umpire would throw me a new ball and I'd throw it in the dugout to Quincy. So finally he just threw me outta the game. Somebody relieved me and got the last man out.

All that kinda stuff just got me disgusted.

You mentioned Wild Bill Wright earlier. Should he be in the Hall of Fame?

You now, I never saw Wild Bill play, but from what they tell me about him he should be. I met him in Monterrey — he was playin' with Monterrey — and I was on my way home from Mexico City. I heard about him. But I never had the pleasure of seein' him play.

You pitched a no-hitter and you faced some great hitters. What do you consider your biggest thrill?

Well, let's see. I think I would have to say … we were playin' the Memphis Red Sox in Belleville, Illinois, on the eve of my 25th birthday. Parnell Woods said, "I'm gonna give you a good birthday present. I'm gonna let you pitch in front of your hometown. Guess who you're pitchin' against." He said, "Keyes."

Now Keyes, he had a good fastball, but it was straight as a string and he had never lasted over three innings against us all the year. So he said, "This should be easy for you."

Let me tell you, he threw hard, but that night he was throwin' bullets. You know, for a long time we were trailin', 1-to-nothin'. Finally, Jethroe got on, stole second and third, and came home on a fly ball and tied the game up. And it stayed tied. I don't know how we got that one run but we won the game, 2-to-1. That was in front of my hometown.

Luke Easter was playin' with the Red Sox. I struck him out three times. [Laughs] I walked for some reason and he said, "Hey, homey, don't be so damn hard on me, man. Gimme a break."

I said, "Hell, man, not hardly." [Laughs] I would think that was the most satisfyin' game, I guess.

What about Luke Easter? Does he belong in the Hall of Fame?

I don't know. When I saw Luke up there hittin' all them home runs, I said,

"How did that happen?" You know? I pitched him high and tight with a good fastball 'cause I had a good fastball. Luke got one hit off of me and that was in '47 when he was with the Clowns. Around home he'd hit a loud foul off of me. [Laughs] I know he could hit a ball a long way, but you had to pitch him up high and tight. But you had to have somethin' on the ball; you couldn't just throw a fastball up there. You had to have somethin' on it. [Laughs]

If you were a young man, would you be a ballplayer again?

I don't think I'd wanna pitch. I see they're gonna let the strike zone come back.

Look here, man, all that armor that they're wearing up there! We had a good remedy for that. We were playin' some team up in Schenectady, New York — I think it was the Black Yankees — and there were times when I would be wild. Sometime my ball would move so much. I came in close to this guy a couple of times and he looked out there. He was known to be a redneck anyway. I came close to him and before I could apologize he made a threatening gesture. I think [Eggie] Clarke was catchin' and they said, "Throw him the goddamn ball, man!" So I stood out there with that ball in my hand and that kinda changed his mind. [Laughs]

They took *all* the pitcher's weapons. Can't throw inside, but they can lean all over the damn plate. They're gonna stand on the inside and lean over the outside. Hell, I gotta have *some* of the plate. Damn. [Laughs]

I got people wanna take me to ballgames and they can't understand why I don't wanna go. They've priced the good fans out of baseball. In our time you could get you a cooler, take a beer and some peanuts, sandwich, and go to the ballpark. But, no-no. You can't do anything like that now. A hot dog costs three dollars and somethin'. It's only the fat cats that's goin' to the ballgames now and they're throwin' beer all over

Ross Davis (Photograph courtesy of Ross Davis.)

It tickles me when they say "quality start." He pitch five innin's, just long enough to get credit for the win. Jesus Christ, man! It took a act of Congress to get us out of the ballgame. The manager'd be halfway scared to come out there. [Laughs] If I was pitchin' a good game — a tight ballgame — and the manager'd take me out, he'd hear it all up and down the line; "Let him lose his own damn game." When that man handed you that ball, that was yours 'til the last man was out.

And then you didn't hear about people gettin' hurt *all* the time. They go through all this weight-liftin' and the other stuff. You don't need that in baseball. We ran *every* day except my day to pitch. Every day I ran around the park, two or three times sometimes. A pitcher needs legs. I never was tired. My arm never hurt 'cause I didn't have that strain on my arm 'cause I was usin' legs and torso, upper torso. I never did have a sore arm. That runnin' was it. Day after you pitched you took a couple of laps around the park, played a little pepper. That third day you pitched a round of battin' practice. Then the *next* day, that was your ball. The man come there with that ball in the box and take it out and rub it up for you and say, "May I present you this beautiful ball from Mr. Spaldin'." [Laughs]

If I really told it like it was — I don't wanna take any glamour away from anybody; right now they're really gettin' the recognition — but a whole lot went down in that baseball that was just not right.

I was livin' up in Berkeley and the phone rang one morning and I picked it up and he said, "Let me speak to Ross Davis."

He said, "Hi, you don't know me, but my name is Larry Lester. I've been lookin'

you. They started caterin' to them people and shrinkin' the strike zone. They don't wanna see no 1-to-nothin' ballgames, or 2-1 ballgames. They wanna see a whole bunch of home runs. So the real fans are sittin' here like me, watchin' it on TV. [Laughs]

And what they're payin' these ballplayers! Good Lord! The owners are paying because a long time ago a ballplayer was a piece of meat. The kept you 'til you couldn't produce anymore and then, "Bye, get the hell away from here," you know.

Now here's a guy with a six earned run average gettin' six million dollars. [Laughs] They gotta do somethin' pretty damn soon. I can't understand. What you wanna sign a guy for ten years for? Look at Albert Belle.

at all these conventions and reunions and those guys gettin' all those accolades, but I don't see your name anywhere. I just happened to stumble across your name and what's wrong with you?"

I said, "I don't know. I guess they just forgot me."

He said, "You won't be forgotten long."

And, sure 'nough, I started gettin' these invitations. He's my champion. If it don't be for him I'll be still out there.

I wasn't a popular guy, except with other teams. Josh used to tell me, "Man, we talk about you *all* the time. You got somethin' on the ball."

He made me go home one night. I was sittin' around drinkin' with some of my teammates and Josh come down to this after-hours joint in Cleveland. He said, "What the hell. What are you doin' down here, you little son of a bitch?"

"What does it look like I'm doin'?"

He said, "You know what you're doin' tomorrow?"

I said, "What?"

"You pitchin' against the Grays."

"So what?"

"It's the Homestead Grays, man! We're the hardest-hittin' team in baseball and you're down here drinkin' with these fools. I'm gonna carry your ass outside and get you a cab."

I'm a grown man but the man's tellin' me right. So he carried me downstairs and that's when he started givin' me a lecture. One of the guys had pitched against 'em in League Park that day and got bombed. He said, "They know that they can't pitch like you, so he's gonna see that you get your so-and-so ass drunk and pitchin' against us tomorrow at Pittsburgh, so you can get your ass kicked, too. We talk about you all the time. We'd rather face any of the son of bitches than you. And you're better-lookin' than all of them other mother-fuckers, too." [Laughs]

So he put me in a cab and I went on back to the Majestic Hotel. Those two

drinks I'd had loosened me up, boy. I was hard on the Grays the next day. We were goin' out after the game and Josh caught up with me, said, "You son of a bitch, I should've left your ass in that place." [Laughs] And he hit me and said, "Good goin', homey. You a bad boy."

The score was 'round about 6-4 or somethin' like that. I didn't shut 'em out, but I had it when I needed it.

Everybody was scared of Josh and Buck, but the boy who would comb my hair was Jerry Benjamin. Good God almighty, he didn't care what I threw! He told me, "I don't give a damn if you throw it out your ass, I'm gonna hit it." And he's hittin' 'em all line drives right back through the box. [Laughs] I could not get that clown out. I don't know what his battin' average was against me. It had to be in the .700s, though.

I can't understand how come Ray Brown ain't in the Hall of Fame. And when he wasn't pitching he was out there in that outfield and he could hit that ball as far as Josh or Buck. I never saw anybody beat him. Like I say, he didn't get the ink.

Jerry Benjamin, I thought he was a hell of a ballplayer. When they sent out that survey wantin' to pick the best ballplayer that I've seen I picked Buck. Most everybody else was in agreement with me. I thought Buck was great, but Ray Brown, I used to look at him and say, "That boy, he's somethin' else."

We played a game against 'em and he played right field and I think he had about 3-out-of-4, a couple of home runs and stuff like that. He was tough.

Hilton Smith, he deserves to be up there. I first saw him in the St. Louis area, relieved Satchel against the Chicago American Giants. I was sittin' there in right field and you could see that curveball from way out there. And threw the ball just as hard as Satchel.

Satchel didn't have no curveball. He

had a little wrinkle, but you know what Satchel's forte was? Control. He could throw that ball *any*where he wanted to. I've seen him. Throw the ball over a matchbox and stuff like that. He could throw that ball anywhere he wanted to. Anywhere.

That's what a lotta pitchers don't know.

It's not how hard you throw. If you can throw the ball close to where it's supposed to be thrown, you can get by. How often do you see Maddux throw in the 90s? He's throwin' the ball where he wants to throw it.

PITCHING RECORD

Year	Team, Lg	G	IP	W	L	Pct	SO	BB	H	ERA
1940	Balt., NNL			2	0	1.000				
	NYBY, NNL									
1943	Cleve., NAL			19	2	.905				
1944–45			Military service							
1946	Boston, USL									
1947	Cleve., NAL			5	1	.833				

Clifford DuBose

Birmingham Black Barons/ Memphis Red Sox 1958

BORN JULY 16, 1937, MONTEVALLO, AL
HT. 5'5" WT. 165 BATTED AND THREW RIGHT

Clifford DuBose played in the Negro leagues for only one season, but he spent a lot longer with baseball. He played and coached sandlot and semipro ball for more than 20 years.

As a result of his community service, he was honored by the local Little League and the city of Birmingham.

How did you get into professional baseball?

DuBose: I played sandlot baseball, so I went to the Brooklyn Dodgers training camp in Vero Beach, Florida. That was when I got out of high school. That was in '57. I wasn't in shape; I hurt my leg and I came back home. Raymond Haggins got me to go play with the Memphis Red Sox. I was with them about three months.

We went 'round and played all down in Mississippi and then played in New York and New Jersey. We were comin' back in July and we were gonna play in Birmingham. Some of the older players that had played with Memphis had went up and they cut 'em. They cut 'bout six of us from the Memphis Red Sox.

I played with Birmingham for a while and they cut me, too. That's why I went to the Memphis Red Sox. I played for about a year.

I played left field and I played third base some, too. I was hittin' 'bout .270 when I was playin' with Memphis.

Does a game stand out?

We was playin' down in Spartandale,

Mississippi. Haggins and I, we had got some new bats and I went 4-for-4 that night. I really remember that. We won the game.

Did any pitch give you trouble?

The curveball. I started hittin' the curveball when I came back and started playin' in the industrial league in Birmingham. I played there for about six years.

Who were some of the players you played with?

I played with Charley Pride. There was Jessie Mitchell and James Ivory. We called him "Sap"; his nickname was "Sap."

Who was the best player you saw?

Let me see. It was quite a few of 'em. Charley Pride, he was a good pitcher.

What are your memories of the travel?

In '58 when I was there, we traveled on the bus and stayed at the motel. They had a motel there in Memphis, their own motel. We rode the bus. That's how I got to know Charley Pride. He was sittin' in the back playin' the guitar.

I didn't know too much. I sat around and listened to the baseball players that was older than I was — how they came out and

Clifford DuBose

how they'd go in restaurants. We didn't go in restaurants much. When we was playin' they'd give us two dollars a day for meals and we would chip in and buy baloney and bread and drinks. That's what we had to do when we was travelin' around. Not many restaurants would accept us.

What was your salary?

I think I got one check for 'round about $200. I got outta high school in '57 and that was in '58. I was 19, 20 years old.

How did the older players accept you?

Well, they accepted me. I got in with 'em and I out-hit lots of 'em. They accepted me. Lots of 'em were teaching me how to hit and everything like that. They were pretty good to me. Raymond Haggins and Eddie Lee Reed, those were two that helped me. I would be with them most all the

time. Raymond Haggins was my room-mate.

What did you do when you left professional baseball?

I came back home and got a job and then I managed sandlot baseball for about 20 years. Boys just gettin' out of high school and some older boys. We had a baseball team around here and we would go to Birmingham, Bessemer, Montgomery, and all places like that. I was playin', too.

Do you have any regrets from your baseball days?

I just regret I didn't come along at the right time. After they cut me I didn't forget about baseball, but I just didn't never go out and try no more, not for the major leagues. I got discouraged.

If you were a young man would you play baseball again?

Yeah. I tell all of 'em right now if I could go back and know what I know now, that's what I would put most of my time in at. In sports and baseball. It's a great opportunity. I know good and well I could do better than some of them what they got up there now playin'.

Did any of your children play?

I got four. I had one try to play. I don't know. They just didn't get interested in baseball. I was talkin' 'bout it the other day. We used to have around here in this little ol' town of Montevallo, where I stayed, we used to have 'round about five teams. Now they can't even get nine baseball players just to play a game.

I think drugs got a lot to do with it. I used to have a team every year and I would have 'bout 15 or 16 young boys and then they got involved in that drugs. I spent my money with 'em. We used to have to sell beer and sandwiches and things like that to buy our uniforms and I was workin' and I spent lots of my money, too. But then a young fella come into town and he got with 'em and they started smokin' that pot and stuff.

We was down at Tuscaloosa down there playin' the Tuscaloosa Yellowjackets down there, and they were smokin' that. When we got through playin' I told 'em, I said, "That's it. Y'all can have it. I'm givin' it up. Y'all don't wanna listen. You can't play baseball smokin' that weed."

BATTING RECORD

Year	Team, Lg	G	AB	R	H	2B	3B	HR	RBI	BA
1958	Birm/Mem, NAL									.270

Lionel Evelyn
New York Cubans 1949
New York Black Yankees 1955
Kansas City Monarchs 1959

BORN JUNE 8, 1929, NEW YORK, NY
HT. 5'9" WT. 160 BATTED AND THREW RIGHT

Lionel Evelyn grew up in New York City with another kid who turned out to be a pretty good ballplayer, too. It was Jim Robinson. They went to school together until high school, when their paths diverged. Evelyn got into professional ball almost by accident; friends asked if he wanted to play on a team coached by the great ballplayer John Beckwith.

From there he was asked to join the New York Cubans in 1949, where he played for a portion of the season. His baseball career was put on a back burner after that, as he joined the Navy and served four years in the Korean War. In 1955, he joined the Indianapolis Clowns on the recommendation of friends, but soon left that team and joined the New York Black Yankees. That was his only full season and he posted a 19-7 record for the two teams.

He again left baseball, this time to work, but the lure of the game remained with him. In 1959 he staged a minor comeback with the Kansas City Monarchs. The league was dying then and the younger players were being signed to minor league contracts. Now 30 years old, he left the game again and went to work with the post office, where he stayed for 37 years.

An interesting note about Evelyn: he played baseball righthanded but he is lefthanded at everything else.

How did you get started in baseball?

EVELYN: As a kid I played around the street. My family came from the islands and my father didn't have any interest in it. He had interest in cricket and things like that. My interest was mainly from my friends I grew up with.

When World War II started we got our chance in the parks because the older fellas — you know, they dominated the diamonds — they left. Then we went out and there and we played.

You joined the New York Cubans when you were 20.

First of all, I played with a team called the Brooklyn Royal Giants. It was coached by John Beckwith; he played in the [Negro] leagues. As kids, we were playing in Central Park and when the war ended they all came back and a lot of players didn't go back to baseball. Jobs were plentiful then around the city. They got older and a lot of them were obligated with their jobs.

I was called one day and one fella said, "Do you wanna go and play with these guys?

46

They want us to play a game. They're gonna pay us."

We didn't know what it was all about. We didn't care; we just liked to go play. They'd take us out and we'd play games out on the [Long] island, like Cedarhurst and New Hyde Park. We played around the area.

Most of the fellas on the team through Beckwith was workin' for Emerson Radio. I went with them one night and I pitched and I was offered a job with Emerson Radio. We was in an industrial league then. I had no idea about the Negro league. I knew about them but I didn't figure they would ever bother with me.

I come to find out a lot of those fellas on the team were from the league, but they settled down because jobs were plentiful then. TV just started and Emerson Radio hired a lot of those players and they played in the industrial league. They took me on and I stayed a year with them and then some of those older fellas said they were gonna go out to Canada and play with Satchel Paige.

I had no idea about those things. I had never left home. Anyway, I took a chance and I went to Cleveland and they folded. They couldn't get off the ground. I came back home and Beckwith still had his team. We stayed in the city and just played around the area. We didn't travel anywhere.

They wouldn't hire me back at Emerson so I played with Beckwith for a while and then he told me, "You know, you can pitch in the league if you like."

He sent me down to a man named [Winfield] Welch. He was the manager [of the Cubans] and he took me on. I stayed about a half a year with them and at the end of the year [Alejandro] Pompez, the owner, said that he's not gonna play anymore, they're losin' money since Jackie got called in.

I want to mention that inspired me: Lyman Bostock at first base; Pat Scantlebury, a pitcher; Impo "Skinny" Barnhill, a

Lionel Evelyn (**Photograph courtesy of Lionel Evelyn.**)

pitcher; Paul Lopez, a pitcher; Pee Wee Jenkins, a pitcher.

So the next year the Korean War started and I was gone. While I was gone a lot of my friends, they went and played. I joined the Navy and I spent four years. After that, I came back and I went to the Indianapolis Clowns. In '54 they told [Syd] Pollack and Bunny Downs about me. In the beginning of '55 they sent the contract to me and I went on with them. The team was loaded with players. Some guys didn't get a chance to play.

A lot of my friends was with the Black Yankees and they said, "Tell them you wanna come over here."

Lionel Evelyn (Photograph courtesy of Lionel Evelyn.)

I still didn't know what it was all about with the contract. I guess they owned everything — Pollack and Ed Hamman. But I asked to go over and I stayed with the Black Yankees. I had fun with my friends over there.

After the year was over I just didn't go back. I couldn't get by livin' in New York and the rent and things like that. I just couldn't make it. My parents were sayin', "What're you gonna do? Baseball doesn't keep you goin'."

At times I had a feelin' to go back. It was hard gettin' a job; they would ask me what was I doin' at my age. They see this baseball and they figured they couldn't depend on me.

I was stationed at Atlantic City Naval Air Station. I played ball on the baseball team; I also played on the local team at Pop Lloyd Stadium.

When I first came out of the Navy, I got a job at Curtiss-Wright. I had a Naval aviation mechanics rate. That's when the contract came; I left Curtiss-Wright to play baseball. I couldn't go back there.

I got another job after that one year and I stayed and I worked with the radio-TV industry. In '59, things got slow and I got laid off. I got another job and I was trained and for some reason I left again. I went out with the Kansas City Monarchs in '59. I stayed there 'til the end of the year.

In the meantime, I took the civil service test and the post office called and I just said, "The heck with it [baseball]." I was called for the Merchant Marines, too. I said, "Why not just settle down?" I had been runnin' all over. My mother called ballplayers "hoboes."

I played throughout the city on little teams but not again in the league. I think I played a half a year with the Cubans, then the whole year with the Black Yankees. I think I played at the most — combined — I would say two years. It was all split up. I spent about 30 years with the post office.

Do you know your won-lost record?

I won about 19 games one year and lost 7. That was the year I stayed with the Black Yankees and the Clowns. But with the Clowns one of the reasons I left there was they had a lot of players that was there before, and they always wanted to show their pitchers off at pitchin'. Some like Wyatt — John Wyatt — and [Jim] Proctor, a fella named [Willie] Gaines. One fella just got up and left. He went to Mexico or somewhere. Ted Richardson, a lefthander. All of those fellas were there from previous years.

Sometimes I would sit a whole week without doing anything, so my friends on the Black Yankees would say, "Tell 'em you wanna come over here. We need pitchers." So I asked and they said, "All right." The team didn't make no difference to me; I just wanted to play.

That year I did pretty good. It was easy to me. I guess I was just born to throw hard for my size. It was easy for me to do things I was taught.

Lionel Evelyn (**Photograph courtesy of Lionel Evelyn.**)

Talk about the travel.

It was fun to us. The singing, jokes, arguments, driving the wrong way at times. The food — we used to carry a lot of can goods with us on the long trips if we got hungry before we made it to the next town. Eating money was two dollars a day.

I remember the hotel in Birmingham that had food for us no matter what time it was at night we came in. They just waited for us.

We used to carry food in the bus — you know, cans of food. Managers of the team knew where to go. Bunny Downs and Dick Lundy. We didn't go where we weren't wanted.

At times, some people would greet you. Like we'd stop for gas, some people would greet you and say, "You boys want something here to eat?"

Bein' from the north, I would do some things and they would tell me, "Don't do that. You'll have trouble here."

Do you remember Emmett Till? He was killed for sayin' something to a white lady down there in Mississippi. That was 1955. We were down there then and do you know we didn't know anything about it. We knew about it when we left there.

I never met anybody that said anything or did anything to me. I heard all the talk and I thought when I got down South somebody would want to shoot me or do something.

I've seen fellas that came from down there who were afraid. I remember one time we went for gas. We had a little dog. King Tut and Bebop had this little dog that they used to put in a box and turn a little handle and little frankfurters would come out. You know, little jokes for the crowd.

While we were gettin' gas, the dog was outside and a little boy came over and he picked the dog up. We were just sittin' there not payin' any attention and it dawned on us that we got the gas. Why is Charlie sittin' there? Why is he waitin'?

So we said, "Charlie, we goin' now?" He won't answer; he just sat there.

So we said, "Charlie, get the dog and come on! The dog's out there."

He said, "That little boy is playing with it. If I take it the sheriff might say something."

He was afraid because he didn't know what the man would do. That was something that was very, very strange to some of us. We had to get off the bus and take the dog from the little boy.

But nobody did anything direct to us. I remember we was goin' to the movie in Mississippi and we went up to buy the ticket and the lady said, "You gotta go around the corner." The movie was like 35 cents or 40 cents. She said, "You can't go in through here."

So we went around the corner and it said, "For blacks only." And it was cheaper; it was 25 cents. We laughed. We said, "Boy, it's a good deal." We had to sit all the way up to the top; they wouldn't let us downstairs.

Who was the best ballplayer you saw?

It was a fella named [George] Wannamaker. He played with the Clowns. For me as a pitcher, it looked like I just couldn't get anything past that guy. He was with some farm team and he was released.

John Wyatt was always determined. He said, "I *know* I could play in the big leagues. I *know* it." He kept tellin' me that. He said all you have to do is keep the ball low.

Richardson was something. We were both about the same size but he was left-handed.

There was another fella named Williams. Stinky Williams. He was with Birmingham. He was a natural hitter. I think he went to the Detroit Tigers. He was up in triple-A and the next thing you know he's back. I don't know what happened.

These were really outstandin' guys. After I left, a lot of 'em went to the minors. Larry LeGrande went to the Florida League and was the leading hitter there.

Have you heard of a fella named Lugo? Lugo played shortstop. He was a Cuban; he was with the Black Yankees. And Roberto Herrera. He caught.

Sometimes we'd go to a town and a fella'd be offered a job and he'd leave the team. And I was offered those things, too. Like in Aliquippa, Pennsylvania; they told me to stay, they'd give me a job in the mill. It was just like Emerson Radio. And in Flint, Michigan, they would do that.

I'd read the stories about old ballplayers and I'd wonder how they raised a family. Bunny Downs, I never knew him to have any children. I'd wonder what they'd do in the winter if they didn't go to Cuba or somewhere else. I wondered what the bulk of the

NEW YORK
BLACK YANKEES
1955

BORN NEW YORK CITY
JUNE 8TH, 1929

LONNIE STARTED WITH JOHN BECKWITHS
BROOKLYN ROYAL GIANTS 1948-1949
THEN WAS SENT TO THE NEW YORK CUBANS

1951 - 1954 US. NAVY
1955 NEW YORK BLACK YANKEES
INDIANAPOLIS CLOWNS
1959 KANSAS CITY MONARCHS

Pitcher
LIONEL
EVELYN

Lionel Evelyn (**Photograph courtesy of Lionel Evelyn.**)

players did after the season was over. What did they do? Do you know anything about that?

Some were bellhops, some were redcaps.

Oh. In New York you couldn't do those things and come back. If you leave a company or a firm, you just don't go in and out. Like when I left that job to go to the Monarchs. They had trained me and I just walked away.

The year I left, they took this fella Choo-Choo Coleman and a fella named [Paul] Casanova. They didn't spend but one year. And Larry LeGrande and Sam Thompson and all them went to the minors. I couldn't live on what they made.

I remember a fella that played with Babe Ruth — Combs, Earle Combs. He was a scout for the Indians and we met him in Indianapolis. He told me, "Let me tell you something. All of you fellas are capable of going but there's not enough room. There's a million guys in this country who think they can make it, but there's no room."

PITCHING RECORD

Year	Team, Lg	G	IP	W	L	PCT	HO	BB	SO	ERA
1949	Cubans, NAL									
1955	Blk Yanks, NAL			19	7	.731				
1959	KC, NAL									

Hubert "Country" Glenn
Philadelphia Stars 1943-1947
New York Black Yankees 1948
Indianapolis Clowns 1949

HT. 6'2 ?" WT. 210 BATTED AND THREW RIGHT

Hubert Glenn is a big man and as such could throw a baseball very hard and fast. He was a strikeout pitcher, as shown by a performance against the Bushwicks of Brooklyn, easily the best semipro team of all time. One Sunday afternoon in Dexter Park in Brooklyn he fanned 15 of them. That just wasn't done.

All together Glenn pitched seven years in the Negro leagues, mostly with the Philadelphia Stars, and three more years in Canada.

How did you begin playing baseball?

GLENN: [Laughs] Way back out there in the country, where I was at at that time, they had a li'l ol' team out there then. A kids' team. I started at a little town called Lewisville, North Carolina. I guess I was around 'bout 13. I was a tall, lanky guy. I started out as a pitcher. I used to play right field a bit.

My nickname was "Country" Glenn 'cause they said they got me out of the country down here.

How did you become a professional ballplayer?

From this team I was tellin' you about out in Lewisville. I moved in to Winston-Salem and that's when I got up with this team. I went to Winston and started playin' with a li'l ol' team down there from R. J. Reynolds Tobacco factory. It was named Pond Giants, the Winston-Salem Pond Giants.

From there I went to Virginia. Bishop, Virginia. That was a coal minin' place; they

had a team there at that time. It was named the Bishop Stateliners. We had somethin' goin' there. I was with them about a year.

I stayed in the coal mines. I was inside the mines. I was a company man; that means goin' and makin' it safe for the coal loaders. They were in a room just like you're sittin' in now. I had to go in and check the room — check the top and if they needed somethin' in there I had to set a post or somethin'.

From there I went to Kentucky. New Benham, Kentucky. That was another coal team. I didn't work in that coal mine, but that was a coal minin' team, too. I just played baseball.

I got in the Negro league through Winston-Salem. They came there one day way back there and we played 'em. The team came in there with Impo Barnhill and a bunch of those guys. I pitched against him that night. And Don Newcombe, too. I did all right. That was back before he came into the majors. I was way up in my teens.

52

You were as big as Newcombe.

No, I wasn't quite as large as he was. I was 6'2".

You eventually joined the Philadelphia Stars.

They played us one time, that team that Barnhill was on. It was barnstormin'; the regular season was over. That's how I got with them; the next few years they sent for me and I went to Philly and I got with the Stars. Ol' Goose Tatum was my manager then. Man, he was somethin'. [Laughs] Bunny Brown was on the team, Jim West was on first base.

Another guy was my manager when I was playin' with the Brooklyn Brown Dodgers. Oscar Charleston. He could play, no question 'bout it. That man could play ball. His home was in Indianapolis, Indiana. He was the manager for the Brooklyn Brown Dodgers the year Jackie Robinson came up. He pinch hit one night when we was playin' in Indianapolis. He knocked a board outta the center field wall. He could hit. That's the truth I'm tellin' you.

Who was the best player you saw?

I played against so *many* good ones. At that time I wasn't pickin' 'em. I was just tryin' to stay there. [Laughs]

Do you know any of your records?

All that stuff got stole from me in 1951 in Philly. I came back to the state [North Carolina] in 1982. I lived in Philly up 'til then. I kept everything — pictures and everything. It all got stole from me.

Oh, boy, Charleston could hit. And he was a good manager. Everybody thought Jackie Robinson was comin' to that team at that time. The Brooklyn Brown Dodgers. That was the United States League. That was Branch Rickey. It didn't last long. Oh, man, there was some good players there.

When we used to go 'round, it was rough back in them days. Oh, man, we went all down through Texas and played; Louisi-ana, Mississippi, Georgia, Alabama. Travelin' was rough. It was *rough*.

We didn't get much meal money. There wasn't much problem for me. They didn't rouse me much.

And I played in 1950 in Alberta, Canada, in the Canadian Wheat Belt League. The name of the team was Clarisse Holm Meteors. The last baseball I played was in '52 in Canada. Three years. We won the championship two years straight up there. My second year was 15-and-4. I was the only black on the team.

What did you do when you left baseball?

I came on back to Philly and I was helpin' to build bridges across rivers. I ran one of them big drillers. I built a bridge across a river there in Philly called Schuylkill River. I did that 'til I retired and I came back to my home state in 1982. I worked on yards. I love that work. I got a great big yard now. I *love* that type of work.

If you were a young man today, would you be a ballplayer?

Yeah, I would 'cause there's money in baseball now. [Laughs]

What were you paid when you played?

Oh, man, just like the rest of the guys: peanuts. It was somethin' in those days. We got by on that little two dollars or three dollars eatin' money. Boy, it was somethin'.

I played along there with Monte Irvin, Don Newcombe, Larry Doby, Roy Campanella. They was playin' with different teams; that was when I was playin' with the Stars. Ol' Satchel Paige. I saw Willie Mays.

And I saw all those guys when the Negro league come to Philly. It was old Shibe Park then, out on 21st and Lehigh Avenue. West Philly.

I guess you remember back there in Brooklyn when they had a team played in Dexter Park called the Bushwicks? I struck out 15 of 'em one Sunday up there. Old ex-major leaguers. And the next Friday night

Clarisse Holm Meteors. Hubert Glenn is on the left in the back row. (Photograph courtesy of Hubert Glenn.)

we was gonna play the Newark Eagles. When they came into Philly, they say, "Who was the guy strikin' out the Bushwicks?" [Laughs] I struck out quite a few as a rule.

Ol' Roy Partlow, I knowed him. Biz Mackey, I knowed him. Catcher. Roy Campanella was a great catcher, too.

Bill Cash was my catcher when I was with the Stars. He handled pitchers good. And they had another catcher come up behind him — he was bringin' him along — named Stanley Glenn. No relation. He wasn't too much with the bat but he could catch now. And had a gun. Cash would whistle. He'd throw that whistle. He could hum! He was somethin'. And he could hit, too, pretty good.

Philly had Frank Austin. And [Ulysses] Mahoney was up from Panama. Frank Austin and Mahoney. Frank was playin' shortstop and Mahoney was a pitcher. Austin played in the Pacific Coast League and Impro Barnhill played out there somewhere. Boy, he was somethin'.

Buck Leonard, Josh Gibson — all them guys. I used to pitch against Josh and Buck. I'd get 'em out a whole lot of times. I can remember one night in Philly, Josh hit one after one hand come off the bat. Next time he come up, you know what I say? I say from the pitchin' mound, "What you gonna do this time?" He didn't do nothin' that time. I throwed him some darts up there that time. He could hit now, no question 'bout it.

That Satchel Paige was somethin'. I didn't never pitch against him. He was playin' for the Kansas City Monarchs along with Jackie Robinson and them. The night we played 'em, a boy named Bill Ricks, he pitched against 'em. From down here in Lexington, Carolina. He was a good pitcher and Garrel Hartman was a good second baseman, too. We three went to Philly together.

I appreciate the experience I did get, the little I did get.

You got more than a little. You were there for seven years.

I enjoyed it when I was doin' it. Listen, I wasn't no hot-headed guy. Guys now tear me up the way they're doin'. Now they're makin' good money and just cuttin' hogs. They're gonna skewer me for sayin' that. It's pitiful. It just hurts me to my heart the way some of 'em are doin'.

PITCHING RECORD

Year	Team, Lg	G	IP	W	L	PCT	H	BB	SO	ERA
1943	Phil, NNL									
1944										
1945										
1946										
1947										
1948	NY BkYanks, NNL									
1949	Indianapolis, NAL									
1950	Clarisse Holm, WtBtLg									
1951				15	4	.589				
1952										

Herald "BeeBop" Gordon
Chicago American Giants 1950
Detroit Stars 1954

BORN MARCH 12, 1925, BIRMINGHAM, AL
HT. 5'9" WT. 150 BATTED AND THREW RIGHT

The Negro leagues' records are hard to find today. We don't have complete stats on most of the thousands of players who played in the leagues. We don't even have *partial* records on some.

Herald Gordon's Negro league records don't exist anymore, but we do have an idea of how good he may have been from the three years (1951–53) he played minor league ball in the Mississippi-Ohio Valley League. In those three seasons, BeeBop had records of 15-6, 18-7, and 12-12. Obviously he was a doggone good pitcher.

Another clue as to his ability: He once outdueled Satchel Paige and the Kansas City Monarchs, 2-1.

At 5'6" and around 160 pounds, he was not an imposing presence on the mound. Until, that is, the game started and the batters tried to cope with his curveball and control. At that point he became *very* imposing. A decade later he might have gotten a better shot in organized ball, but in the early '50s most black pitchers, especially small black pitchers, were not given a second look.

GORDON: I played with the Cincinnati Crescents in 1948 and the San Francisco Sea Lions in 1949. Semipro. Barnstorming teams. Then in 1950 I signed with the Chicago American Giants. Double Duty Radcliffe was my manager and my catcher. Then I played three years with the Paris, Illinois, Lakers in the Mississippi–Ohio Valley League. In 1954 I went back into the Negro American League with the Detroit Stars. That was the last year that I played — 1954.

We did a lot of travelin', played a lotta games, but we didn't make very much money. When I was playin' semipro ball we played on PC — percentage. You now, 60-40. The winner got 60 percent of the gate and the loser got 40 percent. The money

was distributed accordingly. Supposedly. In fact, I broke up in 1949 with the San Francisco Sea Lions. We broke up in Canada because we wasn't gettin' our fair share.

That team was owned by Yellowhorse Morris, a former Kansas City Monarch baseball player. He owned the San Francisco Sea Lions. That was the greatest travelin' team in the world. In 1947 they traveled to Japan and played over there for about a month.

The highlight of my baseball career was playin' against Satchel Paige and winnin' the game. That game was played on August the 15th, 1954, at Tiger Stadium. Well, it was Briggs Stadium then. The reason I remember the date so well, my oldest daughter, Pamela Jill, was born the very next day, August 16.

Satchel Paige was playin' for the Kansas City Monarchs. I pitched for the Detroit Stars. That's the last game that I played. The score was 2-1.

Satchel must have been in his 50s.

[Laughs] I don't know whether Satchel knew how old he was. Satch was one of the greatest pitchers in the history of baseball. He was something else. You can see why that's the highlight of my career.

I had pitched against him before that, but that was the first time I'd ever won a game against him. I pitched against him in 1950; I opened the season against him in Kansas City, Missouri. I don't remember the score.

Who were some of the memorable pitchers you faced?

I pitched against Joe Black. There were several others; I don't remember all the names. With the Memphis Red Sox, Bob Boyd played first base. That was before he went up. Charlie Davis — I pitched against him.

You played in somewhat of a transitional time between when the Negro leagues were at their peak and the time when there were just barnstorming teams left.

Yes. I could see after Branch Rickey brought Jackie Robinson up with the Brooklyn Dodgers, our black fans would go to see one or two — like Jackie Robinson and Larry Doby, who came in a couple of months or so later. Our black fans would go and see one or two blacks on an all white team. That was really the beginning of the breakup of our league. I could kinda see the handwritin' on the wall. That's why I told Ted Rasberry in 1954. I said, "Ted, I have a family now so I got to try to get in one of these factories and try to get me some seniority." I live in Detroit so I went with Ford Motor Company in 1955 and I put in 35½ years with Ford Motor Company. I retired in 1991.

Herald Gordon (Photograph courtesy of Herald Gordon.)

Rasberry tried to keep the Negro leagues going almost single-handedly.

Yes. Ted lost a lot of money, too, after he bought the Kansas City Monarchs from Tom Baird. He had Satchel Paige and Goose Tatum and fellas like that. They demanded big salaries. He told me he got rained out for about three weeks straight and that takes a big toll on the pocketbook. Those guys want their money whether it's rainin' or not. He lost a lot of money. It's quite expensive tryin' to take care of two teams. It's bad enough with one. When you get rained out there's *nothin'* comin' in and those buses, you have to keep them maintained.

[Note: Rasberry owned both the Detroit Stars and the Kansas City Monarchs in the mid 1950s.]

Talk about Double Duty Radcliffe.

You know why he got that nickname, 'cause he'd pitch and catch. He was a good catcher and he was a good manager. He's the oldest livin' ballplayer out there now, I think.

We was at Tiger Stadium together three or four years ago to bring people into the ballpark. They use the term "honoring us," but what it is, is to help to bring people into the ballpark. Double Duty told me he was 96. [Ted "Double Duty" Radcliffe was born in July, 1902.]

Buck O'Neil is 88. He told me that last year in Grand Rapids. They dedicated the baseball diamonds to Ted Rasberry. Ted Rasberry is 86. I'm gonna be 76. I'm considered one of the younger ones.

Duty thinks he should be in the Hall of Fame and a lot of others feel the same way. What do you think?

I think Double Duty should be in the Hall of Fame. He deserves it. He's one of the trailblazers; he was playin' back in the '20s. Although our league was organized in 1920, Double Duty was playin' before then.

Our museum traces the history of Negro baseball players back from the Civil War up until 1960. It goes way back. The league wasn't organized but black players was playin'. They had that Fleetwood Walker. They wanted to bring him up to the majors as an Indian or anything but black. [Laughs]

That stigma was out there. They said at one time that we were three-fifths of a human being. How big a lie can you tell? Then you've got the weak-minded people. There's a lot of stupidity. People believe stuff. If you keep sayin' stuff over and over again, you got some weak-minded people who will believe it.

One player told me about a time when a small

white boy kept following behind him. Whatever way he turned the boy stayed behind him and finally the player asked what he was doing back there. The boy said, "I wanna see your tail." A child isn't going to come up with something like that unless an adult has told him.

They told that same lie durin' World War II in France. The white soldiers told the French women that black folks had tails and their tails come out at night. [Laughs] They've been tellin' lies on us black folks since the beginnin' of time, since they brought our ancestors here in the bottom of the boat.

Talk about travel. You've been everywhere.

Yes. I've traveled all over this nation. In fact, I traveled to Europe since I retired. I like travelin'. I went to Barcelona, Spain. I've been to Rome; I toured Vatican City. I saw the paintings of Michelangelo. It took him three years to paint the ceiling of the Vatican. It's beautiful. And I went to Monte Carlo. I just like travelin', you know.

Did you encounter problems in your baseball travels?

The problems I encountered in baseball was not being able to stay in white hotels. The only times we could stay in white hotels was when we was up around Minot, North Dakota, or International Falls, Minnesota.

Even when I was in the Mississippi-Ohio Valley League; there was three of us blacks in 1951 with the Paris Lakers. We went to Hannibal, Missouri; we was waitin' in the lobby of the Mark Twain Hotel there after our white teammates had been assigned to their rooms. Then our manager — his name was Tom Sunkel; he was a former Dodger and he also pitched for the St. Louis Cardinals — he came to us and said, "Bee-Bop, it's not me, but the manager of the hotel said colored people was not allowed to stay in that hotel, but we have a nice place for you fellas. We found a place with a

Negro family that would put you up. We'll have a cab pick you up from the house and take you to the ballpark and bring you back to the house." That's what we had to do, the three of us.

In 1952 we won the championship there in Paris. But other than that we was treated well by our teammates and the people in the various towns.

Who were your black teammates with Paris?

Clint McCord and Pete Fields. The second year Jim Zapp was there and Fred — I can't think of his last name. Big righthanded pitcher. We wound up with about four or five blacks on the team between '51 and '53. McCord was a good first baseman and a good hitter. Line drive hitter; he could blister that ball.

How was the situation with San Francisco?

I didn't play in San Francisco. The team came out of San Francisco, actually out of Oakland. That's where most of 'em lived. They used the name San Francisco Sea Lions. I don't know whether Yellowhorse Morris lived in San Francisco or Oakland.

They picked me up in Birmingham, Alabama; that's my hometown. I made connections with 'em in 1948 when I played against them when I was with the Cincinnati Crescents. I gave Yellowhorse Morris my address and when he came to Birmingham he got in touch with me and I quit my job. I was workin' in the mines in Birmingham and I left with them in 1949. We traveled all over this nation.

Incidentally, we had a white boy with us named Sparky Anderson. I was thinking the other night, "I wonder if this is the same Sparky Anderson." He had to hide in the bus. We had a big red bus there with "San Francisco Sea Lions" on the very top of each side. "San Francisco Sea Lions — the Greatest Traveling Team in the World."

He came out of San Francisco or Oakland, one. He had to hide when we got to

places like Birmingham or anywhere in the South. He had to hide down in the bus to keep from bein' seen, because durin' that period of time white and black couldn't be together on streetcars and buses and whatnot. Water fountains, toilets. He was a pitcher.

Looking back on your baseball career, do you have any regrets?

No, not really. I had fun. I would've liked to have advanced, but I could kinda see the handwritin' on the wall.

I had an offer to go out to Yakima, Washington. I got a telegram in 1951, the first year I pitched in Paris, Illinois. I had a record of 15-and-6 and I don't know how many games I saved.

But anyway, I got a telegram in '51 to go to Yakima, Washington. Mr. Gibbons — he was one of the stockholders in the Paris Lakers — he called me and told me he had a better deal for me, to forget about the Yakima thing. I went back to Paris and played another couple of years and I wound up back in the Negro American League 'cause I could see I wasn't goin' nowhere.

I had very good control 'cause comin' up I used to throw rocks at cans and bottles. Set 'em up on a post and throw rocks at 'em like people would shoot bb guns or a .22 rifle at a target. I'd throw rocks at a target, like a bottle or can on a post. I had plenty of rocks available where I grew up at, because the road was made out of rock. [Laughs] I didn't have no problem pickin' up a rock.

I played ball all of my life, ever since I was about six or seven years old; playin' with a stick — a broom handle — hittin' a tennis ball. I loved the game.

But I come out of it in 1954 and went on in the factory. Now I see that's the best decision I ever made, because I can see now these guys tryin' to get pensions — tryin' to get some money — so they can try to have a better life. A lot of 'em worked on menial

Herald Gordon (Photograph courtesy of Herald Gordon.)

jobs, around hotels and things durin' the winter, and they wasn't makin' that much money, just enough to survive on. Now they're just out there.

How did you get your nickname?

I was given that nickname of "BeeBop" Gordon by one of my teammates, a guy by the name of Sammy Workman. We called him "Little Sammy" Workman. You can write a book about this guy all by himself. [Laughs] This guy had no hands or feet and

he was one of our featured attractions. We had Little Sammy and Toni — Toni Stone, a woman — in 1949.

I used to wear eyeglasses and the name of the eyeglasses was BeeBop glasses — someone capitalizin' on Dizzy Gillespie's fame. He used to wear the glasses and a lot of musicians started copying his style. I bought a pair. I didn't need 'em at that time; it was just a style, a fad. Anyway, he started callin' me "BeeBop" Gordon and once you were given a nickname in baseball you were stuck with it for the rest of your life.

This guy had no hands or no feet and in the third innin' of each game Yellowhorse Morris, the owner of the San Francisco Sea Lions, would get on the PA system. We would stop playin' in the third innin'. Yellowhorse Morris would get on the PA system and announce to the fans, "Ladies and Gentlemen, I would like to bring to you our featured attraction, Little Sammy Workman, the Wonder Boy, the boy without hands or feet catchin' the ball, throwin' the ball, hittin' the ball, and runnin' around the bases doin' his death slide into third base.

"Incidentally, Ladies and Gentlemen, Little Sammy travels with this ballclub entirely on his own and any kind donation that you might give will be highly appreciated inasmuch as he's workin' his way through college. Incidentally, Ladies and Gentlemen, Little Sammy's hands and feet fell off at the age of two. Without further ado, I will now present to you Little Sammy Workman."

And with that introduction, Little Sammy would run up to the plate. He wore gym shoes turned backwards on his knees. He had on his uniform. He'd run up to the plate and the catcher would give him the catcher's mitt and the pitcher threw the ball and he would catch it. He had little nubs just below his elbows, maybe four or five or six inches. He would put his arm in the catcher's mitt and they'd throw him the ball. He'd catch it, take the ball out, and throw it back to the pitcher. The pitcher'd throw it back to him and he'd throw it to first base, he'd throw it to second base, he'd throw it to third base. *Accurate* throws. He had just enough to crook that elbow over that ball.

Then he would get to bat and the pitcher would throw him the ball. He'd hit the ball, then he'd run around the bases. He'd hit the ball out in the outfield and by the time the outfielder'd get to the ball — he'd have it timed so by the time he'd throw the ball to third base Sammy'd go into the death slide. The ball'd get there just so he'd wind up bein' safe. And that would be the end of his job. The fans would just go wild.

That guy was somethin' else. He could play pool, he could play piano, he could play drums, he could play cards with those nubs. He was strictly a miracle type of guy.

How did he do financially?

They had a box, a little box with a lock on it and slit in the steel box where people put their donations in. People put three dollars, five dollars, ten dollars in it. We had to take it back to Yellowhorse Morris. He's the only one had the key to it. The pitchers that wasn't pitchin' would go around through the audience — through the stands — and take up the collection.

Sammy was amazin'. They couldn't've come up with a better name than "the Wonder Boy." He was something else. The man could do *any*thing just about anybody else could do. He was about 28 years old.

Was he really going to college?

No, he wasn't goin' to college.

Would you go back and be a ballplayer again?

I wish I could. [Laughs] Especially with the amount of money that's bein' paid out there now. They say they're payin' the players too much money. Well, they deserve it. That's what this country is all about: money.

PITCHING RECORD

Year	Team, Lg	G	IP	W	L	PCT	H	BB	SO	ERA
1950	Chicago, NAL									
1951	Paris, MSOHV			15	6	.714				3.92
1952				18	7	.720				3.14
1953				12	12	.500				4.19
1954	Detroit, NAL									

Raymond Haggins
Memphis Red Sox 1953-1955

BORN SEPTEMBER 5, 1929, COLEANOR, AL
HT. 6'1" WT. 187 BATTED AND THREW LEFT

Raymond Haggins played in the Negro American League for three years (1953-55). All three years he was selected to play in the East-West game, the league's all-star showcase.

He was a lefthanded line-drive hitting outfielder who had the potential to play in organized ball, but the owner of the Memphis Red Sox, Dr. W. S. Martin, refused to sell his contract. In 1954, he nonetheless signed with the Chicago White Sox, but when it was learned that he was also under contract to Memphis, he had to return to the NAL club.

When did you begin playing baseball professionally?

HAGGINS: In 1949. I played in the [Negro] Southern League with the Nashville Cubs. That was the year I graduated from high school and I was playing YMCA industrial league ball.

There was an older player who saw me play and knew me when I was playing with U. S. Pipe in Bessemer [Alabama]. He was going to this team and he was wanting me to go, too. So I went in 1949. I played outfield.

The next year I played for the House of David out of Minneapolis, Minnesota. I pitched and played first base and outfield.

In 1951, I was in the United States Army for two years. When I came out of the Army I went to spring training wit the Birmingham Black Barons. From there I went to the Memphis Red Sox. I played with them in '53 and '54 and I was being scouted by the Giants and Cincinnati Reds and the White Sox. But the team wouldn't sell my contract. Dr. W. S. Martin was

the owner. He was a tough man. [Laughs] He was stubborn; if he believed he wasn't getting' a fair price for his players, he said, "I don't have to sell no players. I'll let 'em play on my team." He's thinking 'bout his pride and everything, but he didn't think about players so he didn't sell anybody. We had quite a few promising and talented players.

Who were some of your teammates in Memphis?

Ed Reed and Willie Sheelor, Casey Jones, Pat Patterson, Fate Simms, Charlie Davis.

You were an All-Star three years.

I was selected to play in three East-West All-Star games in Chicago. It's been a while. [Laughs] I vaguely remember. We left Chicago before I could get any clippings or records of the games. I think we [the West] won two of the three. I played right field.

I barnstormed against major leaguers. I faced Connie Johnson, Don Newcombe, Joe Black, Bob Trice, and Brooks Lawrence. I hit 'em pretty good.

(l-r) Ray Haggins, Eddie Reed, Willie Sheelor (Photograph courtesy of Raymond Haggins.)

I was a line drive hitter. I hit some home runs, but I didn't have a home run swing, you know. I took what the pitcher gave me.

I think I have some clippings. In Black History Month the kids at my church had to do projects and I let 'em have some of my clippings. Let me look in my scrapbook and see what I have left.

Here's one clipping against the major league all-stars. I got 3-for-4. I think I hit a home run on Brooks Lawrence and I hit a single and a double. Here's one where we played them again. They beat us, 4-to-3, and I had one RBI; I had a double and a single.

Here's the stats for the beginning of the season in 1953. At this time we hadn't played very many games. I had 75 at bats; I had 13 RBIs, 23 hits, and two home runs, batting .307 at that time.

Here's a clipping where we played Birmingham Black Barons. We beat 'em in a double header; we beat 'em, 5-1 and 3-2.

In the first game I had 2-for-4 and I was 1-for-2 in the second game.

Here's one where the Campanella All-Stars beat us, 1-to-nothin'. We played 'em in Louisiana. I don't have the box score, but here's the write-up. I was involved in one play where Larry Doby was thrown out. I relayed the ball to the shortstop, and he threw him out trying to stretch a play into an extra base hit. I could throw pretty good.

Here's a clipping where we beat Detroit in a double header, 14-to-8 and 11-to-1; and I went 3-for-5 in the first game. In the second game I had 1-for-3, an RBI, and two runs scored.

Here's a clipping where I played on the Army team. We were playing the playoff for the championship. It said, "The playoff had superb pitching on the part of the Lions, held the Clips to a score of 2-to-nothin' until the fifth inning when Ray Haggins strode to the plate. A rousing cheer went up in the stands when Haggins slammed a home run with one man on to tie the score." Then in the ninth inning with the score tied, I drove in the winning run.

Who were the best players you saw?

I played high school ball against Willie Mays. I knew him as a basketball player and football player before he played baseball. I didn't know him as a baseball player. When I first saw him as a baseball player, he had a good arm and he could catch everything, but he wasn't that great a hitter. That was right out of high school. But he worked hard and developed real fast. He learned to hit. He had good reflexes. I never saw him throw to a wrong base. He was always in the game. I never saw him make a mental error. He's that type of ballplayer.

He was a good basketball player. He was a good athlete. He played football — quarterback — in high school at Fairfield Industrial High. Whatever sport he played he was good.

Another one I played with was Ernie Banks. Ed Reed and him and I, we all come out of the Army at the same time. Banks was a good ballplayer. Reed had a terrific arm.

There was another player played for the Kansas City Monarchs. Ernie Johnson. He played outfield and he was a good ballplayer.

Who was the best pitcher you saw and who was the toughest on you?

The toughest pitcher on me was a left-hander named [Hiram] Gaston. He played with Birmingham. They had another one named Kelly Searcy, but his ball didn't move like Gaston's did. Searcy's ball I could see real good. It was straight, but he could throw hard. But Gaston, he could throw hard and he had good movement on his ball. I could hit him but I had to take what he give me.

The best pitcher I saw — Newcombe wasn't hard for me to hit because he didn't have a very good curveball. He could throw hard and he was trying to learn to throw a changeup. I hit him real well.

Connie Johnson, I hit him pretty good but you had to take what he give you. He had a good curveball and he had a good fastball.

Sam Jones was about the most difficult to hit. He had the best curveball I ever saw. When I come to the plate he'd turn his back and start laughin'. He'd throw me the knuckleball or junk up there. [Laughs]

Joe Black was a relief pitcher with the Dodgers. He come up there and say, "Well, I'm gonna pitch you inside." I guess he was experimentin', workin' on his control. He'd throw the ball over the outside corner, over the inside corner. You know, move the ball around. He gave me the first insert helmet I had. You know, back then we didn't have helmets, so he gave me the first insert to go in my cap. I guess he knew pitchers was gonna be throwin' at me if I got in organized ball.

Knockdown pitches never did bother me. I was more determined when they threw at me than I ordinarily would be. When I was growing up, my brother and I — he's about a year-and-a-half older than I was — he never would want to play on the same team with me. We'd be playin' on opposite teams and sometimes he'd pitch and he'd get a little upset if I hit him. [Laughs] He would knock me down. That's where I first got introduced to the knockdown pitch. [Laughs] So the knockdown pitch never did bother me.

Did your brother ever play professionally?

No, he didn't. He lost interest in baseball. He went in the service. He put up his age to get a job when he was about 15 and they drafted him. He was in Cleveland workin' at the time. He had to go in the Army. When he came out he played a little but he wasn't committed.

I had a good family life. I had one brother and one sister. My sister was about 18 years younger than I was. [Laughs] We always got along well and she was our little boss when she came along. [Laughs]

Does one game stand out?

I was playing for the House of David. We was playing against a local team and I hit about three home runs one game. I remember that game.

In another game we were playing in Yankee Stadium and I hit a home run there. I think we was playing Detroit Stars there. The pitcher was a guy named Mason, I believe. I'm not sure.

Do you have any regrets from baseball?

No. I'd do it again. I loved to play.

One thing I would have done differently, I would've completed my education. I would've gone to college. I finished high school, but I didn't go to college. I took classes since I've been out and raisin' a family. I went to night school and got a degree in religious education. I don't use it professionally, but I use it at my church.

Are there any ballplayers among your children?

My boys, I didn't force 'em into sports, but both of 'em liked basketball and that's what they played. All of 'em went to college and graduated but one. I have five.

What did you do after you left baseball?

I came back home and got a job in a steel mill. I worked there 39 years.

Back to baseball. How much did you pitch?

I pitched quite a bit when I was playing with this barnstorming team out in Minneapolis. But after then — when I came out of the service — I didn't pitch any more. If I could stay in the lineup every day that's where I wanted to be.

Where did you bat in the order?

I batted third, fourth, and fifth.

What about the conditions?

Playing in those days, we had difficulty finding places to stay. There were towns that did have accommodations and there were towns that didn't. Sometimes you'd get to a town where you were gonna play and you couldn't find accommodations. You just slept on the bus.

And back then, just like they have roadside rest areas, you couldn't use these accommodations, either.

I remember a town we played in here in Alabama — Culman, Alabama. We played ball there but we couldn't even go to town to get some food. A guy went and got us some. They went and got some sandwiches.

Life was pretty rough for years after they integrated baseball in the South. The black ballplayers, the teams that they assigned them to play at — South Carolina, Alabama, Georgia — it was rough on those players.

I signed in '54 on my own after Martin wouldn't sell me. I signed with the Chicago White Sox and they assigned me to Colorado Springs Sky Sox in Class A ball. We trained in Hollywood, Florida, in 1954. They had to find accommodations in black homes there, and the other players, they stayed at Holiday Inn. The only time we met was when we came to the ballfield.

Some [players] accepted you, some didn't. You had problems because they felt that you were taking their jobs. You were a threat. Back then you got knocked down more and the guys would take you out. We accepted that as part of the game. To me, it wasn't a threat. I could take it. Most of the black players could take it.

They [Memphis] found out where I was before I got a chance to go to Colorado Springs. When they signed me they wasn't supposed to publicize it and there was a write-up in *Jet* magazine 'bout me signing. Dr. Martin's brother, the president of the league, he lived in Chicago, and they got hold of him. He called minor league baseball — whoever was the head — and they called and told 'em I had to come back to Memphis.

The same thing happened to Ed Reed. He was with the Cleveland Indians down at Daytona Beach. That almost took my will to play baseball away from me. I stopped there where he was at Daytona Beach and I talked with him, told him what had happened. I come on back to Memphis and I was in town I guess about a week before I went back to the team.

I told Dr. Martin, "I'm gonna play this season and if you don't sell me I'm leavin' baseball." That was in 1954.

I thought I might go down to South America and play a year. I thought about it and I said, "I missed two years in the Army and now I've hit a roadblock here. I've gotta get established. I've gotta get some security

somewhere. I can't stay out here in minor league baseball until I get too old to do anything else and don't have any kind of security." So I had to make up my mind to leave baseball and go to work and that's what I did.

I was kind of bitter at baseball. I didn't even talk about it. Guys I worked with, they didn't know I played professional baseball. A guy came down from the *Birmingham News* and interviewed me just before I retired and they had a write-up and that's how they all found out that I had played professional ball. They were comin' around, "Why didn't you tell me you played professional ball?" [Laughs] I said, "Well, I didn't wanna talk about it."

I was bitter for a long time, but now I understand. When I was a youngster I was so sure I was gonna succeed in baseball. Instead of goin' to college, I decided I'd just go into baseball. But I didn't know then about the things that *could* happen. I could've had a disablin' injury or anything.

Then the career itself is short-lived, you know. You've got so many years to play. You've gotta have something to do after that. You're still a young man when you're too old to play baseball.

My advice to young athletes would be to complete their education and then if they're good enough, give professional sports a try.

Also, I would advise them to make room for Christ in their life so that they would have some guidance or direction in their lives. This would help them to avoid the many pitfalls and bad influences they will encounter.

BATTING RECORD

Year	Team, Lg	G	AB	R	H	2B	3B	HR	RBI	BA
1949	N'shv'le, NSL									
1950	House of David, ind									
1995-52	Military service									
1953	Memphis, NAL									
1954										
1955										

J. C. Hartman
Kansas City Monarchs 1954-1955

BORN APRIL 15, 1934, COTTONTON, AL
HT. 6' WT. 175 BATTED AND THREW RIGHT

"Good field, no hit" is a favorite description for many shortstops, and one of the prototypical ones was J. C. Hartman. But that was only at the major league level; in the minors he batted over .300 a couple of times. He must have hit well with the Kansas City Monarchs, because he was selected to play in the East-West All-Star game in his only season with the team.

He might have done better in the major leagues but he was up and down with the Houston Colt .45s a couple of years and was never in the lineup regularly enough to get into a groove. But, as he points out, he made it to the major leagues, and that's something that most people can't say.

HARTMAN: I initially started with the Kansas City Monarchs in 1954 when I first went up for a tryout with them in Swayne Field in Toledo, Ohio. The Kansas City Monarchs were playing there and Buck O'Neil was the manager of the team at the time. I was living in Inkster, Michigan, which is only about 52 miles from Swayne Field.

The manager of my team I was playing with at the time, which was the Inkster Panthers, took me over to Swayne Field to meet Buck. We had a little workout just before the game and you wouldn't believe it. I was *shocked* when I looked at the lineup and I was playing in the game. [Laughs] That's the way I started.

The season was almost over, so he told me, "Listen. I will send for you for next year. This year's almost over."

The following year I went to spring training in Atlanta, Georgia. I was the shortstop for the Kansas City Monarchs that year. I was shortstop in the East-West All-

Star game. Satchel Paige was there, too. We won it, 2-to-nothing. I had two at bats; I didn't get any hits, but I think I made a couple pretty good plays in the field.

I was more defensive than offensive, I guarantee you. [Laughs] I played 13 years of pro ball, so I had to do something.

I was purchased by the Chicago Cubs. I'd been following Ernie Banks around. I was behind Banks approximately five years in the Cubs' organization. You know, Banks was a shortstop for the Kansas City Monarchs at one time, also. He was a tremendous ballplayer.

Originally, when I went with the Cubs, I was bought in a three-player deal. George Altman and Lou Johnson were the others. They paid $12,000 for the three of us. Believe it or not, I didn't get any of the money. I never got a dime. I was more concerned about opportunity at the time. I said, "I'll eventually get mine some kind of way. I want to get to the majors some way."

How was the travel with the Monarchs?

J. C. Hartman (Photograph courtesy of J. C. Hartman.)

The travel conditions were kind of bad. Jackie Robinson and Larry Doby and guys like that had migrated into the major leagues and we couldn't really draw. We didn't have the fans. As a matter of fact, Satchel Paige was our drawing attraction and we couldn't start the game until he got there. That was a problem.

The actual conditions — I played many a game when my uniform was still damp. Wet. And the pay wasn't quite what it should've been. I don't remember exactly what I made, but I usually equated it with schoolteachers' salaries.

Who was the best player with Kansas City?

We had a catcher named Juan Armenteros. He was a tremendous catcher. Then we had a guy named Hank Bayliss; he was a tremendous ballplayer. And even

Buck O'Neil, at his age he could still hit that ball. He'd look around for a pinch hitter and he'd say, "Wait a minute. Hand me my wood." [Laughs]

I played behind Banks but I never did actually play with the Cubs' major league team. The Colt .45s bought me from the Cubs. I played one year in Houston prior to that; I played with the old Houston Buffs. That was triple-A. The following year I played with the Colt .45s. That was a patented name; it was a gun company or a beer company, and they said they'd have to pay if they were going to use that name. So they changed the name to the Houston Astros.

I was in the Houston organization four or five years. On-and-off, I was in the major leagues a couple of years

Who was the best pitcher?

Satchel Paige was our attraction. I faced guys like Bob Gibson and Sandy Koufax, [Jim] Maloney, [Don] Drysdale — I faced all of 'em.

With your speed, did you bunt a lot?

Not really. Most of the time I was leading off; I didn't do a lot of bunting. Didn't do a whole lot of hitting. I do recall getting some key hits on occasion.

My game wasn't really offensive; it was defensive. I was always struggling to get hits. But defensively, it makes me feel good to know that I used to take guys like Joe Morgan and work 'em out. Paul Richards paid me extra to take Joe Morgan on the field. And Jim Wynn was a shortstop — the Toy Cannon — and show them defensively how to keep from getting killed around second base.

When Joe first came in as a raw rookie, I was paid extra to do that and that's what I did. I bought an apartment building with some of that money.

The thing that really used to get me, when I was going real, real good — like when I came up from Oklahoma City I was

J. C. Hartman with the Houston Colt .45s (Photograph courtesy of J. C. Hartman.)

really hitting the ball good and the first thing they did was sit me on the bench for about four or five games. My rhythm and everything was off. Then they put me in against Koufax and the next guy was Drysdale and I never did get on track. It doesn't take long for your timing to go. I said, "My goodness, man! Let me play!"

I remember one game I got two or three hits, played excellent defense and next day I'm on the bench. Bob Lillis and I mostly shared the position. At least I was in the majors.

He got more hits than I did, but actually neither one of us was in the class of some of these superstars that they have nowadays.

Does one game with Kansas City stand out?

No, other than the East-West All-Star game. That was a thrill. Enrique Maroto had a clipping of that. We won the game, 2-to-nothing, and Satchel Paige was the winning pitcher.

Maroto was a good ballplayer. He was a competitor. He was a fiery little guy.

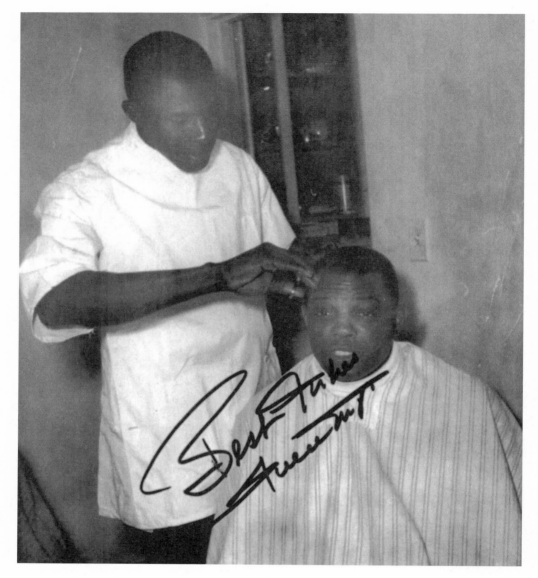

J. C. Hartman cutting Willie Mays' hair. (Photograph courtesy of J. C. Hartman.)

How about a game with Houston?

I can remember one time I made three errors in a game. [Laughs] I'd like to forget that one.

The game that stands out was a game that Don Nottebart pitched a no-hitter. Tony Gonzalez hit a *blue-darter*— I mean, you could hardly see the ball. I just got a glimpse of it. I got over and dropped my glove, but by that time it was in center field.

They called it an error. I'm glad they called it an error because it would've been a hit. That's the one game I can remember.

During my career I helped to break in Ron Santo. Billy Williams and I were on the same team together. Billy Williams and I are just like brothers, even today. Ron Santo came to us and he could hit the fastball but he couldn't hit the curveball. When he first came he had yellow shoestrings in his spikes.

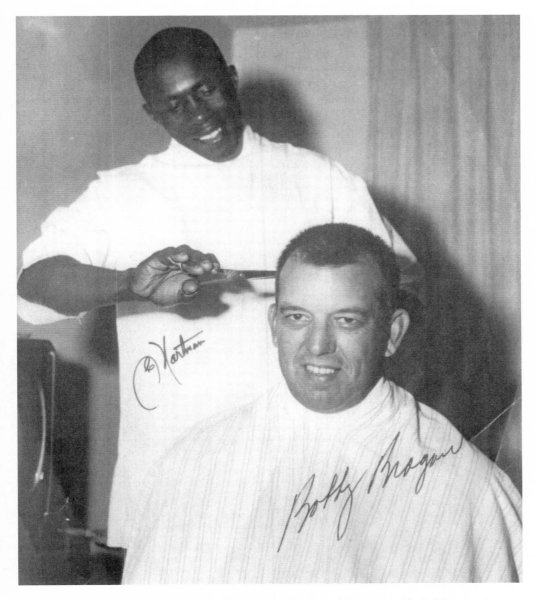

J. C. Hartman cutting Bobby Bragan's hair. (Photograph courtesy of J. C. Hartman.)

I said, "Oh, no. You're gonna have to change this." We laugh about it now when we see each other. [Laughs]

Billy Williams was a first baseman at first. Grady Hatton and I worked with him. He was so bad when he first went to the outfield he almost had to wear a hard hat. He was that bad, but he became a good one. He's a Hall of Famer.

I could write a book on just my roommates. Charley Pride, we were in the service together. All-Army team together. Lou Brock, Billy Williams. We were roommates, shared apartments coming up through the ranks.

In high school one of my classmates was Leon Wagner. Leon Wagner and I are just like brothers. We grew up together; we went to the prom together. Lou Johnson was the best man at my wedding. We found Lou in Lexington, Kentucky, when I was with the Kansas City Monarchs. Roman Mejias was my roommate.

I have pictures of me cutting Willie Mays' hair and stuff like that. One of my best friends is Orlando Cepeda. Ferguson Jenkins is a dear friend. Pat Kelly and I were roommates. Aaron Pointer, he was the Pointer Sisters' brother. He was an official in the NFL recently.

Would you do it again?

Oh, that's the love of my life. I *love* baseball. But, you know, I was a better football player, I thought. I earned four letters in high school. Baseball and track used to run together. Sometimes I'd run track and play baseball the same day.

BATTING RECORD

Year	Team, Lg	G	AB	R	H	2B	3B	HR	RBI	BA
1955	KC, NAL									
1956	Magic Valley, Pioneer	132	508	63	139	25	3	0	52	.274
1957-1958	Did not play									
1959	San Antonio, TxL	142	545	80	150	17	3	5	48	.275
1960		143	581	94	170	24	3	3	49	.293
1961	Houston, AA	144	599	64	155	19	3	6	53	,259
1962	Houston, NL	51	148	11	33	5	0	0	5	.223
	Okla City, AA	90	388	54	126	12	2	4	40	.325
1963	Houston, NL	39	90	2	11	1	0	0	3	.122
	San Antonio, TxL									
		67	278	60	85	11	4	3	24	.306
1964	Hawaii, PCL	84	301	30	79	10	3	2	26	.262
	San Antonio, TxL	49	183	24	42	5	0	0	12	.230
1965	Amarillo, TxL	17	68	7	16	3	0	1	4	.235
	Okla City, PCL	82	216	30	54	7	1	2	17	.250
1966	Amarillo, TxL	71	264	39	77	11	2	5	20	.292
	Okla City, PCL	41	133	15	34	2	0	0	6	.256
1967	Amarillo, TxL	24	83	17	22	2	1	1	9	.265
	Denver, PCL	107	353	47	109	10	5	0	37	.309

Prince Joe Henry
Memphis Red Sox 1950-51
Indianapolis Clowns 1955
Detroit Clowns 1958

BORN OCTOBER 4, 1930, LOVEJOY, IL
HT. 6' WT. 190 BATTED LEFT, THREW RIGHT

Joe Henry was raised a softball player, oblivious to the existence of the Negro leagues. His ability at softball, however, attracted the attention of some who thought he could make it in baseball, and they were right. Not only did he make it in the Negro American League, he also made it in the minor leagues. He might have made it all the way, but a knee injury led to an arm injury that ended his serious baseball career.

He still made a living from baseball, though. He returned to the Negro league, now a mere shadow of what it had once been, and joined the Indianapolis Clowns, where he was, indeed, a clown, originating many gags and other innovations that we take for granted today. It was here that he was given the title of "Prince."

Although he clowned with the Clowns, Joe Henry took the history and heritage of the Negro leagues and of blacks in America seriously. Listening to him is a history lesson in itself.

HENRY: I had a discussion with a person recently and he told me his name was Joseph. I said, "I can't stand that name Joseph." And, oh, he wanted to explain to me how great that name was and he was telling me about the Bible, etc., and I told him, "I don't think you can promote the idea, especially to me, about accepting that name Joseph." That's why I cut it short to "Joe", but really Joseph is my first name.

I'm from Brooklyn or Lovejoy, Illinois. Lovejoy is rather an adopted name. The school was named Lovejoy and the post office was named Lovejoy and both of these names were from Elijah P. Lovejoy, the great abolitionist from Alton, Illinois, about 20 miles from here.

When I played 12-inch fast pitch soft-

ball I played around the infield — second, third, first, catch. That was my game. I never cared for baseball as far as playing it. It all started with the moving of Jackie Robinson from the Kansas City Monarchs to the Dodgers. Then I began playing baseball with the encouragement from other people, especially Mr. Josh Johnson. He managed a semipro team right about three minutes from here in Madison, Illinois. He used to see me play this 12-inch fast pitch and he began to talk about converting myself to playing baseball. I never even thought of the idea of playing baseball because I just had no interest in it and didn't know a thing about the Negro leagues. Not at all.

I could have gone to Los Angeles, California, to work out with the Los Angeles

73

Joe Henry (r) (Photograph courtesy of Larry Lester.)

Angels, at that time in the Pacific Coast League. This happened because of the black columnist from the *Chicago Defender*, A. S. "Doc" Young. My friend, Eugene Critten-den, we grew up together from six, seven years old. He, in the latter part of the '40s, asked me if I thought I could play in the Negro league. Just to show you that I was completely unaware of the Negro league, prior I had only heard of Satchel Paige or Goose Tatum.

The reason he asked me this was because of Elston Howard, who lived just across the bridge from us and starred in high school in baseball and basketball against him. At that time Elston Howard — about '49 — had come to the Kansas City Monarchs. My friend thought that I could play anywhere that I wanted to play and he asked me if I thought I could play in the Negro league.

Prior to that, the opening of my intelligence in regards to the Negro league had come with Jackie Robinson, but I had not gotten all into it at that point. My friend had brought the Negro league to my attention. So he asked and I said, "Heck, yes, I can play."

After I had contacted the columnist in Chicago, I mentioned Mr. Johnson and the columnist was in California at that time. He set up a tryout with the Los Angeles Angels. He contacted Mr. Johnson and Mr. Johnson came down to Brooklyn [Illinois] here to tell me about it.

Mr. Johnson and I, we discussed the possibility of going to California because I knew I needed some assistance at that time. Mr. Johnson knew Goose Curry — Homer "Goose" Curry, who was manager of the Memphis Red Sox at that time. After we

Joe Henry (Photograph courtesy of Larry Lester.)

had talked about the different things — the distance involved, etc. — we thought it was a pretty good idea to go into the Negro league because the Negro league represented a history that I had become very interested in. So I decided to go to Memphis.

At that time, Goose Curry was holding the first and only black baseball school in Greenville, Mississippi. After the baseball school was over and I was to return back to Memphis, which was only about 300 miles from where I lived, he included Vernell Jackson and a catcher named Booker Butler.

My story is pretty deep dealing with the Negro leagues. My story dates back to when I was very, very young — 11, 12 — and getting knothole tickets to go see the Cardinals and Browns in St. Louis and being led away to a little isolated section in the left field stands where blacks were seated. I suppose the disdain of a young kid at that time was sorta like my friend and I, we did a lot of little things because we knew some-

thing was going on wrong but we really couldn't put our fingers on it because we were too young.

One thing we did do was want every team to come in there against the Cardinals and Browns and run 'em to death. To look out there on that ballfield and all that beautiful green grass and the way things were set up and structured, it just seemed as if a miracle would have to happen for you to be out there playing on that field. This is at a time when he and I were *completely* oblivious to there being a Negro league.

All of those great black players, that was a history that we were unaware of so we had to choose people such as Ted Williams for our hero, or Terry Moore, Stan Musial. So I guess this is why the historical aspect of the Negro league meant so much to me. It geared my attention to the Negro league because of the history that was there and I said that to get back to this: batting averages, to me, they were unimportant. I went there and the things that I first started seeing I said to myself at the time I sat in that little isolated section in Sportsman's Park and watched the ballplayers play. I would pick out what ballplayer I thought was really productive, such as Marty Marion, Whitey Kurowski, people like that.

When I got to Memphis and these players started coming in from different places, and after hearing about the Negro league, I was under the impression that it consisted of blacks or black Americans. When guys started coming in from Cuba and Puerto Rico and different places like that along with black Americans, I started seeing things that I had never before saw in my life.

I saw guys like Neal Robinson, Willie Wells — the last part of Willie Wells, Sr., and at that time Junior was also playing with the Red Sox. Neal Robinson, how he could hitch his left hip and shoot balls out of the park. I mean, bam-bam! The same way like playing 12-inch fast pitch. If I happened to be playing third base and off the bat of some guy standing at the plate the ball would come at you, bam-bam! One move to get it — this is the way I saw guys like Neal Robinson, who was the left fielder, drive balls out of the park.

I saw guys like Bunny Serrell, Kansas City Monarchs, who was playing second base, range to his left. Whereas you would see a second baseman reach and get a ball and make that clockwise turn to go to first base, a guy like Bunny Serrell would go over, pick it up with his left hand — glove the ball — and take it out of the glove and go behind his back to first base. All kinds of things like this.

I saw Willie Wells, who was gone at that time, and his son, who could skip and time grounders to perfection. And I'm saying, "This is unbelievable! This is really unbelievable!"

And everybody from here thought that I can't miss. "He's going to be back in one of these parks one day, either at Sportsman's Park or some other park." I became afraid

to even go out and take infield practice. I'm just being honest with you. I thought that I was hot as fire when I first went there but when all of these different players started coming in ... Bob Boyd — oh, my goodness! This man hit line drives so devastating!

I'm a part of a Negro league that at that time in 1950 was *dead*. From 1947, when Jackie Robinson went from the Kansas City Monarchs to the Dodgers, a few years later the Negro league was dead. Teams like the Philadelphia Stars — just hanging on to drop out; the Cleveland Buckeyes — I think I played against them one time. I'm saying to myself, "What if I had followed this league when all of these teams were playing against each other before the advent of Jackie Robinson, there is no telling what kinds of ballplayers I would have been able to be with." The guys that I saw, like Double Duty Radcliffe, his time was over. Lundy, that was a heck of a shortstop — Dick Lundy. Oscar Charleston. All of these type of people. I've seen the last bit of them.

And do you know what? When people would ask me if I ever faced Satchel Paige — yes. *Five* times going to the plate. After he had left Cleveland [Indians] and joined the Chicago American Giants, where Double Duty was, and Winfield Welch and some members of the Harlem Globetrotters; the nucleus of the Harlem Globetrotters came from within the Negro league.

And do you know that the five times that I faced Satchel in that game he struck me out four times! And this was when he didn't have this blazing fastball. He was dealing with me from a standpoint of knowledge. Do you follow me?

And do you know that I lost the friendship of Goose Curry, who believed that I was capable of doing anything in baseball at the time? On that particular day, Goose Curry bet Satchel Paige, who was his buddy, that there was a kid from around St. Louis who was gonna wear him out. [Laughs] All of this was without my knowledge.

Ted Strong and Joe Henry (r) (Photograph courtesy of Larry Lester.)

The only thing that I could think of in regards to Satchel was those placards that I used to see at times about Satchel Paige and Goose Tatum. You know, guys like that who they promoted in the league.

They had this little bet going without

my knowledge. But don't you know what? *Every* time Satch struck me out and I headed back to the dugout, I could hear Satch holler, "Goose!" But I didn't know it was related to what *I* was doing at the plate.

I grounded out weakly back to him

[the fifth time] and I felt due proud of myself that at least I got the ball on the bat.

After the game in the clubhouse when I was walking around so happy with my clothes off getting ready to take a shower, thinking after I finished I was gonna call my dad to tell him I hit Satchel Paige, Goose was sitting in a chair with half his clothes off, watching my every move. So I just happened to pass him and I hollered, "Goose, how you doing?"

He said, "Not worth a *damn.*"

I asked him what's wrong and he said, "Boy, you can't hit a goddamn thing, can you?" And Goose believed that I could hit anybody before I faced Satchel Paige.

I asked him, "What do you mean I can't hit a damn thing?"

"Goddamn it, you know. The man struck your ass out four times today."

I said, "You can't get mad at me for that. The man's been striking people out when I was a youngster."

But don't you know for some reason I never did mend that friendship that I had prior to that.

He didn't know that I was thinking of the greatness of this man and that I happened to be on the same field playing against this man. This is why I said my thing about the Negro league is very deep, because I've always found it so great to me to be associated with people as great as Satchel Paige. I would seek these people out to try to have pictures taken with them.

I wanted a picture with Brown. Willard Brown. Just every great person that I could think of. Great black person out there on the ballfield, I wanted pictures. And history became much more to my involvement in the Negro leagues than anything else. It's a mixture of the history of blacks playing at that time and me being a part of one of the greatest organizations I've ever known. In fact, blacks in America today don't have another viable organization as powerful as was the Negro league.

It was out of this world and I am proud at any time to sit and talk about the Negro league because at that time the majority of black owners are entrepreneurs. They provided everything for a young black kid interested in baseball and from that experience a black kid could travel the country free. You don't have anything close to that today. At that particular time when somebody would mention the fact that Mr. Martin—W. S.—just walked in the stadium, there was nothing but respect, because I would say here's a man who has granted me the opportunity to ride this country, to see it firsthand.

Talk about the travel. A black ballplayer in the days of the Negro leagues saw North America.

Oh, you better believe it. That's what I'm talking about, see. And just like me, I'm so ... hung up on black history that it's a part of my lifestyle. I'm always ready—cocked—to talk about it.

Just like in Daytona Beach, Florida, I stood at the gravesite of Mary McCloud Bethune. In Hazelhurst, Mississippi, the name Richard Wright popped into my mind and just like in Durham, North Carolina, when we had spring training at one time with the Indianapolis Clowns, I used to sit out and watch Lee Calhoun, that great hurdler that went to the Olympics. I was always *seeking out* great blacks. Like New York, when I first met Sugar Ray Robinson. He put his arm around me and my knees buckled. [Laughs] All of these type of great blacks, whether in music or not. I had a chance to meet Danny "Bang-Bang" Wambaugh, who at one time had beaten Kid Gavilan.

I looked up the hotel for this song "Jumpin' at the Woodside." The Woodside Hotel. The Teresa Hotel. Small's Paradise in New York. All of these things associated with blacks—this is what I was out there observing. Birdland. Everywhere we played where there was a great black school like Morehouse in Atlanta.

I was traveling the country at the expense of black owners and I was gaining all of this knowledge from this great black history. It became more important to me than baseball. After awhile I was out there playing baseball in organized baseball — I guess so-called organized baseball because I always said it was organized like most other places throughout the country at the time: to keep blacks *out*. But, anyway, all of this became part of me.

If you heard of Ted Rasberry, he was a great black man. I even see Larry Lester as a great black man. I have all of this admiration for great black men. I mean *Men*. I'm not talking about lackeys. I'm talking about *men*.

When I was scheduled to go back to the Indianapolis Clowns — this was after the knee injury that I received in so-called organized baseball against a Philadelphia Phillies [team] when I was playing with Mount Vernon — I thought I was well enough to return to playing but I began to favor this knee of mine and ruined my arm.

At that time I was originating all of these different gimmicks. One was used in this movie that I thought was the worst depiction of the Negro leagues you'd ever want to see, *The Bingo Long Traveling All-Stars*.

Here recently I had a little bit part in this movie, *Soul of the Game*. I heard so many people say, "Is that the right depiction? Was this a part of the Negro league?"

I say, "Hey, I heard of the catcher, Josh Gibson. We've heard of Jackie Robinson and Satchel Paige, but this argument among the three of them about who goes first I was completely unaware of any such thing ever happening." Sometimes movies exaggerate things to grasp the viewers' minds.

Getting back to Ted Rasberry, I chose not to go back with the Indianapolis Clowns because of hearing about Ted Rasberry and

his enterprises, such as the basketball team, the New York Harlem Satellites, which featured Rookie Brown from the Harlem Globetrotters. He played in the movie *The Harlem Globetrotter Story* with Dorothy Dandridge.

Ted had employed Goose Tatum to come back, the original showman for the Harlem Globetrotters. Along with Goose Tatum came Nat "Sweetwater" Clifton, one of the first three blacks to go into the NBA. I wouldn't miss that opportunity of being there with these two guys.

At a young age after seeing *The Harlem Globetrotter Story* I had this hang-up about Rookie Brown, why he would call a black college "jerkwater." That's a part of the plot. But the plot of that movie was one that you don't see too often today because it was talking about the togetherness of blacks at that particular time. It was really focused upon Rookie Brown, who wanted to individually be the star of the Harlem Globetrotters after leaving a black college. Because of his inability to come together with the rest of the team, the Trotters lost to the Boston Celtics in the plot, I think. It was a teaching experience after that loss that in order to win you *must* be together.

All of these things were very important to me and I was upset about Rookie. And do you know what? Once I met Rookie Brown — and I'm telling you about guys with *class*— this guy was the sweetest guy you've ever met in your life. And he would always tell me after I voiced my feelings towards him in that movie, he said, "Joe, you must always remember that that was an illusion. That was a part of the plot."

This guy, as well as Goose Tatum and Nat "Sweetwater" Clifton, they were *class*. I'm talking about *class*. And when you speak of the Negro leagues as a whole at that time before I became a part of it, nothing but *class*. The Kansas City Monarchs — I mean, they talk about the New York Yankees and the class they have; hey, there was no difference between the New York Yankees and Kansas City Monarchs. How guys would keep their dressware so neat in a cramped situation all the time. How they would carry irons to iron their clothes.

I mean, I met nothing but men, guys like Lonnie Summers. He was among such guys as Double Duty, Satchel Paige. When he had come back into the Negro league with the Chicago American Giants, I can remember I was playing third base and Lonnie Summers stood at the plate and I think I was playing a bit shallow. This guy could hit as hard as Willard Brown. See, they talk about the Josh Gibsons and the home runs that Josh produced — there were *numerous* fellows that could hit that ball as equally hard.

Lonnie Summers pulled one of those inside pitches straight down the line to me playing shallow and the only thing that I could do was throw my glove up in front of my face and put my arm across my waist and try to keep me from being killed. The ball was hit so hard it was just like a knuckleball coming at me. The only thing I could do was holler, "Aaagh!"

And do you know what? All of a sudden it dawned on me that that ball did not hit me. It went past me so hard that Lonnie Summers tripled and he was laughing *so* hard when he got to third base he had to fall out on the ground. He just let his arm be in contact with a part of the third base bag. He was laughing so hard and he asked me not to get upset with him. [Laughs] He said, "Son, tell your manager that you couldn't help yourself." He said, "Tell your manager that you did the best you could."

And do you know, I began to look at *all* these different players and I couldn't believe it. A young black player had to love Jackie Robinson. You know why? Had not it been for Jackie Robinson coming back to the Kansas City Monarchs and then moving forward with the Dodgers, a lot of guys like Joe Henry would've never been heard

of. Had Jackie Robinson not made it, had Jackie Robinson not gone from the Kansas City Monarchs to the Dodgers, those teams would've still been intact in 1950. There were guys 45 years old could perform as well almost as a guy 20. But by Robinson going from Kansas City to the Dodgers, it created openings throughout the Negro league for guys being purchased.

You'd be surprised at the guys that I knew could've gone straight to one of those teams at that time, like Chicago White Sox, Chicago Cubs. Bob Wilson, Bob Harvey — I could just name 'em from now on. They could've did the same thing Ernie Banks did, to step off the Kansas City Monarchs' bus and step into a Chicago Cubs' uniform.

Banks and I were very close. We used to run around together, Ernie, Ollie Brantley, and myself, looking at the town and things like that. Sightseeing before game time. Ollie would tell Ernie, "I'm gonna strike you out every time you come up." They'd joke around.

And then Mays; I think I got a little scar on my leg from Willie Mays. When they were advertising him — the Birmingham Black Barons: "Willie Howard Mays." And this guy right here was just completely out of this world.

But then I saw so many more guys. Everywhere I looked there was a potential guy who could've been playing what was *called* major league baseball. Sometimes interviewers get awful upset with me for saying the things that I say, but before the advent of Jackie Robinson there was no major league baseball. I mean, there was Negro leagues and white leagues, because the best had not yet come together. When the integration occurred, then the best ballplayers began to come together. Not only then did it become "major," but it transcended just being major. It became big business. Look at it today.

I'm being honest to goodness truthful when I say this to you: I have almost lost respect for most blacks in basketball, baseball, and football. Because when Jackie Robinson went to the Dodgers, I thought at that point the turn of feelings among blacks and whites in America would begin to change.

But I just don't feel from the sacrifice of so many guys *long* before Joe Henry, I don't feel like the majority of those baseball players [today] have did anything for the black community. The Negro league, during its time, was just as important within the black community as the St. Louis Cardinals or the St. Louis Rams to St. Louis, or Atlanta Braves or Atlanta Falcons to Atlanta. They have contributed nothing, and with *all* of this money explosion, it is terrible.

Until the Negro leagues just completely folded from existence — I understand it could have been around the early '60s — do you know with the money that these blacks are getting that every black former Negro leaguer existing should be getting $25,000 a year from 'em.

There's a lotta ignorance among some of those players, too, you know. I played against Joe Black. How could they stop or have a cutoff point of '47 when two or three of your greatest ballplayers happened in the '50s? That was Ernie Banks, Willie Mays, and Henry Aaron. Just like this $10,000 per year that some players are getting, do you know even if they started that at a certain point it should've been phased out? Say if guys from '47 to '50 — $10,000; maybe guys from '50 to '55 — $5,000; maybe guys from '55 to '60 — $2,500. These people were a part of the Negro league and they kept the Negro league in existence although all of the teams had gone.

You have to tip your hat to Ed Hamman and Syd Pollack. Like when I was with the Indianapolis Clowns. That's where I started my showing after the injury in organized baseball. It was a part of history that if the average person knew about it that at that time black owners and white owners came together to put together a masterpiece.

It should tell Americans that black owners and white owners and blacks and whites could have been getting done perfectly at that time. The Negro league had an opportunity to really bring about the point that we can all work together.

When you look at the overall picture, although the great sacrifice was made by so many blacks playing ball at the time and where other blacks were a part of it, such as bus drivers, etc., do you know that, really, the demise of that league brought destruction to a lot of players and a lot of team owners.

In 1975 I started a manuscript but at the time we didn't have all the literature on the Negro league then as we do now. When I started this manuscript I didn't have it set up or structured just to deal with baseball. It was a book dealing with America. It was from a psychological standpoint, a philosophical standpoint. It was dealing with society. It was dealing with all of these things. It was entitled *Big Niggah Catchin', Little Niggah Pitchin'*, which actually happened in a game where I played with the Memphis Red Sox.

Casey Jones was about six-five. We had a pitcher, his name was Frank Thompson. His nickname was Frank "Groundhog" Thompson. He was about five-five. This was during the time when the baseball school that Goose had put together was going on.

There weren't many players for the Memphis Red Sox there, but what Goose did, he put the youngsters who were coming to that school to try to make the Red Sox and he formed a team — a mixed team — and promoted it as the Negro leaguers and an all-star team.

There was a white fella on the PA system and he called the regular lineup — the shortstop, first baseman, etc. — and he got to the battery — the pitcher and the catcher. This combination was there that night: Casey and Frank "Groundhog" Thompson.

The PA announcer said when he got to the battery, "The battery for the Memphis Red Sox tonight will be a big niggah catchin' and a little niggah pitchin'. Now you niggahs can get it on."

This is a book that will deal with America and all aspects. I'm always interested in trying to get a message out that could be very meaningful. We are so programmed in America, we are so oriented to the fact that this is the way this is done — there is no other way to do it.

The way that I originated so many different things on the ballfield. When you see guys hitting a home run and walking from home plate, watching it sail outta the park — I was doing that in 1955. Clowning. I'm not saying that I hit home runs all the time, but with my back to the plate I took a picture with a tuxedo and tails on. There had been several times when I spun around before the ball reached me and hit home runs.

And do you know what I'd do after hitting that home run? I wouldn't even look at it because you can just about tell from the impact whether a ball is going out or not. Some might fool you. But then I would throw out both hands for the catcher to slap my hands and then I would step back to the umpire and do likewise. Then I would walk over to the stands and might joke with somebody there and then jog around the bases. I was doing that *then*. I guess they said Reggie Jackson originated that. No, no. Joe Henry originated that thing in '55 while clowning with the Indianapolis Clowns.

In fact, one night we were in Paducah, Kentucky, at the old Army base. Bill White was in service at the time. He went on to play with the St. Louis Cardinals, then he became president of the [National] league. I did that in a game where he was playing with the local team.

Just like wearing your pants long. I was doing that in 1955. When it was not acceptable for a person to have a mustache, I

was trying to grow a mustache. I'd take a wooden matchstick and burn it and put it in a little water and try to make me a mustache, so everything that really was outlawed for players to do, I was *doing* that. I have pictures to show that.

I always looked at the league from a different standpoint. Just like I was gonna say before the advent of Jackie Robinson, I didn't see it as just this guy isn't good enough to play ball on this particular team. I saw it as a means of not accepting blacks from the standpoint of jobs, because that's what it was all about: jobs.

The thing that hurt me very badly, the columnist from Chicago, after all the things that he did for me to get me started in the right direction, after Mr. Johnson and I had arrived at a decision, I never ever gave him the courtesy of knowing how much I appreciated everything he did for me. That was a hurting point in my life because I never got back to him to let him know exactly what my intentions were at that particular time. He had set it out for me even to the point of the only thing I needed was money to get to Los Angeles. Once there, he had everything else arranged for me. If I did not make the Angels I would be farmed to a lower team and work myself back up.

I played against Leon Wagner in the Mississippi–Ohio Valley League. This guy started off liking me after we played against each other the first time because he would talk about the cut I would take. This guy had the most vicious cut you'd ever wanna see.

You should see four display boards that I have — 40 by 60 — with all the pictures and everything. It is really out of sight. I have James Earl Jones' picture, and Billy Dee Williams'. I have these pictures included because I was saying that movie stars — black movie stars, that is — should know the history of *their* nationality. This is the first thing that I told Michael T. Williamson in St. Louis when I had a bit part in that *Soul of the Game.* It's not the best depiction of the Negro leagues but it's the only thing that's been closer to it, other than *The Jackie Robinson Story.*

Little Edwin Morrow, who played the role of the young Willie Mays, used to go with me to lecture. He's making another movie. He's from East St. Louis. He went to school at Lincoln High School where Lafonso Ellis, the kid with the Minnesota Timberwolves, went. And he's such a nice little kid. Very intelligent.

I know that you would prefer to talk about my batting average and all of these things but I just don't know. I saw one book that's supposed to be the history, that encyclopedia pertaining to the Negro leagues, talking about I hit .285 and I struck out more. When somebody showed me that I had to really laugh about it, but it keeps ol' Joe's name in there. It did serve a purpose, though; it did resurrect the Negro leagues.

Talk about your time in white baseball.

That goes along with being black in America at that particular time. There were people of an unintelligent type of lifestyle, especially where a black was concerned. We had places we couldn't go into. We'd ask some of the white players to bring different things back to you. Some of the fellas would get fed up with that and I couldn't blame 'em. They would take a position, "Wait a minute. I'm sick of this now. Let's *all* go in." And you had white players out there that would stand toe-to-toe with any restaurant owner, etc., who would deny a black player who played with them an opportunity to come in and eat or whatever.

On our team there were three of four blacks in 1952 when I went to Mount Vernon. I was traded to Mount Vernon. That Mississippi–Ohio Valley League was a strong league.

Where did "Prince Joe" come from?

After my injury, even doing shows that I put on with the Indianapolis Clowns,

there were still scouts from the Giants and different teams that were interested in me, but Ed Hamman would make it known very quickly, "Oh, his arm is gone. His leg is messed up." He was making sure that he was gonna hang on to this guy as a performer, not as just a serious-minded baseball player.

So I began to originate the gimmicks. The tuxedo was a part of the Negro league, like King Tut, and I took that top hat and tails. At one time I used to put about 18 bats down through the pants legs and go up to the plate. I'd pull out one and look at it. I'd throw it away and then I'd pull out another one. I might try to take a cut. Now, you can't take too good a cut because of all these bats, but I'd go through the motions pretty good. After that I'd pick out two or three more and look at 'em and throw 'em away. Every time I'd pull out more and more; and more the people in the stands, they would just go completely wild.

Okay, all of a sudden here comes that label "Prince." That was some of Ed Hammond's doings. "Prince Joe Henry — this guy believes that baseball is a gentleman's game and he wants to come dressed formal." Different things like that. That's how I acquired the name "Prince."

I did a lot of things out there originating gimmicks. I'd take a lead off first base and the pitcher would throw to pick me off. I had that way of falling backwards and sliding; I don't know how I did it. Don't ask me 'cause I can hardly stand up, but always my beaten-up derby on my head would be touching the bag. There was some timing involved.

To be a showman out there, you really need the aid of the people around you and those guys were very, very considerate of me putting on a show. I tried to do a pretty good job of playing and putting on a show, too. My arm was sort of bad because of favoring my leg. At third base if I got a shot off the bat of a guy at the plate, knowing how bad the pain was — just the thought of me turning that ball loose hard — I would take off running across the diamond straight toward the pitcher's mound. About the time I felt I was close enough to deliver that ball to get the runner out, that's what I would do. People in the stands would think I was trying to outrun the batter. No, I was trying to get close to first base before I turned that ball loose.

I used to take a glove and tuck it up under my arm in that coat and stand at the plate like that and take one hell of a cut at the ball and miss it three or four feet. Then, maybe the next time, I'd have my arm folded with my hand in the glove without the people in the audience seeing it. When the guy came down through there with a fastball I'd slap that glove out, catch the ball, take a step up, throw the ball up in the air, and just like you're fungoing, I'd hit that ball. In Yankee Stadium one time I turned my back to Charley Pride and hit it up against that right field wall there.

BATTING RECORD

Year	Team, Lg	G	AB	R	H	2B	3B	HR	RBI	BA
1950	Mem, NAL	48	183	30	52	4	4	0	15	.284
1951										
1952	Canton, MOV	89	343	68	104	15	4	9	43	.303
	Mem, NAL									
1953	MtVern, MOV	92	363	60	100	12	4	3	30	.275
1954		30	106	20	29	6	1	1	15	.274
1955	Ind, NAL									
1958	Detr, NAL	41	109	12	31	2		3	15	.284

Carl Holden
Birmingham Black Barons 1960

Born August 22, 1941, Madison, AL
Ht. 5'11" Wt. 200 Batted and Threw Right

By 1960 the Negro leagues had just about played out. A few teams tried to hold on, and did for another year or two, but it was a hand-to-mouth existence. More and more blacks were being signed to professional contracts, but still it was a tough road for the black ballplayers. The final major league team had just integrated in 1959 (the Boston Red Sox), and an African-American ballplayer had to be outstanding to be considered. An injury could mean the end of the line, and such was the case with Carl Holden.

Holden: I started out *real* young. We played sandlot; we started picking teams up. We actually started throwing a hardball when I was about 10 or 11 years old. We'd been playing stickball before that.

Back in those days I played infield and I played some outfield, but as I got bigger everybody was wanting me to catch. With that stature, everybody automatically wanted to make a catcher out of you.

Back in 1960 I had a tryout with Baltimore — the Baltimore Orioles — and Fred Hofman, he was the chief scout for the southeast. I was reading *The Sporting News* or something; somehow I got his name and address in Dunedin, Florida and I just dropped him a letter. When he got the letter, he had me to come up to Pensacola. They had this guy they called a birdwatcher; it was something like an audition in the middle of the winter. He had you running and he clocked you and he'd have you throwing a ball — checking skills like that. Didn't do any hitting. He timed us like home plate to first.

Four of my friends went with me. Out of the four, he sent me on to Thomasville, Georgia. I had hurt my knee earlier and I hurt it while I was down there and it kind of throwed me back. Some of the guys came in from the college world series and I got caught up in the numbers, because they had spent money on those guys.

They wanted to do surgery and I turned that down. I wound up coming back home, but I had an option. I could've come and rested up and they had the rookie league in Bluefield, West Virginia. I could've went there. Harry Dalton was over that stuff.

After I came back home, a few weeks later a guy that kind of watched out for ballplayers for the Negro league saw me. He sent ballplayers to Birmingham and Kansas City and those teams. He saw me and he sent me to Birmingham and that's how I wound up with Birmingham in 1960.

You played only one year. Why?
It was breaking down. I came back home and got a job. Out there on the road some days you didn't get your meal money. The money started drying up.

They signed me for $300 a month. That was pretty good, but they knew they weren't gonna pay it. [Laughs] They could've told me $500 a month knowing they weren't gonna pay. We got the meal money pretty regular. Sometimes we'd have a good crowd and they'd give us some cash, but they didn't stick to the contract. Most of the time they had trouble meeting the payroll.

I don't know if it was so bad. They was giving us something and then the hotels was free and I was doing something I enjoyed doing. You're 18 years old and you get to go all over — that's pretty good.

We went by bus. We had an old clinker but we got around. We had some problems with the bus, but we went all over the southeast. That year they really didn't do nothing up north. We got to most of the southern states — Tennessee, Alabama, some in Florida, Mississippi a lot.

Do you know your stats?

No, I didn't keep up with that, but I always hit .300 about everywhere I ever played.

Who was the best player you saw?

I think the best player I played with was Willie Smith with Birmingham. I caught him.

Was he the best pitcher?

He was the best pitcher I ever caught. Best pitcher I ever caught and played against was probably Stacy Acklin. He was an old Negro league player back years ago. The first time I caught Stacy I was like 18 years old and he was 42 years old. He'd throw three balls at you and then throw three on the outside corner. [Laughs] That's how good he was. We fought for possession of that plate and he'd back you off the plate and he had enough speed to do it.

Does one game stand out in your memory?

I think the game that stands out most in my memory was when I was like 14, 15

years old in high school. They had this boy named Johnny-Boy Childress; he pitched in the Negro league for the Detroit Stars and I think he played for Memphis and a couple of other teams. I hit back-to-back triples off of him and he didn't give up a whole lot of hits. He was one of them guys that was cocky. He was good and he knew he was good. When you played against him you better bring your best game because you wasn't gonna score a whole lot of runs off of him. I guess he was in his mid 20s when I played against him.

You hit back-to-back triples. Were you fast?

Well, I didn't think I was, but when I went to the Orioles camp we were running with the catchers. A friend of mine from Southern University was also a catcher, and we ran off and left all the catchers so they made us run with the outfielders. But the guys I grew up with, we was playing football and they was halfbacks and I was a lineman and they'd always run off and leave me and I didn't think I was running that fast. But when I got into camp running with guys that played the same position, I was as fast as they were or a little faster.

Would you be a ballplayer if you were a young man today?

I'd do it in a heartbeat and I'd make me some money doing it this time. [Laughs] Nice smooth diamonds, lights.

You see, back then a ball would go out of the lights and you'd have to wait 'til the ball came back in the lights to go after it. Now they've got all that stuff taken care of. Most people didn't realize back then it was a lot harder playing a game than it is today.

Any regrets from baseball?

No. I just wish I could've played longer and not had any injuries. I felt like when I was at the training camp, if it hadn't slowed me up I think I would've got signed to a contract.

I was a catcher and they started working me out at first base and third base. Most of 'em looked at you being kind of short for a first baseman. McGraw was a first baseman at Baltimore I think and that was unusual 'cause he was about 5-10 and for a first baseman that's kind of short.

What did you do when you left the Black Barons?

After I came back to Huntsville, Alabama, I played up until 1968. I tore my ankle up; that's when I stopped playing. It was maybe a step behind playing with Birmingham but it wasn't that far behind because they had some good athletes. A lot of those guys, they had played semipro and stuff and some played professionally. Like Willie Smith; he played after he had been to the majors.

What kind of job did you have?

Back then I kept stock for a bunch of cafeterias. I always worked around food and beverages — wait tables, tend bar. It kind of led up to the position I'm in now. For the past 28 years I've had a beverage store.

We've done fairly good. We've educated both our kids. My son, he's got his doctoral degree and my daughter, she'll finish her Master's soon.

Top: Buck O'Neil (l) and Carl Holden (Photograph courtesy of Carl Holden.)
Bottom: Mr. and Mrs. Carl Holden with Mrs. Jackie (Rachel) Robinson (center). (Photograph courtesy of Carl Holden.)

At this age now, I'm ready to do a little traveling. I hope to go on some of those baseball trips. Scruggs and I, we usually travel together. We've had a lot of fun. We stay in much better hotels than we stayed at when we was playing ball. [Laughs]

Every now and then you'd get a nice rooming house and occasionally a hotel, but most times they weren't much or either you were on the bus and that bus would get a little congested. When you got back to Birmingham everybody'd be a little rank and that shower would get a good workout. [Laughs]

Carl Holden (Photograph courtesy of Carl Holden.)

BATTING RECORD

Year	Team, Lg	G	AB	R	H	2B	3B	HR	RBI	BA
1960	Birm, NAL									

Vernell Jackson
Memphis Red Sox 1950-1951
Houston Eagles 1951

BORN MARCH 1, 1930, MADISON, IL
HT. 6'1" WT. 180 BATTED AND THREW RIGHT

When I met Vernell Jackson I thought he was some other ballplayer's son. He looks as if he's in his mid to late 40s; when he told me he was 70 I couldn't believe it. Some folks just age better than others do.

He received early coaching from the late Josh Johnson, a catcher in the Negro leagues and later an educator. From there, Jackson went to a top-level semipro team in St. Louis and then to the Negro American League's Memphis Red Sox. His professional career was only two years, however. He might have gone on to be a household name because the Boston Red Sox were high on him, but the Korean War was going on and he was drafted into the Marine Corps. An injury ended his playing career (and almost his life), but he managed semipro teams and umpired from 1955 through 2000.

JACKSON: I got started on the Y team in the schoolyard when I was seven here in Madison, Illinois. Then coach Josh Johnson came to town in 1946 and formed a team around us. I had three other cousins. I was about 12 years old then. He just let us play 'til we got to 15.

When we got to 15 he put us in a league over in St. Louis. We done so good in the league in St. Louis that the teams over there asked us if me and my cousins and a couple more guys, if we would not play together. On Sunday we played on different teams.

When I got in high school we didn't have no high school baseball team because the school was too small, so I played with a team in East St. Louis called the East St. Louis Colts. Bigger fellas. These were men, but I was in high school. At that time Mr. Wallace was the coach and on that team was Sam Jethroe, who played with the Braves,

and Al Smith, who played with the Chicago White Sox. I played with them until 1948.

Then in 1949 I barnstormed with Satchel Paige. He picked me up in Sportsman's Park. I barnstormed with him for six weeks. I came back home and went to college down at North Carolina State. It was then called the Colored Intercollegiate Athletic Association. I played down there for that summer.

I come back and Mr. Johnson sent me down to Memphis and I made the Memphis Red Sox in 1950. I played 'til '52 when I went in the service. When I came back out I didn't play no more ball. I just managed 'cause I was wounded. I managed from '55 'til 1971. Semipro. We traveled around. In '72 I started umpiring semipro. I did that up until 2000, then that was it.

I played with Memphis from 1950 to 1951 and I went to Houston in June. Then

89

Vernell Jackson (Photograph courtesy of Vernell Jackson.)

in September that's when I went in the service.

Do any games stand out?

Quite a few with Memphis. I had one good one with Houston.

One that I had with Memphis, we were playing in Kansas City. Elston Howard was playing for Kansas City. We beat Kansas City, 2-to-1, and Ellie hit a home run off me in the ninth inning. It kinda broke my heart. [Laughs] We talked about that 'til he passed. He was a good ballplayer. I played with him; he played with me with the Colts. Mr. Johnson sent him to Kansas City and me to Memphis. I wish we'd've went together. Then we played together in the Marines.

You were drafted into the Marines?

Yeah.

How were you wounded?

I was in combat. I got wounded on the line. I got hit with a mortar shell. I was lucky. Four of us out of the whole company lived out of that. Korea.

Who were some of the other players you faced?

I faced all of the teams we played. Willie Mays was in the league with Birmingham. Ernie [Banks] was with Kansas City. Ernie and Ellie played together. Monte Irvin was with Newark. One of the Bankhead boys was pitching. It was Sam. With the Clowns was Archie Ware and the lady that played second base, Toni Stone. That was the only female that I played against in the league.

Some of the other players I can remember playing against back then are Luis Tiant, Earl Wilson, Earl Battey, Donn Clendenon, Tommy Harper, Lou Johnson, Vic Power, Sam "Toothpick" Jones, Tony Taylor, and John Roseboro.

I played with Bobby Boyd, who played first base; he went on with the White Sox. Josh Gibson's son — he didn't go nowhere but he was with the Homestead Grays. Pittsburgh Crawfords — they had a pitcher that went to the Braves, a lefthander. A Cuban. He went to Schenectady, New York, and pitched.

Was there a batter who gave you a lot of trouble?

Monte Irvin gave me a whole *lot* of trouble. He hit the ball.

I thought I could handle all of 'em. You know, when you play against one another you see what they're doing in batting practice and when you get your chance to pitch, you try to do what you think can get 'em out. I can say this much for myself: I had successful luck.

Do you know your record?

Yeah. My record for my first year in 1950 was 13-and-3. I got picked for the East-West All-Star game. I didn't pitch. In the East-West All-Star game in Chicago they very seldom let a rookie pitch.

The following year the Boston Red Sox picked me up in San Antonio, Texas, and followed me all the way back to Memphis as we made out little tour. They picked me up in '51 and they wanted to put me on their farm team in Sacramento. That was Triple-A at that time. I left there and I went to Houston, and when I went to Houston they still followed me. I went to Sacramento just before I got drafted in the service and I stayed there for about three weeks and I had to come home. I got a letter that said I had to come home to see my draft board. I couldn't see the draft people out there.

On that team was Walt Dropo. I remember a lefthanded pitcher named Ted Schuster. Billy Higgins was the coach. He was the fella that picked me up, an old fella. He took me to the airport and when I got here they told me I had to go in the service.

I got in one game for Sacramento. I did good.

When I was young I always wondered why the Negro league never went out there and played. I guess it was too far to travel. They had some good teams out there, all up and down that coast.

How were the travel conditions with Memphis?

[Laughs] That ol' raggedy bus. The veteran players, they had a seat, but the rookies had to sit on the floor in the middle of the bus. You worked your way to a seat. If they get rid of a guy and then they bring in one, then you get a seat. [Laughs]

It was a pretty good bus. It wasn't good as a Greyhound or it wasn't good as a Trailways, but it got you from city to city, from state to state, 'til it broke down. Then you'd just have to wait 'til they'd get it fixed. [Laughs]

Was there a bus driver or did one of the players drive?

There was a bus driver, but then sometimes the captain or the secretary — one of the three — would be the driver.

How was the housing on the road?

We all stayed at different places when we'd go into cities. They'd house you — two players here, three players there. You ate with the people where you stayed or they had little places where you'd go to eat. They knew where to eat it in different places in every city. You eat on the run. They give you that little two dollars and fifty cents that had to last you all day long. [Laughs]

You covered the whole eastern half of the country. Where were the best and worst places?

Well, the worst places was in the southern part. The Midwest was nice. A few places out east were bad, like we couldn't play in Fenway Park, but we could play in Braves Field. When you came to Chicago we couldn't play in Wrigley Field but we could play in Comiskey Park. Out of the original 16 we could play in every park except Fenway Park in Boston and Wrigley Field in Chicago.

Pumpsie Green was with me on that team, played second base. He was the first [black] with Boston and there was another infielder out of Texas. I never will forget Walt Dropo. He put his arms around us and said, "We'll try to make it to the majors." And he made it. Big Walt.

If you were a young man would you be a ballplayer again?

Yes. I would do the same thing over again. I enjoyed it. The only thing that I disliked is when Uncle Sam grabbed me and put me in the service.

Who was your manager with Memphis?

Goose Curry. He was a character. [Laughs] If they ain't bothering the players and letting 'em play he was all right, but if the umpires were not giving the benefit of the doubt, he's got to come out and say something. He just couldn't sit in the dugout. If the game was going good he'll sit there but, like I said, if he thought the umpire was kinda giving us a raw deal Goose would come out of the dugout and give the umpires what he thought was right. Then he'd go back to the dugout.

None of the players couldn't cool him down. Casey Jones, the catcher; Bobby Boyd, the first baseman; and Neal, the third baseman, they could really cool him down. He would listen to those three fellas. They'd know when he got mad and they'd put their arm around him and say, "C'mon into the dugout." He'd get in the dugout and throw bats, break bats, throw balls. [Laughs] You'd be ducking. [Laughs]

And all the teams were playing for 60/40 percentage of the gate. He would always want to win that 60 percent.

How much were you paid?

When they signed me, they signed me for $550 a month. Guys like Boyd, Neal, and Casey, they were getting right at $750 or almost a thousand. And they gave $2.50 for meals a day when you were on the road. When you were at home you did your own.

The pitchers when I left there were Buddy Woods, Frank Barnes, Willie Hutchinson, Ollie Brantley, Sam Bankhead, Dan Bankhead's brother, a boy named Isiah Harris from Monroe, Louisiana, lefthander, a good pitcher. I think we had a staff of eight or either nine pitchers.

We had to play more than one position. You didn't make the team playing just your position. I played outfield; when I started out, I started as an outfielder and they made a pitcher out of me in St. Louis. Goose never did put me in the outfield, but he knew I could play it. We carried 15 to 18 ballplayers.

PITCHING RECORD

Year	Team, Lg	G	IP	W	L	Pct	SO	BB	H	ERA
1950	Mem, NAL			13	3	.813				
1951	Mem-Hou, NAL									
	Sac, PCL	1		0	0	—				

Clarence Jenkins
Memphis Red Sox 1946-1947

BORN FEBRUARY 20,1927, VERONA, MS
HT. 5'5" WT. 145 BATTED LEFT, THREW RIGHT

What are the odds of three men with the same name playing baseball?

If the name is John Smith or Bob Jones, maybe the odds are good, but Clarence Jenkins is a lot less common. Yet three men named Clarence Jenkins played in the Negro leagues.

The first was Clarence "Fats" Jenkins, an outstanding outfielder for several teams from 1920 through 1940. The second was Clarence "Barney" Jenkins, a catcher who performed for the Detroit Stars in 1929. The third, and the one of concern to us now, is Clarence "Full Bosom" Jenkins, a speedy, strong-armed, five-foot five-inch tall shortstop who played for the Memphis Red Sox in 1946 and 1947.

After leaving the Red Sox, Jenkins did not leave baseball. He played on for decades, first in semipro and then in old-timers leagues. Along the way he founded the International Afro-American Sports Hall of Fame and is a member as well as founder. Today he remains active, making appearances on behalf of baseball.

JENKINS: I played shortstop. I could play second base. I played all the infield and the outfield; the only thing I couldn't do was pitch.

How did you get started in professional baseball?

All my life, even when I was a kid in Verona, Mississippi, where I was born, I always liked baseball. Me and the kids used to play with a rag ball.

I played a little in high school, not too much. Most of the time I played was in the Navy. I went in in 1943 and I played around the base there. We played the Army and the Marines.

I played with the Memphis Red Sox, Tupelo Tigers, and Verona Blue Jays. I started with the Verona Blue Jays. It was just a hometown team. Then the Tupelo Tigers. Then Memphis.

How much did the Red Sox pay you?

$250 a month. It wasn't too bad. If we played we got paid. If we missed games we didn't get paid. I played two years.

Who were some of your teammates?

Casey Jones was one. There's a lot of 'em. I can't think of all of 'em now. I'm gettin' old — 74 years old now. I feel pretty good to be a old man.

I got two sons, two grandsons, two granddaughters, two great grandsons, and two great granddaughters. I love 'em all. I got some in Memphis and the others stay here [Detroit].

Did any of them play ball?

Both of my sons played ball, and my grandsons. They played from the Little League up to the Pony League. They quit there. My baby son, he had a chance to go to the Cardinals. He was scouted by the

Clarence Jenkins (Photograph courtesy of Clarence Jenkins.)

Cardinals, but he said he didn't wanna go so he stayed home. My grandson, he was a catcher but that basketball got him. That's what they want to play.

What kind of hitter were you?

My lifetime battin' average was .300.

When I quit playin' ball with Memphis and I moved to Detroit I played with the 8-Mile Road Eagles. That was semipro and they played in the recreation league. We played a lotta games up in Canada and up in Petoskey and up in northern Michigan, Ohio, Indiana. We had a good team. We won the championship in 1950.

Then I started playin' with the old-timers. That was the International Old-Timers — 50 and up.

The 8-Mile Road Eagles, we had us a good team. We played the Pittsburgh Crawfords and we beat 'em. Cecil Kaiser pitched and William Doody was the catcher. We had a guy named Dee Jenkins. Robert Carter, Sonny Kitchen, and all them. Back when we was playin' in '49 and '50 and on up it was baseball. That was all.

Then I started workin' with the Little League and I went with the Little League up until '64, '65. That's when I started with the old-timers and we played up until about '89. We still get out there and run a little bit sometime.

I was inducted into the International Afro-American Hall of Fame in 1994.

What did you do when you left baseball?

I worked at Ford Motor Company and I left there and went to Chrysler. I got laid off and I went to Kelsey-Hayes and I retired from there in 1979. I got hurt. I retired as a supervisor. I had a pretty good life. I've taken care of myself and I go to church.

Do any games stand out from your playing days?

I never will forget when I was with Memphis. We were playin' Satchel Paige in Kansas City. Satchel Paige used to throw! I always liked to play — I was funny — and he used to call me "Full Bosom" 'cause I was short and had a high chest.

Satchel Paige threw at my head and I ducked. I shook the bat at him; I told him, "You can't get by me. I'm gonna hit you if you throw the ball."

So he tried to strike me out and he couldn't do it. He had to walk me. He was a strikeout pitcher and if you wasn't careful he would get you. I fouled the ball and fouled the ball and popped up. I told him; I used to be mental with him. I said, "You can't pitch to me 'cause I'm better than you is." [Laughs] I used to play with him and he'd get angry, you know.

When I did all that, he became a pretty good guy, a pretty good friend of mine. He kept on playin' ball; he played with the St. Louis Browns and the Cleveland Indians.

The Cleveland Indians done drafted me but Lou Boudreau kept me outta the majors. He played shortstop, I played shortstop, and he was the manager. They wasn't gonna put me out there for him, so that kept me outta the majors. He was a good one. I knowed he was a good one. They brought me up and I stayed a while and they got rid of me.

Who was the best ballplayer you saw?

They all was good, you know. Satchel Paige, Double Duty. Buck O'Neil was a pretty good ballplayer — long, tall first baseman. He was a pretty good guy.

Red House — he was one of the greatest third basemen that I have seen in a long time. He didn't get the recognition that he should have got.

I don't know. There was a lotta good ballplayers. I just couldn't say one. The reason I could say Red House is because I played around him so long. We played against each other when I was with the 8-Mile Road Eagles. He was a good third baseman.

But all the Negro leaguers could play some ball. They could hit, they could run, and everything. Turkey Stearnes — he was another one. I don't believe nobody could hit a ball any better. Between him and Josh. They tell me Josh was a good ballplayer, but I don't know. Turkey Stearnes was a good one, too. He could hit the ball, but they say Josh was a good one, too. I don't know. I just missed Josh.

I love all these guys. I call 'em young

Clarence Jenkins (Photograph courtesy of Clarence Jenkins.)

guys now, you know, 'cause they get around and they look well. We just got through bein' together. We was down in Louisiana. We had a beautiful time.

Was there a pitcher who was particularly tough on you?

They had a guy they called — let's see, what was his name? I done forgot now. He was with the Birmingham Black Barons, a lefthander. That guy had a curve on him! It looked like I was steppin' in the bucket every time. I could hit him, but I just had to bunt the ball. I could bunt the ball and get a hit like that 'cause I could run. That's one thing I could do: I could run.

A boy named Smith — he's dead now; we used to call him "Rabbit" — he was a catcher. He used to tell me, "You can't hit him." They'd say, "What you know, li'l boy? You can't hit no ball."

Clarence Jenkins (Photograph courtesy of Clarence Jenkins.)

They used to tease me. The girls used to say, "Don't mess with my li'l honey." [Laughs]

I started tryin' to bat righthanded. I could do pretty good, but I couldn't get outta the way battin' righthanded like I could lefthanded, so I said I'll just stick with lefthanded.

Willie Mays was young and Hank Aaron was young. I played against 'em down there. I didn't know they were gonna make the majors and do that good. Mays wasn't much of a hitter when he started. He becomed to be a hitter when he got in the majors.

Talk about the travel.

We traveled at night, played in the daytime. Sleep in the car, eat in the car. Sometime we'd be down in different places and we'd have to sleep with the guys we played. Some of us stayed with them.

The old bus'd break down. I forgot the guy's name; he fixed it with barbwire and all that stuff. He fixed it with barbwire to keep it runnin'. It was a good bus but we never could keep it runnin'. He was a mechanic and everything.

Sometime we had to push that bus. It'd break down. It looked like it had more wire on it than anything else on the motor.

Travel was pretty good. We liked it. We couldn't stay in no hotel; we couldn't do a lotta things. I was born and raised down South; I was used to it. It didn't bother me.

Was there much overt racism?

Oh, yeah. Quite a bit. Some of the guys, they didn't wanna take it, but we went on. They threw at us and called us names and stuff like that.

I guess Jackie Robinson was the one they picked because I don't believe nobody else coulda stood what they did to us. He was the best man for that job. It wouldn'ta never happened if somebody else had been there.

I made a lotta money. White guys in my hometown called me "Full Bosom". That's all they ever knowed. They used to say, "My nigger can hit your pitcher" and stiff like that. That's all they knowed. They talked that stuff and everything, you know.

Was the racism tougher on the boys from the North than it was on you guys from the South?

Yeah, because they wasn't used to that. When the people messed with them, they wants to fight 'em. It didn't bother us because we was used to it. It was harder on the guys up North. There wasn't too many of Northern guys would take that stuff. But they had to take it then.

I never will forget. We was in Nashville and we was playin'. Some of them guys started that stuff and it almost got outta hand. But the police broke it up. We didn't stay there long. We had to leave there.

Some of 'em just got overbearin' about it. Some white guy just kept on. They pt a young kid up to do it. It got outta hand. The police broke it up and we had to leave there.

Did you find fewer problems when you moved to Detroit?

You know, I thought it was rough down South, but when I got to Detroit it was worse here. To me it were. There was so much favoritism. I couldn't play 'cause when I got hold of the 8-Mile Road Eagles team my brother stayed while they practiced 'cross the street and I went out there and I talked to the manager, George LeGrand. I talked to him and I said, "Do you need another ballplayer?"

He said, "Come on out for a trial."

They didn't like it 'cause I see 'em whisperin' to each other and they was talkin' "Who was he?" and all that and everything. I went on out and they kept me on the bench a whole year. Onliest thing I did was practice with 'em.

On the weekend they'd go out to play — semipro — and they was gettin' a dollar or two, a few dollars. And I couldn't play. I said if I can play durin' the week and can't play on weekends I might as well be goin' on to somewhere else.

Every weekend I'd go back to Memphis and play. Then I'd come back and go to work. I was workin' afternoons at Ford. I could fly down there and be back Monday. If they was playin' outta town I would go there. I did that 'bout a half a season.

One of the boys got hurt on 8-Mile Road Eagles and then they put me in and he couldn't get back. The guy was a good shortstop; he had a great arm, but if you got a good arm and don't know where you're gonna throw the ball that don't mean much. I was throwin' the ball accurate. When I got in there he couldn't get back.

I played with the 8-Mile Road Eagles up until I think it was '63. A long time. I played up into my 40s. Then I played with the old-timers. They played every once in a while. They traveled a lot, too. We used to go all up in Mackinaw and up in Petoskey. In Ohio. We played against Ferguson Jenkins over there in Canada.

I loved the game. That's all I do now: talk about it. When I get with somebody to talk about baseball, that's all.

I'm the founder of the Universal Sports Hall of Fame and Gallery. The onliest thing, we can't get a building. Our mayor, he ain't gonna help you do nothin'. He helped the white but he ain't gonna help the black.

I've been tryin'. I could take it to Mississippi to my hometown, but my friends, they don't wanna go. They want it in North Carolina or somewhere over there.

I said, "We need to move this Hall of Fame." I think they done found a builder. They haven't talked to me about it, but she was tellin' me about it. They might have something and if they do they gonna find the land and build a Hall of Fame. We need that.

Would you go back as a young man and play baseball again?

If I could. [Laughs] I really would. I love the game. I likes to travel anyway.

BATTING RECORD

Year	Team, Lg	G	AB	R	H	2B	3B	HR	RBI	BA
1946	Memphis, NAL									
1947										

Ernest Johnson
Kansas City Monarchs 1949-1953

BORN NOVEMBER 4, 1929, CLINTON, MS
HT. 6'3" WT. 170 BATTED LEFT, THREW RIGHT

Ernest Johnson began as a pitcher for the House of David in 1947 at the age of 17, and it was at that position that he joined the Kansas City Monarchs two years later. But he could hit and soon he became an outfielder. In 1953 the Monarchs' manager, Buck O'Neil, called him the best hitter on the team, a team which also had Ernie Banks and Pancho Herrera on its roster.

It was as an outfielder that the Monarchs sold him to the St. Louis Browns after the 1953 season. He played six years in the minor leagues, compiling seasonal averages of .320, .308, and .300. Only once did he bat lower than .288.

But when he reached 30 and found that the major leagues were still far away, he decided to retire, heeding the advice of a manager he had in his first year in the minors. He looks back at his career with no regrets.

You began playing professionally with the Kansas City Monarchs. Is that correct?

JOHNSON: No. I originally started with the Van Dyke House of David in 1947. I was around 18.

We lived in Chicago, and my mom had a friend that was rooming at the house of a gentleman named George Bennett, who was an ex–Negro league ballplayer. He was the business manager for the House of David. I had been playing in the Chicago Industrial League and he knew about me and he wanted to take me on the road with them, so that's how I got started. I was with them '47 'til '49.

The House of David traveled everywhere.

Well, mainly we covered more of the Midwest. We played everybody. Back in those days just about every town of any size had their own baseball team. During that time, especially in Minnesota and Iowa, you had a lot of teams that were stocked with college ballplayers and guys that had been to the major leagues or been in minor league ball and they were playing in these smaller towns. That's who we played.

With the House of David we were paid on a percentage: 60-40. No meal money, just 60-40.

Do you know any of your House of David stats?

No, I really don't. It was so long ago and, really, we didn't keep accurate statistics.

How did you get from the House of David to the Kansas City Monarchs?

The House of David and the Monarchs happened to be in the same town, which was Des Moines. We were going through. And if you were a decent ballplayer back in those days someone knew about you. "This guy here, he's a good ballplayer."

Dizzy Dismukes, who was the business manager for the Monarchs, had heard about me. We talked while we were here in Des Moines. That was in '48, and then in '49 he sent me a ticket to go to spring training with the Monarchs.

Was it agreed that you would make the team?

No. It was just you take your chance.

You were a big boy. You must have been pretty impressive out there on the mound.

No, really I wasn't because I only weighed about 160 pounds. I was tall.

With the Monarchs you received a salary.

Yeah. I got paid a set salary plus meal money. I think it was something like three dollars a day; my salary was $200 a month.

The first year I went to the Monarchs was in '49 and, for some reason or other, I didn't really like being there, so I went back to the House of David in '49 to finish out the season. In 1950 I was in the service at Fort Riley, Kansas, which is a hop, skip, and a jump from Kansas City, and whenever the Monarchs were in town I would go into Kansas City and I would be in the rotation. I would play with the Monarchs.

You were a pitcher then. Did you play outfield, also?

Yes. That was my position after I got out of service.

You stayed with Kansas City through 1953. The Monarchs were a high-profile, well-run team. How were the facilities?

Oh, we had wonderful facilities, as far as traveling. We had some of the best buses. We had top-notch travel facilities, I'll put it that way. We stayed in the better hotels than the Negroes could stay in. It was good.

How far did you travel?

As far east as New York and all over the South and the southern part of the country. And I think we played as far west as Denver.

Did you enjoy it?

Oh, yes. Hey, that was, to me, the best part of my life, playing with the Monarchs.

You had some famous teammates there.

Yeah. I played with Elston Howard and Curt Roberts and I guess the most famous would be Ernie Banks. He was a pretty good country ballplayer.

How did you get into the minor leagues?

I was old to the old St. Louis Browns, which turned out to be the Baltimore Orioles.

You spent six years in the minors. How did that compare with Kansas City?

The conditions were rough. The caliber of ball I would say, the team [Kansas City] that we had in '53 I think we could've beat *any*one in the minor leagues. We had that much talent.

Who were some of your other teammates there?

As I say, Ernie Banks. There was a gentleman named Henry Mason, who pitched for the Philadelphia Phillies; Francisco Herrera; Sherwood Brewer, who had been in the league for several years and he was an outstanding second baseman; and Henry Bayliss, Tom Cooper. We had a pitcher named John Jackson, who eventually pitched for the Cincinnati Reds. That's about all I can think of right now, off the top of my head.

Kansas City sent more players into professional ball than any of the Negro leagues teams.

That's true.

The Browns at the time you were sold to them were hand-to-mouth. Were there any problems?

I didn't have any problems with the Browns. I only played in their organization one year and I played that year in Canada in the Provincial League. I injured my knee and then I was released by them and the Cubs picked me up after that, the next year. Wid Matthews, who was the director of minor league ball, he called. At that time I was living in Chicago. He called and asked me if I would like to go to spring training with the Cubs' minor league. I said yeah and he said, "I can't guarantee you will make the team but we'll pay all your expenses."

I said, "That's fine." That's all I wanted, was just a chance to play.

We had Pepper Martin as our manager down there in spring training, and he took two of us to Macon, Georgia, where they never had integrated baseball before. Henry Aaron played the previous year for Jacksonville, but within the city of Macon they had never had integrated sports. It was rough there.

You had close to a .300 career average in the minors and had some punch. The numbers look as if you should have advanced further than you did. What happened?

Oh, I don't know. Maybe the Cubs gave up on me because in '57 I went to Portland in the Pacific Coast League for spring training. At that time Portland was owned by the Cubs and they started sending major league ballplayers down, like Monte Irvin and Solly Drake and these guys, and they had to make a place for 'em.

The next level was double-A, which was Fort Worth in the Texas League. At that time Shreveport was in the Texas League, also, and they still had this law: no integration. If you go into Shreveport for a four-game series, then I would have to sit on the bench. No, I couldn't even sit on the bench; I couldn't even be in the dugout.

I never went to Fort Worth because at that time I had just gotten married. I married a lady from Des Moines. I knew I could go back to Des Moines and play and I'd be with my wife. I told 'em, "I don't want to go to Fort Worth. Send me back to Des Moines." So that's what they did.

Then the next year they sold me to an independent team in the Western League, which was Sioux City.

The Western League cities were pretty advanced for the time in accepting players on ability rather than color. Did you encounter any problems?

In Des Moines and Sioux City—and you had Topeka, Kansas, and Amarillo and Colorado Springs, Pueblo, Albuquerque. Those cities were pretty receptive to the change. I didn't have that much trouble. The only trouble, some places—I remember in Topeka, Kansas—they refused to serve me in a restaurant, but as far as hotel accommodations and stuff like that, I didn't have any problems.

Does a game stand out?

Oh, no, not really. I can't say that there's one game. I enjoyed each day. I would go out there and enjoy what I was doing.

Which did you prefer, outfield or pitching?

I liked outfield because I liked to hit.

What did you do when you left baseball?

I went into retail for a couple of years, then I worked for the State of Iowa for five years. From there I went to Armstrong Tire and Rubber and I stayed there 28 years.

Who was the best player you saw?

Oh, golly. That's hard to say because I was never in awe of any one of 'em. I always felt that I was just as good as they were. [Laughs] Or better. As a matter of fact, playing with Ernie—although he is a gentleman and a good ballplayer—I read a letter from Buck O'Neil that was written to Tom Baird [Monarchs' owner], and he was giving him some insight on the 1953 team. Buck has me hitting third and the notation he put on there, he said, "Ernest Johnson can pitch and play the outfield. He is the best hitter on our team." [Laughs] That's pretty good.

As a batter, was there a pitcher who gave you a hard time?

There was a pitcher out in Colorado; he was a lefthander and I can't think of his name. He gave me problems. And then there was a kid that played for the Indianapolis Clowns; his name was [Ted] Richardson and he gave me problems. He was a lefthander, too.

As a pitcher, was there a batter who was tough?
No.

If you were a young man again, would you be a ballplayer?
Oh, yeah. Definitely. I liked baseball. I tell some people, "I played baseball and I got a chance to travel this whole country." People live their whole lives and don't see the country like I've seen it and I got paid to do it.

Do you have any regrets from baseball?
None. As a matter of fact, things that are happening to me now I never even visualized them happening once I stopped playing baseball. I felt that once I had quit that was just another facet of my life and I had to go on to something else. Now, through the [Negro Leagues Baseball] Museum some of the events that I have taken part in, like the reunions, let me see guys I hadn't seen in years and years and years.

Then there's a lot of things that's happening here with Des Moines, as far as public attention that I'm getting here. I never thought this would happen to me. I just feel that I'm blessed.

Why did you stop playing when you did?
EJ: I had a manager who told us, "Once you get to the point in baseball that you feel that you can't make it to the major

Ernest Johnson (**Photograph courtesy of Larry Lester.**)

leagues, stop playing. Because that's where the money is. Money's not in the minor leagues. I think only a few guys like Steve Bilko and those guys are making money in the minor leagues." He said, "Once you get to the point in life where you feel that you cannot make it to the major leagues, go home, get you a lunch pail, and go to work. Do something else." And that's what I did.

His name was Bill Krueger. He was the manager of Thetford Miners in the Provincial League. Fifty-nine was my last year.

BATTING RECORD

Year	Team, Lg	G	AB	R	H	2B	3B	HR	RBI	BA
1949	KC, NAL									
1950										
1951										
1952										
1953		62	260	43	77	12	5	11	43	.296
1954	Thetford, Prov	88	285	38	82	12	2	9	54	.288
1955	Macon, SAL	30	110	11	32	6	1	0	15	.291
	MgcVal, Pio	98	384	63	112	19	10	6	61	.292
1956	DesMns, WL	134	566	100	180	32	6	8	67	.318
1957		147	590	89	177	23	7	8	68	.300
1958	SiouxCity, WL	130	533	83	164	24	6	15	92	.308
1959	Chrlstn, SAL	107	339	42	90	12	1	10	43	.265

Tom Johnson
Philadelphia Stars 1940
Indianapolis Clowns 1950

BORN MARCH 10, 1917, PHILADELPHIA, PA
HT. 5'10" WT. 185 BATTED AND THREW RIGHT

Tom Johnson is one of the most unusual baseball players of all time. First, his career consisted of two seasons, ten years apart. That's something no one else ever did.

Second, he is one of the most educated men ever to play the game. He has a bachelor's degree from Springfield College, a master's degree from New York University, and a Ph.D. in physiology from the University of Maryland. In between, Dr. Johnson had stints at Tufts University and Howard University.

While attending Springfield College, he was a member of the baseball squad. He was probably the first Negro pitcher at the school. Following graduation in 1940, he was signed by the Philadelphia Stars. That fall, because of his YMCA and athletic training in college, he was recruited for service in the USO rather than entering the Army. He remained in that position for the duration of the war. He established USO camps both stateside and in Hawaii and he played baseball on several island teams.

When he returned home after the war, he became an instructor at Howard University, where he stayed for 32 years. He also developed and coached both baseball and swimming teams at the university, and coached the football team.

In 1950 he joined the Indianapolis Clowns and played during his summer break from school. Later, he played for the Black Sox, a local barnstorming team in the Washington, D.C.–Maryland area. Still later, he was a scout for the Pittsburgh Pirates.

He left baseball to work on his Ph.D. at the University of Maryland, then became Associate Professor in the medical school. He retired in 1978 as Associate Dean of Student Affairs in the graduate school. After retirement he and his wife toured the country, visiting every state. Today he spends his time reading and watching baseball on TV.

JOHNSON: I lived in Camden, New Jersey, which is right across the river from Philly. There was a gentleman who was a policeman and he was interested in the high school players at Camden High. It was he who was instrumental in my going to Philadelphia.

I was probably better known at the time as a track athlete, particularly in the Penn Relays. I was a good 440 runner. Camden High had an *outstanding* relay team, so that was part of the introduction.

Then I played sandlot ball for a while. It grew from there. I pitched for our school team and was always a pitcher.

If you could, envision the ellipse down right across from the White House. Baseball was played in the evenings when people were getting off from work. Our sandlot team played on the ellipse, which had about four diamonds in action at the same time. I have an old clipping from a *Washington Post* sports writer which talks about Johnson pitching. We were kind of an outstanding team.

And then when I joined the Black Sox, which was a sandlot team, a guy we called Dofie was the manager and he had some very good ballclubs down there that played through southern Maryland. I eventually was recruited by him and that's where I played quite a bit at the sandlot level. I was still in high school when I started with them.

I graduated from Springfield College in Springfield, Massachusetts, and I finally got to the Philadelphia Stars through that route. I pitched for Springfield. I was perhaps the first Negro pitcher for Springfield College. At that time, we didn't have many on the teams. I know when we went South, I couldn't go. Our team used to go on spring break — Easter time — and the New England teams would all head south. I was not able to go. The color barrier had not been broken at that time.

We had one [Negro] fellow — Ben Hargraves — who played first base, but he was a little bit behind me. I believe he did play my last year. I graduated in 1940. He was a good player.

I was in Philadelphia with Jim West. [Gene] Benson was the center fielder. Webster McDonald was the manager for a while; he was a submarine pitcher and he was from around Philadelphia. Henry McHenry was one of our stellar righthanded pitchers. He was good. Some of them would go to the islands in the winter. [Red] Parnell. [Leon] Ruffin was a catcher. [Robert] Palm played with the New York Black Yankees and he joined us. Jim West was my roommate. [Mahlon] Duckett was there.

I was with them just that one season after I got out of school.

How did you join the Clowns a decade later?

The owner, Syd Pollack, became interested in me and I was picked up in Camden and traveled with them. From Camden we went south. We barnstormed through Tennessee and ended up in Calgary. Most of the time there were night games. We played there at the chariot races and then we stayed at Brandon, Manitoba, for a while. From Brandon we went to several towns not too far from there.

Buster Haywood was our manager. Harry Butts, Jim Cohen, [Verdes] Drake in center field. Sam Hairston was a catcher. Henry Merchant was the right fielder.

Were you tempted to play longer?

No. I started teaching.

During the war I was in Hawaii and played there. I was detailed to the USO clubs and I came back stateside near the end of the war. They were going to transfer a number of the USO workers to places like Georgia and Mississippi and so on, so I decided I would not accept those appointments.

In the meantime, I was invited to join my colleague from Springfield College, Eddie Jackson. He was the athletic director at Howard University. I became a member of his staff and, of course, baseball was in that picture.

If you were a young man again, would you be a baseball player or would you devote your time to education?

[Laughs] That's a tough one 'cause I'm in love with both of them. Education would be a priority for me. I didn't put baseball first, but it was high on the list. Whenever there was an opportunity and I was invited to barnstorm, I'd play for a weekend. I had split loyalties, I guess. [Laughs] I loved the game. I still do.

I've been a Brooklyn Dodger fan and I was friendly with some of those ballplayers, even during the war when they were up in Maryland. I had a chance to play against some of the Dodgers.

With the Clowns, I was friendly with the [business] manager, Bunny Downs. I had an opportunity to chat with him from time to time on the bus as we barnstormed.

Dr. Thomas Johnson

Former Pitcher for the 1940 Phila. Star.

Signing February 19th, 2000
Noon to 2 PM # 4
MEGA Baseball Card Show
February 18, 19 & 20, 2000
Cherry Hill Mall
An affiliate of THE ROUSE COMPANY
Cherry Hill, NJ
WWW.BellmanEvents.COM / 1-800-676-2188
9 -FILE: MP/ CHERRY HILL MALL SIGNERS 02-00 Page 7--Tuesday, February 01, 2000

Tom Johnson (Photograph courtesy of Dr. Thomas Johnson.)

PITCHING RECORD

Year	Team, Lg	G	IP	W	L	PCT	HO	BB	SO	ERA
1940	Phi, NNL									
1950	Ind, NAL									

Marvin Jones
Kansas City Monarchs 1954–1955

BORN NOVEMBER 22, 1932, ATLANTA, GA
HT. 5'11½" WT. 190 BATTED AND THREW LEFT

Before the Milwaukee Braves moved to Atlanta and became the Atlanta Braves, there was another Atlanta Braves. It was a semipro team and this is where Othello "Chico" Renfroe discovered the young Marvin Jones. Renfroe recommended the youthful southpaw to his old friend and former teammate Buck O'Neil, and that's how Jones became a Kansas City Monarch.

JONES: I started playin' around Atlanta at an early age, about nine or ten. We played stickball. The first team I played on was the year after Larry Doby broke into the major leagues. I played for a team called the Doby Indians. I was 16.

Othello Renfroe was from Atlanta, Georgia, and after his playin' days was over he moved back to Atlanta and Othello scouted me. I was playin' for the Atlanta Braves, which was a team that he played for. A lot of the baseball players that came off of the old Atlanta Black Crackers, which was a professional team, came to the Atlanta Braves, and I got a chance to play with most of those guys.

He was a scout. Othello played for Kansas City and him and Buck O'Neil, bein' friends, any time he scouted a player he thought had good potential, he sent 'em to Kansas City. Willie Clyde Bennett played with Kansas City. Joe Douse, he played with Kansas City. Richard Phillips is still in Atlanta; he played for Kansas City. So Othello sent several players from Atlanta to the Kansas City Monarchs.

I was considered above average and when I first got there, Buck O'Neil used me mostly as a relief pitcher. Sometimes I would pitch maybe one innin', two innin's at the most.

Do you remember your first game?

Yes, the first day I got there. I left Atlanta and they was up in North Carolina somewhere. I just happened to get there about 12:00 that day. I hopped a cab and went right straight to the ballpark. I was given a uniform, and some of the guys from Atlanta I knew. Buck O'Neil sent me to the bullpen and around the seventh or eighth innin' he called down there and requested me to come in in relief. The ballgame was lost when I got in. I think the score was like about 4-to-1. We never could regroup. I think we lost the game maybe about 5-to-1 or 5-to-2. But I pitched the very first day I reported for duty.

You still had butterflies, didn't you?

[Laughs] Hey! Tell me about it! [Laughs] Scared to death. It was good for me, though, the fact that I didn't have to sit around and wait a week or two before I got a chance. That helped me a lot.

He didn't use me very much. Like I say, he only used me comin' out of the bullpen

107

for maybe one or two innings; very seldom did I start a game.

I started a ballgame in Nashville one night and I didn't do too good at all. A game that stands out in my mind the most was after Satchel Paige joined us. I was pitchin' a game in Philadelphia and we was playin' a doubleheader. They started gettin' to me. Satchel Paige was scheduled to pitch the second ballgame and Buck O'Neil took me out and put Satchel in, hopin' that Satchel could come in and close the door.

I never will forget it. [Laughs] I was on my way up the tunnel goin' to the clubhouse and I just happened to stop to listen to see the echo from the crowd, to see how Satchel was doin'. And let me tell you, they hit him harder than they hit me. [Laughs] I said, "Boy, I left a mess."

I think we was playin' the Indianapolis Clowns. We lost that game; I don't know what the score was. They beat me up pretty good and when Buck O'Neil put Satchel in there to put the fire out, they hit him just as hard as they hit me. [Laughs]

You guys saw the country in your travels.

Yes. It was too much for me. I don't like to travel today because of that. We played baseball in a different city about six days a week, some weeks seven. We played baseball *every* night and we didn't hardly have a off-day. We might get a couple off-days a month.

How were the accommodations and meals on the road?

The years of '54 and '55, we did, on a few occasions, run into restaurants that didn't wanna serve us, but as a rule we didn't have no problem. We went into cities like Detroit where we was predominately in black neighborhoods.

But we played baseball out in Texas and Kansas and Nebraska and you didn't have too many black hotels that could accommodate us, but the restaurants was nice

to us. I think they had accepted the fact that we gotta serve you guys and we gotta let 'em have rooms, like in the hotels. It was real nice the two years that I played. We was turned down a few times in restaurants, you know, "You guys can eat but you gotta take it with you." If we couldn't find a restaurant, we would go to a supermarket and get cold cuts and what have you.

With Kansas City we were really treated nice. A lot of people wanted to talk, wanted autographs and they remembered some of the old ballplayers that had come through there. They remembered Satchel Paige, Josh Gibson, [Joe] Black, and all of 'em. These guys went through them places and when we came through in '54 and '55 a lot of people wanted to talk to us and find out what happened to them guys. So we was welcome.

You just mentioned some awfully good ball-players. Who was the best you saw?

Oh, my goodness. I played with George Altman; he left us and went to the Cubs. Francisco — we called him "Pancho" — Herrera, a first baseman, was a good ballplayer. I don't know what happened to [Juan] Armenteros. He was a catcher. He was a *good* catcher and could hit. Enrique Maroto, lefthanded pitcher, was good and he could pitch and he could *hit*.

The littlest man on the team — [Dagoberto] Nunez — he didn't weigh 80 pounds. Now he was a pitcher could throw hard as Joe Black and he could hit a ball out of a ballpark. He was with the Monarchs in1953.

That was the last year they took a team photo was in '53. We did not make a team picture in '54 or '55. In '54 we was on our way to Miami, and the only pictures that I can remember bein' made was when the bus caught fire. We lost everything; we lost our clothes, uniforms, everything. We was in route to Miami, Florida. Some pictures was taken durin' the fire. I did get some of 'em and I sent 'em to my family in Atlanta and heaven knows where they're at today. Nobody was hurt; we ran like crazy. [Laughs]

How much were you paid?

The first year I played I made $250 [a month]. The second year I got a raise; I went up to $300.

The second year we wasn't makin' any money and Buck O'Neil told me they was gonna have to cut salaries. He said, "We're gonna have to cut your salary from 300 to 250."

A friend of mine lived here in Detroit and it just so happened we was playin' here. He told me, "There's a steel mill here in Michigan and you can play ball on their team and that's all you gotta do, and get paid." So I talked to Buck O'Neil about the move and he told me that it was a good move because Detroit is a good baseball town and I still got a chance.

I took my bags of the bus here in Detroit and got a job at Great lakes Steel, where I worked 41 years. I ended up getting a motor mechanic job. I ended up bein' a diesel motor mechanic. I was trained; I came up through the ranks.

If you were a young man, would you play ball again?

Yes. I didn't really get serious about baseball until I started playin' old-timers baseball. I think what happened to me comin' along as a youngster I knew that there was no place for me to go, so I felt I'd just play good enough to play here with the Atlanta Braves. But if I knew the day might come, if I would've devoted myself and tried to learn, I would've did it a little different.

One thing I will emphasize. We only had a manager when I played with Kansas City. We had 25 ballplayers. It's impossible for one man to coach 25 ballplayers. We didn't have no pitchin' coach. The only pitchin' help that the pitchers got was from some of the old-timers.

Buck O'Neil is a wonderful guy, but it's impossible for one man to coach 25 ballplayers. He did the best that he could do, but it's just impossible. If I could've went to maybe some major league farm club and got me some schoolin' like at double-A or class A where they got more than one guy, then my baseball might've been turned around.

That's the way it was with all the clubs I played against in the Negro league. They only had one manager and they had like a business manager and a bus driver, and that's all we had.

You find yourself bein' lazy. Like Buck O'Neil is doin' infield or whatever, the pitchers are sittin' over there or down in the bullpen laughin' and talkin', where you could've had somebody teachin' you. But we were just sittin' there watchin' the other guys, you know.

PITCHING RECORD

Year	Team, Lg	G	IP	W	L	PCT	HO	BB	SO	ERA
1954	KC, NAL									
1955										

Ezell King
Detroit Stars 1955

BORN MARCH 18, 1930, WINFIELD, LA
HT. 6'5" WT. 195 BATTED AND THREW RIGHT

Ezell King's teammate, Henry Saverson, with the Detroit Stars, describes King as "rangy." That's a very fitting description because King stands 6'5" and weighs less than 200 pounds.

The Stars were not King's first professional team; in 1952 he played for Hutchinson in the Western Association, then played the next two seasons with the Harlem Globetrotters baseball team and Satchel Paige's barnstorming team.

After spending 1955 with Detroit, the Baltimore Orioles signed him and sent him to Phoenix in the Arizona-Mexico League, where he was injured and released. Tucson of the same league signed him immediately, and for the season, he batted .282 with 16 home runs and 74 runs batted in.

Then the Boston Red Sox bought him and sent him to Eugene in the Northwest League, where he put up .295-9-84 numbers in 1957. Nine home runs do not sound like many, but he led the team in a ballpark not suited to power hitters (the entire team hit only 34 that year).

Then, in 1958, he had his best year while playing with Waterloo in the Midwest League: .315-24-80. The 24 home runs were second in the league. The next stop was Allentown in the Eastern League, where he was .242-20-68. Allentown was his last stop; he began the 1960 season with the team but had only eight at bats and only one hit, a home run, and was released.

How did you begin playing baseball as a boy?

KING: Just playin' stickball and stuff among the kids around the community. There were no organized teams, just playin' among ourselves.

You first played professionally in 1952.

I was signed out of Grambling College. After that I played with the Globetrotters baseball team, traveled with Satchel Paige for a season, and after that I joined the Detroit Stars. Durin' the time with the travelin' team they'd see me and picked me up. I did fairly well. I hit okay, I think.

Then I went to the Orioles, training with the Orioles out in Arizona. I played with Phoenix and Tucson. I was released from Phoenix, and Tucson picked me up the next day. I went on and finished the season there.

After that, they sold my contract to the [Boston] Red Sox.

You played at Eugene the next season and did well.

Salem, Oregon, was in that league. I know we went there. We were always talkin' about the witch thing. There were teams in Washington. Wenatchee.

Then I went to Waterloo, Iowa. I thought I had a pretty good year there and I spent the winter there after that season. I went from Waterloo to Allentown, Pennsylvania.

Then I got released again. At that time, if your battin' average went down or you got injured, like happened in Phoenix, they'd let you go. I had been doin' pretty good in Phoenix and I got injured, but they kept me in the lineup and my average was goin' down, down, down and eventually I was released. I hurt my wrist; I was playin' first base and a guy jammed my wrist. I could play but I couldn't swing the bat like I should.

What did you do when you left baseball?

I went to the waterfront here in Houston and I worked part-time there and eventually I just stayed there.

Who was the best ballplayer you saw while you were with the Detroit Stars?

I guess J. C. Hartman; he was with Kansas City and Buck O'Neil. J. C. made the majors here in Houston.

Who were some of the best players you saw in the minor leagues?

I played against [Juan] Marichal, a couple of the Alou brothers, and quite a few guys that made the majors in the Giants' organization. In the Red Sox organization there was Tracy Stallard, the one that gave up that 61st home run [to Roger Maris].

Marichal was with Springfield. He was

Sheriff Robinson, manager (l), and Ezell King with Allentown. (Photograph courtesy of Ezell King.)

tough as he was when he got to the majors. [Laughs]

If you were a young man again, would you play baseball?

Oh, yeah. I was just an athlete, period. I just liked sports. I played basketball for a while; I played at Grambling and I joined the Globetrotters for a couple of years. They had about three farm teams and I toured with them for two years.

I had a family and I started to get older. I was 25-26 and I just gave it up.

BATTING RECORD

Year	Team, Lg	G	AB	R	H	2B	3B	HR	RBI	BA
1952	Hutchinson, WA							1	18	.210
1953	Globetrotters, Ind.									
1954	Satchel Paige AS									

Year	Team, Lg	G	AB	R	H	2B	3B	HR	RBI	BA
1955	Detroit Stars, NAL									
1956	Phoenix–Tucson, AML							16	74	.282
1957	Eugene, NWL							9	84	.295
1958	Waterloo, MWL							24	80	.315
1959	Allentown, EL							20	68	.242
1960								1	1	.125

Willie Lee
Birmingham Black Barons 1956
Kansas City Monarchs 1956-1958

BORN MARCH 19, 1935, BIRMINGHAM, AL
HT. 6'2½" WT. 185 BATTED AND THREW RIGHT

Willie Lee was a big, slugging outfielder who might have made it to the major leagues, if a hose had been put away. He tells about how he injured a ligament by stepping on the offending hose in the minor leagues in the interview that follows. He had the power; he hit more than 20 home runs in a season twice — once in the Negro leagues and once in the minor leagues — and had double figures in home runs in three of his four minor league seasons.

LEE: I used to go around with a broomstick and we had a neighborhood and most of the kids, they followed me. I was interested in playing ball and other activities. I'd make up a basketball goal or a ping-pong table — whatever else as long as it was sports. I was really a sports-minded person. I'd get a broomstick and whip a tennis ball, like most kids with a love of the game, like Willie Mays used to do in New York.

I would go to Rickwood ballpark here in Birmingham, which is the oldest ballpark in the United States — it's a historical park — and I would go to the games there. They had the Southern Association; that was before they would allow the blacks to play with the whites. I would go out during batting practice and get baseballs that way, to play with. Sometimes I would get cracked bats and nail 'em together and so forth.

From there, they had local teams here. Industrial teams, sandlot some people would call 'em. I'd go for tryouts and they told me I was good enough to play 'cause my talents were good enough.

Then I saw an ad in the paper where they were looking for ballplayers. That was the Black Barons. That was in 1956. I went for the tryout and I made the team. My first road trip was down in Mobile. We played against Tommie Aaron's team. That's Hank Aaron's brother.

I came back to Birmingham and I saw another ad in the paper. The Kansas City Monarchs were downtown in Birmingham. Mr. Ted Rasberry from Grand Rapids, Michigan, was looking for ballplayers. So I came down for another tryout. I made that team and that's where I played my most baseball in the Negro league, from '56 through '58. I played a little bit with the Black Barons in '56.

After I retired from the Negro league in '58, I made my home in Grand Rapids, Michigan, where I played with Mr. Rasberry's team up there in Grand Rapids, the Grand Rapids Black Sox. Another fellow up there in Grand Rapids named Bob Sullivan had a semipro team. He gave me a job with him just to play ball. I found out he was the

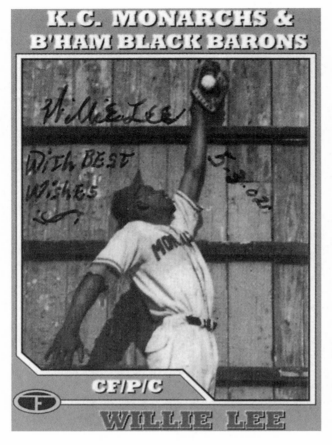

Willie Lee (Photograph courtesy of Willie Lee.)

chief scout for the Detroit Tigers. I had some good years with him and that's when I got to meet Willie Horton and Gates Brown and fellows like that.

So I signed with the Detroit Tigers in '59 and went to spring training. They were going to take me up with the parent club my first year. I had never batted against Iron Mike — a pitching machine. Everything was new to me. I was used to live pitching.

I had a good spring training. They were going to take me with the parent club and I stretched a ligament in my left knee. I stepped on a water hose. We were playing against Cincinnati's farm team and the ground crew manager left a water hose down on the right field line and I went over after a foul ball and stepped on that.

After that I limped around and they decided they'd send me out to Class D, the 3-I League in Decatur, Illinois. Illinois, Iowa, and Indiana. So I played in Decatur, Illinois, my first year and I came back to spring training and my second year they sent me up to Duluth — the Duluth Dukes — up in Minnesota. That was in the Northern League.

Then on a slide into second base on a pickoff play I jammed my shoulder and they sent me back down because the weather was so cold there they told me I would do better to go back down to Decatur. When I went back to Decatur I didn't do too well. They had to operate on my shoulder — just a small operation.

After that, I went back there in '61, I think it was, to spring training and my arm didn't come around. I couldn't even bat right. That's when I got released by the Detroit Tigers.

I came back to Grand Rapids, Michigan, where I resided and played for Bob Sullivan again. After I gave my arm rest it came around. He asked me if I would like to go back into pro ball and I got re-signed by the Minnesota Twins. I played a couple of seasons and they outright released me. I had my best seasons with the Twins. I played with Pat Kelly and George Scott. I played at Erie in the New York–Pennsylvania League and Wilson in the Carolina League. My last year in organized ball was '63.

Then after I came back to Grand Rapids I played with local teams. I played fast pitch softball, slow pitch softball, bowled — just kept myself active in sports.

Was there any problem with acceptance when you played in the minor leagues?

No, not really. Guys in spring training like Dick McAuliffe, Don Wert, and all of 'em were okay. They put me up against Triple-A teams down there and I played real good. They just figured I had natural ability.

I was in Bismarck, North Dakota, my first year I got signed with Minnesota. Northern League. I had some good times up there. Some of the players when I played in the Twins organization were sort of prejudiced. I heard prejudiced remarks about *other* players, like George Scott, who later played for Boston. I'm sitting on the bench next to 'em and when he'd make a good play they'd call him bad names. They'd look over at me and say, "I'm sorry, Willie." But I was used to it, being born in the South. It's still around.

But I still love the game. We do speaking engagements at schools and baseball clinics for kids at church and so forth. We have an organization here in the city called The Alabama Negro League Baseball Players Association. We've got about 30-some-odd players here in Birmingham and Mobile.

Who was the best player you saw?

Willie Mays. He was my idol. I had a shirt; I used to wear that shirt to bed. It had "Willie Mays" on the front of it.

And I loved baseball cards. My mother got hold of 'em. She didn't know I collected baseball cards back then. I used to buy Bazooka bubble gum and stuff like that.

Who was the toughest pitcher you came up against?

It was a tall righthander in the Washington Senators organization at the time. That was up in Geneva, New York, I believe. A *tall* righthander. I don't remember his name; I know Paul Casanova was catching. He would always give me trouble with that sidearm. I tried not to step in the bucket, but, *man,* he'd come around there and I backed off a couple of times. I never shied too much but I was kind of leery of him.

I traveled with the Al Kaline All-Stars when I was in Grand Rapids. Al Cicotte and Joe Ginsberg and Al Kaline and a bunch of the other guys. Jim Rivera. Bob Sullivan was a good one for having me play with the pro ballplayers as much as possible.

We had the NBC tournament every year there in Michigan. The winner goes to Wichita, so I did go to Wichita.

Do you know any of your statistics with the Monarchs?

Sort of. I think it was .311 and 26 home runs one season. I think the Tigers were high on me then. We used to go out West. I used to hit a lot of home runs; I was mostly a long ball hitter. I played center field, pitched, and caught.

I pitched a one-hitter in Mound Bayou, Mississippi. I never will forget that. It was against the Memphis Red Sox. I think Rufus Gibson got the hit. The only reason he got that hit, the catcher called for a changeup curveball. It was an all black town — Mound Bayou, Mississippi — not too far from Memphis.

My most exciting thing in the Negro league was playing in the East-West games. That was in '57; we played in Yankee Stadium in Newark, New Jersey. I hit a grand slam home run to win the game. It was a doubleheader; we lost the first game.

What did you do when you left baseball?

I went to work in a factory in Grand Rapids. That's where I retired from. Then I came back here to Birmingham in 1985. I'm seeing after my mother, who is 93.

Would you play baseball if you were a young man today?

Oh, my God! Yes! With the conditions now, I wish I could. I had a knee replacement here about a couple of years ago. My left knee.

Eugene Scruggs did, too. We hadn't seen each other for 25 years. We lived together in Grand Rapids. He got my phone number for Mr. Ted Rasberry, who was a

wonderful man. We went to his funeral. He was a good man. I remember Bill Veeck used to run the Chicago White Sox. He and Ted were pretty tight.

I try to tell the kids to get into sports, to get into baseball. I know it's only a game, but it teaches you different things.

I really enjoyed myself throughout the traveling and meeting different people. I look back on it at times and think about it. Some of the guys made it and I didn't, but it just wasn't my time.

It's still in my blood. I love sports. It kept me out of trouble.

Willie Lee (Photograph courtesy of Willie Lee.)

BATTING RECORD

Year	Team, Lg	G	AB	R	H	2B	3B	HR	RBI	BA
1956	Birm, NAL									
	KC, NAL									
1957	KC, NAL							26		.311
1958	KC, NAL									
1959	Decatur, MWL							12	64	.241
1960	Decatur, MWL							3	16	.266
	Duluth, NoL							2	13	.309
1961	Bismarck, NoL							14	74	.270
1962	Wilson, CarL							1	4	.174
	Erie, NYPL							24	87	.253

Larry LeGrande

Memphis Red Sox 1957
Detroit Stars 1958
Kansas City Monarchs 1959-1962
Minor leagues 1960
Satchel Paige All-Stars 1963

BORN MAY 25, 1939, ROANOKE, VA
HT' 5'9" WT. 160 BATTED LEFT, THREW RIGHT

Larry LeGrande was a .300 hitter with a strong, accurate arm. He did not get a fair chance in the New York Yankees' minor league system, but he showed his merit in the Negro league in its waning days. He batted .300 or better every season and led the league in outfield assists twice.

He left baseball because there was no place for him to play. The league ended, the teams died out, and he had a family, so he went to work for General Electric in his hometown of Roanoke, Virginia. It was a good job; he stayed at it for 33 years.

LeGrande: I played with a local team here in Roanoke. I was 14 years old and the rest of the players were in their late 20s and 30s and early 40s. I was the youngest on the team. God gave me that ability and I could throw a baseball like a bullet. I was a catcher, then I played right field.

I was with the Webster's All-Stars here in Roanoke. The Memphis Red Sox and the Birmingham Black Barons played a Negro league game in Salem, Virginia, and I lived in Roanoke County, Virginia, but I went to high school in Salem. I saw the placards nailed to the telegraph poles around town. I was a junior in high school, so I caught a ride with someone. I didn't have a car.

I went up there and I saw a man named Homer "Goose" Curry. He was the man-ager of the Memphis Red Sox baseball team. [Laughs] Everybody knows about him. I asked him if I could come to Memphis for a tryout and he looked at me with those big red bloodshot eyes and said, "How old are you, boy?"

I told him I was 17 but I'd turn 18 in May. He asked me when would I finish high school. I told him I was a senior and I would be finishing this summer. He told me to let him know when I finished high school and I did. I called him and told him that I had finished high school.

So he wrote me a letter right back. He was also a slickster. He told me that I could come to spring training but I would have to pay a fee of $35 and if I made the team I would be reimbursed.

Larry LeGrande (Photograph courtesy of Larry LeGrande.)

My father, who worked for the N and W Railroad — Norfolk and Western — he got me a pass to go to Memphis by train. I never saw such a long train ride in my life. When I got to Memphis, he was there to meet me and took me to Martin Stadium. I never saw anything like it. They had rooms like a motel underneath the grandstand there.

Martin Stadium was owned by a group of dentists and doctors. Two brothers was a dentist, one was the head of a hospital there in Memphis, and one bigshot dentist brother lived in Chicago. He was president of the Negro league. It was amazin'; they looked like white people; they were highly educated. That's who owned the Memphis Red Sox.

When I got there, some of the baseball players were standin' outside of the stadium and one of those guys was Charley Pride. We all shook hands and I was shown to my room. We had spring training; did some runnin' the next day but we didn't throw — just getting' your body in shape. That went on for about two weeks and he called us all

to the infield and told us who would make the team. You know, that's a sad day. I was one that made the team.

I played one year. I didn't get to play much because I was a rookie and that team was already put together. But, hey, that was a stepping-stone to the major leagues for black people. That was the major leagues to me and all the black people who ever played.

He never did reimburse me my money. You know how that goes. That was a lotta money back then. Later on during the season I found out that he had done several players like that.

He was fired after all those years of playin' and managin' in the Negro leagues. They hired a manager named Rufus Ligon, a tall lefthanded pitcher from Texas. He became manager of the Memphis Red Sox.

They had the All-Star game. It was always played in Chicago in Comiskey Park. We all went there because we were a travelin' team. I just set up there in the stands because I wasn't picked to play in the All-Star game.

Whilst I was there I met a man named Ted Rasberry. I asked him if I could come to try out for his baseball team. He owned the Detroit Stars and the Kansas City Monarchs and told me that he'd be glad to have me. He knew I could throw; he knew I was a good ballplayer.

So he sent me a bus ticket and I rode the bus to Birmingham, Alabama, to spring training. He had both teams there; he had the Kansas City Monarchs and the Detroit Stars. We both trained in Birmingham. That way he could divide; he could pick out what players he wanted for the world-famous Monarchs, what players he wanted for the Detroit Stars.

This was my second year. He picked me for the Detroit Stars and on that team we had one of the most greatest home run hitters who ever played: Willie Washington. He usually hit about 50 or 60 home runs a year. I mean, he was great! He became the new Josh Gibson of the Negro league.

On that team we had Satchel Paige; we had Reece "Goose" Tatum, who played first base for the Indianapolis Clowns and for Philadelphia Stars. He was a fine athlete. He became famous with the Globetrotters. And he had his own team, traveled the world over. Most traveled athlete who ever lived. He was a famous athlete who's not in *any* hall of game. He should be in every hall of fame there is. The man thrilled kings and queens all over the world.

Satchel Paige pitched three innings. He was an amazing man. I caught him. It was special. I'm one of the few now who caught the greatest pitcher that ever lived, I think. If he's not, I want somebody to tell me who the greatest is.

Did you ever bat against him?

Yeah, and I grounded out. He used to tell me, "I don't know whether you're catchin' or playin' right field tonight, but I'm gonna tell you this: don't forget that I don't pitch inside. I'll never let one of these kids pull me out of the ballpark and brag about how they hit ol' Satch." He always told me that.

That year went on pretty good for me. I was havin' a great year. At that time, there was about seven teams interested in me.

We went to Canada, toured five provinces. Played in Louisville at the Fairgrounds. We had about 20,000 people out there.

We all got put in jail out there in Louisville. There was a lot of racism goin' on back them. What happened was, our bus driver didn't have that sticker on the bus. You know, when you enter a state there's a sticker — a state sticker — that you gotta get on a vehicle. We didn't have that so the police pulled us over and carried us to downtown Louisville and locked us up in the inside of a chain link fence about eight feet tall.

Larry LeGrande (Photograph courtesy of Larry LeGrande.)

We had to play there that night. [Laughs] Locked us all up downtown at the police station. About an hour before game time they let us go and we went to the Fairgrounds. That's where they played baseball; they had boxin' matches there. There were several buildings on those grounds. That's where we played.

Like I told you, I had several teams interested in me. The next year I was moved up to the Kansas City Monarchs. That's the team that got all the recognition. The Monarchs sent more players to the major leagues than anybody. That was 1959. I led the league in outfield assists; I hit over .300. I had a good year. I hit .334. I hit about .318 for Detroit Stars. I could hit the ball out of the ballpark. I could hit, run, and throw.

At the All-Star game I went 2-for-3 at

Comiskey Park. We had about 35,000. They used to have 50-plus thousand there.

The New York Yankees were followin' me all over the country. You know, they had district scouts pick us up because we traveled. We played in Washington, D.C., at Griffith Stadium and the owner, Ted Rasberry, motioned to me to come down behind the dugout there. He hollered to me on the field and asked me to come over to the dugout, so when I went over to the dugout he said, "Come to the dressin' room."

I noticed a lot of women out there and we all liked women and I wondered, "What in the hell he want with me. What did I do?" When I got to the dressing room, here were these two white guys and they had great big diamond rings on their fingers. I thought, "What in the devil is goin' on?"

We left the dressin' room and we walked up about two flights of stairs. When we got up there, here was all of this plush office and I saw Washington Senators' pictures of former players. Jim Lemon, Camilo Pascual — all those guys that had played there. Ted Rasberry introduced me to these two men and they were New York Yankees' scouts. Are you a preacher?

No, sir.

I liked to shit bricks. [Laughs] I said, "What!?"

And they said, "Larry, we've been following you and we really like the way you play and we'd like to sign you." Man, that was about the happiest I've ever been.

I knew that they were such great teams because they used to kill the Dodgers. The Dodgers won twice in my time: '59 and '55. But, anyway, Lord have mercy! I wanted to sign with them, so I did.

At the end of that season — the Monarchs' season — they called me and asked me if I objected to flyin'. I told them, "No." I didn't know whether I objected or not; I had never flown before but I wasn't gonna tell

them that. [Laughs] I was scared to death. Now I *am* scared for a reason.

I got on an Eastern Airlines four-motor airplane here in Roanoke Municipal Field. Now it's called Woodrum Field. And I flew to Tampa, Florida.

When you're playin' in the Negro league, you take care of your own luggage, you carry your own luggage to your rooms. You do everything for yourself.

If it wasn't broke you had to ride. If it was broke, you still hade to ride. You know, we couldn't leave you behind because we traveled all over the country, so they had to put the cast on whatever was broken and you had to ride with your legs propped up. Moanin' — you never heard so much moanin' and groanin' in your life.

So, anyway, I went to Tampa, Florida, and a limousine was waiting for me. Put my luggage in, carried me across the Tampa Bay bridge to St. Petersburg to my motel. I never will forget. I stayed on what I called black street. A black motel — I never will forget the lady's name. Her name was Dorothy Blanton; she owned the motel.

That was the first time I had roomed by myself 'cause in the Negro leagues we had two or three or four in the rooms. Sometimes we played in towns where there was no black business and we had to stay with private families. And if they did allow us in white hotels they put us all on the same floor so they could watch us, so they could keep a eye on us. Sometimes we got put out in the middle of the night.

Let me tell you this. We had the greatest bus driver who ever lived. His name was McAllister Keen. He was from Memphis, Tennessee. He was the greatest mechanic–bus driver in the world. I wanted to tell you that before I get back to St. Pete. If we got put out, he was ready to drive is 'til we could find a motel or hotel that would accept us, 'til we could find a city where there was black people with a hotel.

Back to St. Pete. The next mornin' this

station wagon came for me, picked me up, and carried me to Miller Huggins Field. There, when I got out of the station wagon, the first person I met was Jerry Coleman, who played second base for the Yankees in those championship years. There was Ed Lopat, who pitched for the Yankees; there was Bill Dickey, who was a Hall of Fame catcher, and Johnny Neun, a famous base stealer. I met those people and I put my first Yankees uniform on in November of 1959. That was winter ball; I played in the winter instructional league. I was one of the most talked-about players in the Yankees' camp. I could hit, run, and throw.

I've been tryin' to find some of my old teammates so I could get a book. At the end of that instructional season we got a book with all of our pictures in it and I've been lookin' for that so I could get a picture of me in my Yankees uniform.

Joe Pepitone was one of my teammates. Boyd Coffie, who is from Tennessee, is a scout now. He used to catch. [Boyd Coffie played from 1959 through 1966; he was about a .260 hitter.]

We played from November to December and we left just before Christmas. The following year I was in the Florida State League; I was hittin' .304, tied for the lead in triples, leadin' the league in runs batted in, and they released me. Had the best throwin' arm in baseball; I could throw the ball belt-buckle high from right field. I had a tremendously strong arm.

So then I came back here and called Ted Rasberry and I went back to the Monarchs. And in 1963 I played with Satchel Paige All-Stars. That was about the most fun in baseball I ever had. Talk about havin' fun!

Why were you released?

They said they didn't think I could hit the ball out of Yankee Stadium. Isn't that a poor excuse? Who has? Mickey Mantle came close to hittin' one out. Josh Gibson

Larry LeGrande (Photograph courtesy of Larry LeGrande.)

is the only one. Ain't that a whole lotta people? Luke Easter came close to hittin' one out of center field there.

I got released. Man, I tell you, I never got over that.

I got pictures of me in my Satchel Paige jersey. I got a picture in my Satchel Paige jacket.

In the six years you played, who was the best player you saw?

Man, there was several of those. Oh, man. Willie Washington was the best. I played with him both with Detroit and with Kansas City. He was a great hitter. Jessie Mitchell, with Birmingham Black Barons, was the next best. He was a good ballplayer. There was a whole lot of good ballplayers I played with and played against. [Laughs] It's a long list.

With Satchel Paige All-Stars, we got paid every day, accordin' to what the gate was. With the Monarchs I was paid 300 a month. Pretty decent money. Sometimes, though, the money was short. [Laughs] Sometimes we got rained out two or three days.

Larry LeGrande (Photograph courtesy of Larry LeGrande.)

You know, it's a funny thing. I want you to print this. The white people refused us and the black people raised the prices on us. Thought we had plenty of money. "Here come the baseball players. They got money."

Does one game stand out?

Yeah. Quite a few. I caught Satchel Paige for nine innings in Indiana and I went 3-for-4 and I hit two home runs and we won the game. I went 2-for-3 in the East-West All-Star game at Comiskey Park in Chicago. We had 35,000 people there.

Why did you leave baseball when you did?

The league folded and I went to work for G.E. I was startin' a family. I should've caught on with somebody else. I really should have, but I didn't have anybody to catch on to. I spent my good playin' days workin' for G.E. company for 33 years.

Would you be a ballplayer again if you were a young man?

I sure would. Man, I'll tell you, I'm ready to go now. What I'm lookin' for is a scoutin' job.

I'm going to be inducted into the Salem, Virginia — Roanoke Hall of Fame. My cousin is Billy Sample; he played for the Texas Rangers, Atlanta, and then he spent a year with the Yankees. He'll be there. Maury Wills is gonna be the speaker.

BATTING RECORD

Year	Team, Lg.	G	AB	R	H	2B	3B	HR	RBI	BA
1957	Mem, NAL									
1958	Det., NAL									.318
1959	KC, NAL									.334
1960	St. Pete, FSL									.304
	KC, NAL									
1961										
1962										
1963	Satchel Paige AS									

William Little

Memphis Red Sox 1952-1957
Kansas City Monarchs 1957-1958

BORN DECEMBER 6, 1934, MEMPHIS, TN
HT. 5'9" WT. 158 BATTED AND THREW RIGHT

William Little served as batboy for his hometown Memphis Red Sox for several years before playing for the team. His first appearance in a game came when he was a senior in high school and he remained with the team into 1957.

During the off-seasons, Little attended LeMoyne College in Memphis, where he earned his bachelor's degree. Then he attended Memphis State University and earned a master's degree in education. In addition to teaching, he was a highly successful high school baseball and basketball coach for many years.

LITTLE: I was the mascot — batboy — for the team here [Memphis] and I wanted some day to do the same things as these guys I was picking up bats for.

There were some [players] who took the time out to help me, guys like Marlin Carter, who was an infielder — he passed away a few years ago — and one of the Bankhead brothers — a brother of Dan Bankhead. Fred Bankhead — he was an infielder — took time out and kind of showed me the ropes. I played from '52 to '57 with the Red Sox; '57 and '58 I was with the Kansas City Monarchs.

Is there a game that stands out?

Probably being able to travel with the team one spring. We had a lot of Latin ballplayers and they hadn't arrived and the team was ready to go down to play some exhibition games in Texas. I was a senior in high school and I got a chance to break in the lineup until those guys got back. I played second base and spent a lot of time as a utility infielder.

Also, the single most memorable game that stands out in my career was when we were down in Greenville, Mississippi. Charley Pride was on our team and Goose Curry was the manager and the catchers were banged up. He said, "I need somebody to catch." And I said, "I'll catch." It was just because I wanted to get into the lineup; I'd never caught a game in my life. We were playing the Birmingham Black Barons and we beat Birmingham, 6-3. Charley Pride was the winning pitcher. That incident sticks out.

Charley Pride was in town several years ago and I was talking about this. I still have the final out ball and they wanted to take it to Nashville and put it in the Country Music Hall of Fame. I said, "No, you won't get a chance to do that. I'm going to keep this one."

Did you catch any more games after that one?

Yeah. I left Memphis and I caught a few games with the Kansas City Monarchs.

What happened with me was that I got

in on the tail-end of the Negro league as a player, but unlike a lot of others, coming up as a batboy, I go way back, like with Verdell Mathis. I saw Willie Mays starting out, Casey Jones, Larry Brown. You might have heard some stories about Brown, how the New York Giants wanted to say that he was Latin so that they could sign him.

I remember some of the guys who were at the top of their game when the league was considered at least triple-A baseball. It was predictable that it was going to just kind of peter out. I went out to California and played some semipro baseball in San Mateo, California, in the El Camino League. This was '58 to about '62, '63. Jim Fregosi was a senior in high school and we drafted him to play with us down in Santa Clara in the state semipro championships.

You mentioned Verdell Mathis. He was an outstanding pitcher. Does he belong in the Hall of Fame?

Oh, yeah. Definitely.

Who was the best pitcher you saw?

You have to include Verdell Mathis among them. Dan Bankhead. And there was a host of good pitchers. One fellow in the Hall of Fame from the Kansas City Monarchs was Hilton Smith.

Was there one pitcher who was especially hard on you?

No, no one just stands out. I was not a hell of a hitter. I had my problems with most of them. Those coming from the side gave me problems. If they had a good hook coming from the side they were tough. No one particular person stands out.

Who was the best player you saw?

I would say Willie Mays. He was just such a natural. But I saw some great guys, like Willie Wells, Sr. He was an *old* guy and made things look easy. Ernie Banks is another that comes to mind. Of course, I didn't see enough of Hank [Aaron]. He just came through and mesmerized the pitchers

and the league. He came through as an unknown at one period; the next time he came through they had developed a shift for him. They had a lot of respect for an 18, 19 year old.

Who was your favorite player?

I would say Buck O'Neil. He's been around so long, involved with various things. We just had a kind of camaraderie that started when I used to travel with the team as a batboy. We had a favorite eating place that most of the teams ate at in Little Rock.

I played basketball in college and when I got out of school and got my coaching job—I coached baseball here in Memphis for a good while—I used to run into him all the time coming to town as a scout. We probably ran into each other, even though he was with Kansas City, longer than any of the guys other than maybe Verdell. Verdell was very close because his family and ours were close right down to his death.

But Buck, I saw him in a lot of different capacities and was able to relate with him as a result of that. Ironically, my first teaching job I took the position of his brother-in-law. He married a girl from Memphis and I replaced his brother-in-law, who got an administrative job.

When we had the reunion in 2000 in Kansas City, he was the chairman of that.

Did you attend college in the off-seasons?

Yeah. At that time, baseball wasn't large-scale so I put my education ahead of baseball. I went on and finished in five years. I went to LeMoyne.

Talk about the travel.

There were long jumps. I remember one night we left Lincoln, Nebraska, on Friday night and played Sunday in Birmingham, Alabama. Along the way we hit a deer. That was typical of those long jumps—Memphis to Kansas City and like that. I remember we left Martin Stadium here in

Memphis to go to New York. Occasionally we'd have breakdowns. I'll never forget one in Pauls Valley, Oklahoma. We must've hung around there two or three days.

You ate a lot out of the grocery stores — cold cuts and stuff. You were fortunate if you got a warm meal once in a while. Hotels were restricted and some places you didn't have good accommodations.

A lot of the ballplayers were not from wealthy homes so it was easy to live with some of that. You didn't think about it at the time you were doing it. You look back and say, "We did all of this."

You got two dollars a day to eat. In Birmingham, there used to be a place where we used to have breakfast. We got two pieces of chicken and rice — I don't remember if they threw in an egg or not — for half-a-dollar.

What was your salary?

The last salary I remember was 200 a month. Some of those guys, when the league was in its heyday, made as much as eight to a thousand a month. They were the frontline guys and that was just before Jackie made it.

Did you see him play?

Only when he barnstormed, when he came back with the major league all-stars.

Do you know any of your stats?

No, but if I had to fathom a guess, I'd say I was probably a .260 to .280 hitter. Just occasional power.

If you were a young man again, would you play baseball?

Oh, yeah.

Any regrets?

None whatsoever. I consider myself one of the lucky ones.

Tell about your coaching.

My coaching has a baseball tie up. Ironically, I first started teaching as a sixth-grade teacher. The Black Barons owner was from Memphis — Tom Hayes — and he sent

William Little (Photograph courtesy of William Little.)

a Joe Atkins from here to be the traveling secretary for the Birmingham Black Barons team. He was a math teacher in the high school here and at the school where he worked he got the principal to hire me. He felt that I could do the job as basketball coach. I was hired my second year of teaching as the basketball coach at Douglas High School and I also became the baseball coach. I coached both on the high school level and stayed there about ten years.

I got a chance to move over to where Verdell went to school and where I went to school. I coached at Booker T. Washington for 18 years, baseball and basketball.

We won several district championships. I guess I had about a 158-108 record [in baseball]. I had a little bit of an edge over most of the coaches with my professional background.

In basketball, I was about 340-something and maybe 132. I thought I had a pretty good coaching career.

And I officiated college football and basketball. I stopped officiating in the Southwestern Athletic Conference — the conference with Grambling and Texas Southern and those schools — in about 1997.

I got a chance to officiate in three New York-area stadiums: Yankee Stadium, Shea, and the Meadowlands. Transworld Dome in St. Louis, the Superdome in New Orleans, Orange Bowl Stadium. I got a chance to travel across the country.

Ironically, I never was interested in umpiring. Primarily because, by the time that the baseball season rolled around after I was done playing and coaching, I didn't want to fill up a whole summer umpiring. I umpired maybe one or two ballgames in an emergency situation.

BATTING RECORD

Year	Team, Lg	G	AB	R	H	2B	3B	HR	RBI	BA
1952	Memphis, NAL									
1953										
1954										
1955										
1956										
1957	Mem-KC, NAL									
1958	KC, NAL									

Nathaniel McClinic
Chattanooga Choo-Choos 1945-1946
Cleveland Buckeyes 1946-1948

BORN APRIL 26, 1924, LINDALE, GA
HT. 5'11" WT. 165 BATTED AND THREW RIGHT

Nathaniel McClinic didn't play professional baseball until after he served in World War II. He began in the Negro Southern League with the Chattanooga Choo-Choos, not far from his home in Rome, in northern Georgia. He played there in 1945 and part of 1946, when he joined the Cleveland Buckeyes, where he played through 1948. When he left the Buckeyes, he moved back to north Georgia where he continued to play with a local team.

How did you get into baseball?

McCLINIC: I was in the Army overseas. I was on Iwo Jima playin' in the baseball league there and I won the island's Most Valuable Player. I was with the 442nd amphibious company. I was in the service three years.

When I got out, I came home. We had a little ol' team here and I managed them for a couple of years. And then I went to the Chattanooga Choo-Choos of the Negro Southern League. From there, when Jethroe got drafted from the Cleveland Buckeyes, I went to them. I was with the Buckeyes 'bout two and a half years.

Does one game stand out?

Yeah. The biggest game was when I was with the Chattanooga Choo-Choos in the Negro Southern League. We had a flight from Indianapolis, Indiana, to Raleigh, North Carolina. It was the first time I'd ever been on a plane. I had a bad shoulder and I asked them not to send me there, but the skip sent me anyway. Just ten of us went over there. I was playin' center field.

I couldn't hit the curveball too well and that's all they'd feed me. I hit a grand slam. That was the greatest hit in my life. We won the game against the Raleigh Tigers.

When I was with Cleveland, I guess the most memorable game I had was my worst game. We were playin' in Knoxville, Tennessee; it was the first time I ever faced Satchel Paige. At that time, he had the hesitation pitch. People ask me, did I hit Satchel Paige. In the first place, I couldn't hardly see him. [Laughs] That was the most memorable game. I faced him twice; one time there in Knoxville, Tennessee, and then another time when we was in Cleveland.

Who was the best pitcher you saw?

[Jimmy] Newberry. He played with the Birmingham Black Barons. The reason I say he was the best, I couldn't hit the curveball and he had a hell of a curveball. [Laughs] Best baseball player I saw was the short-stop of the Birmingham Black Barons: Artie Wilson. He was tops in my book. That's just my opinion now.

The best player I played with was Sam Jones. Sad Sam Jones. From my hometown was Ernest Long; he recommended me [to the Buckeyes]. He was there, too. He's passed now.

Do you know any of your statistics?

I didn't have much statistics 'cause I couldn't hit the curveball. But as far as throwin' and speed, I had it all. When I hit the ball, if I had a single it was a double or if I hit a double it was a triple.

When did you leave the Buckeyes?

I disremember the year, but that was when all the players started breakin' into the major leagues, '48 or '49.

What did you do when you left the Buck-eyes?

I came home and got me a league team and managed it. Semipro. I managed and played. I did that for about seven or eight years.

What did you do for a living?

I worked in a cotton mill. Pepperell Manufacturing Company. And I went to work at a high school. I was a trainer for the Pepperell High School there in Lindale, Georgia. At the time, I believe I was the only black trainer there was.

Then I was the first black Floyd County policeman and I was the only black investigator Floyd County has ever had. I believe that was the reason I got along so well with the whites here.

Would you be a baseball player again if you were a young man?

Yes, if the time had changed I would, but if the time had not changed, the answer would be no, because we caught hell. It was

Nathaniel McClinic (Photograph courtesy of Nathaniel McClinic.)

pretty rough on us. It wasn't too rough up North, but down South it was. Like we're goin' to Jacksonville, Florida, or comin' to play the Atlanta Black Crackers and all them, we'd get to the [Mason-Dixon] line and we couldn't stop nowhere.

We traveled by bus. We had to get our sack lunches once we got to the South. We couldn't use the restrooms, couldn't drink out of the fountains or anything like that. It was rough, but it was baseball.

Up North the livin' conditions was better. You could go wherever you wanted to to eat, sleep, things like this. But when you got down to my hometown, down through the South, we couldn't eat at the cafes. If we did, we had to go to the black cafes or people's homes or things like that.

Rome [Georgia] has treated me wonderful. I was the trainer for this white football team and they had a gatherin' recently and they honored two people: me and the secretary of that school. She was white.

I worked in the cotton mill and everybody say I was a pretty good ballplayer.

Most of the whites say I was a good guy, a fair guy. I trained the Pepperell team all down through the years and we'd go to different places. Some places we'd go to they wouldn't let 'em because of me. I'm the onliest black there on the bus.

It has changed. It has changed tremendously. From back then it has changed triple.

BATTING RECORD

Year	Team, Lg	G	AB	R	H	2B	3B	HR	RBI	BA
1945	Chat, NSL									
1946	Chat, NSL									
	Clev, NAL									
1947	Clev, NAL									
1948										

John Mitchell
Detroit Stars 1957
Birmingham Black Barons
1958-1962

BORN DECEMBER 25, 1937, AUTAUGA COUNTY, AL
HT. 5'11" WT. 175 BATTED AND THREW RIGHT

Several former players say that Jessie Mitchell was one of the best ballplayers they saw. There's no denying that Jessie was good, but he had an awfully good younger brother. John Mitchell played six years in the waning days of Negro league baseball and was good enough to be an all-star. A power-hitting center fielder, he was also an outstanding defensive player and was scouted by the major leagues. An arm injury and a growing family ended his playing days.

MITCHELL: I got started in sandlot. I was playin' for the 24th Street Red Sox. I played for Fairfield for a while. Fairfield Tigers in Fairfield, Alabama, that's where Willie Mays was from. After I was playin' with them, I was playin' for the 24th Street Red Sox when the Birmingham Barons' manager saw me playin' with them and asked me, did I want to travel with them.

I was about 16 years old. I told 'em yeah, but my mother didn't want me to go 'cause I was so young; I was still in school. She asked the manager would he take care of me. He said, "Yeah, I'll take care of him."

I started with Detroit. I played with them a year. Detroit Stars. Then Birmingham picked me up in 1958. I played with them about five years.

Does one game stand out?

I was playin' in Memphis, playin' the Memphis Red Sox. I hit two home runs. I hit a grand slam in the nightcap and won the game. And I hit a home run the first game, too. That stands out most in my mind.

I played in the Comiskey ballpark. That was a great thing. And I played in Yankee Stadium. I played in Ebbets Field, too. I played in a lot of major league ballparks.

You were an all-star.

Yeah. I played in the All-Star game in '59. I got a hit, but I made a catch — an overhead catch in center field. They said, "He's just like Willie Mays out there." [Laughs]

How were the travel conditions?

It wasn't that good 'cause some of the time we had to change on the bus 'cause we didn't have nowhere to change clothes at. Didn't have no shower. A lot of times we didn't have nowhere to go eat. We had to eat on the bus sometimes. We'd get to a town that didn't have no restaurants. It was bad sometimes. Sometimes it was good, accordin' to what town you was in.

The farther north you go it was better, but in the South you had a lot of problems. We had to stay in roomin' houses most places; we couldn't stay in a motel. That was pretty bad. You had people call you names, that's about it. There wasn't no real serious things, like a fight or nothin' like that. It didn't bother me, people callin' names. That made me want to hit the ball further. [Laughs]

Do you know any of your batting statistics?

I batted .295. I hit 15 home runs in '59. I hit a home run practically every night; I was hittin' the ball good. They had a scout — Joe Sewell, a scout for the Cleveland Indians — he wanted to sign me up. I don't know what happened. He was a scout for the University of Alabama, too.

Who was the best player you saw?

I've seen some good ones. Willie Smith was a good ballplayer. We played ball together. He played for the Cubs for a while, and California Angels. We played together in '59. He could pitch, man, and hit.

Willie Washington was a good ballplayer. He could hit that ball a long ways. Another player named [Juan] Armenteros; he was a Cuban. He was a catcher for the Kansas City Monarchs. He was a good catcher. My brother, he was a good ballplayer.

Did you two ever play on the same team?

Yeah, one year we did. I played center and he played left.

How much were you paid?

$200 a month. That was pretty good. We got eatin' money. We got two dollars a day; you could eat on two dollars. You could get a breakfast for about 30 cents. You could get a dinner for about 35, 40 cents. Times have changed.

Why did you leave baseball when you did?

I hurt my arm. I messed my arm up in that cold weather. I got married, too, and my wife was expectin', so I gave up. We had four children. I had a boy played football and run track. He was good.

What did you do when you left baseball?

I went to work in a steel mill for 37 years. I kept that job 37 years.

If you were a young man today, would you play baseball again?

Yeah. I love it. I would play again.

My son said, "Daddy, you must've *loved* that baseball," 'cause that's all I ever look at on TV in baseball season. He says, "I bet you wish you were 16 again." [Laughs] With all that money goin' around, I'd be rich. Right now they've got ballplayers in the majors that couldn't touch the ballplayers we played with.

Do you have any regrets from your baseball days?

No, I don't. I enjoyed it. It was a great experience, travelin' and seein' the world like that. We'd meet a lot of interestin' people, a lot of dignitaries, a lot of superstars, like singers, bandleaders, and stuff like that. It was great.

Charley Pride was playin' the same time I was playin'. He was playin' with Memphis and I was playin' with Birmingham. He was a good ballplayer, too.

BATTING RECORD

Year	Team, Lg	G	AB	R	H	2B	3B	HR	RBI	BA
1957	Detroit, NAL									
1958	Birmingham, NAL									
1959								15		.295
1960										
1961										
1962										

Grady Montgomery
Chicago American Giants 1950-1951

BORN AUGUST 8, 1931, GASTONIA, NC
HT. 5'11" WT. 180 BATTED AND THREW RIGHT

"Montgomery" is a lengthy name and box scores don't have room for that many letters, so Grady Montgomery was known as "Monty" much of the time,

There are those who say timing is everything. Montgomery feels that he came along too early, and that is probably true for most black ballplayers until very recent times. The opportunities weren't there when he was a player.

Wedding bells and an injury to his shoulder caused him to leave the game at the tender age of 20, but he enjoyed it while it lasted.

MONTGOMERY: After high school my first encounter with professional baseball was with a southern division team of the Negro league called the Asheville Blues. I got out of high school in 1948 and that summer I started touring with them through '49. In an all-star game up in Asheville in the summer of '50, the scouts for the Chicago American Giants were there and they signed me to a contract. I played with Chicago American Giants for a couple of years, '50 and '51. I hurt my arm so I didn't play the '52 season. I went to spring training with 'em but my arm never came around.

How were you accepted when you joined the American Giants?

'Bout like all rookies. At the time I was 18 years old. You were just a rookie. It was quite an experience for me. It was something I was wantin' to do. I would've did it if I hadn't been paid anything.

What were you paid?

I think the last year I played I was making two-fifty or two-seventy-five a month, plus expenses. Meal money was like a dollar-and-a-half a day, or maybe two-and-a-quarter. It was adequate back then.

How was the travel?

You can imagine an 18 or 19 year old. It was exciting gettin' on these busses and goin' from city to city. At the time, it was just an exciting time for me. I was wide-eyed and googly-eyed at the things that went on. As I think back on it now, it should've been tiring but it wasn't. The bus rides wasn't bad for a young person.

The facilities that you were afforded wasn't the best, as far as hotels and all, because a lot of places you just couldn't get a hotel to house a black outfit. A lot of times you got in a black neighborhood and rented a room for the guys.

And we slept on the bus. I remember one little ol' place, the hotel was so infested I stayed on the bus. One night, I think it was in Georgia, it was such a nice night we slept in the ballpark. [Laughs] Right on the field.

It was a wonderful time. The only re-

Grady Montgomery (Photograph courtesy of Grady Montgomery.)

gret I have is I came along a little bit too early.

We had one incident where we pulled up to the hotel in Asheville, North Carolina, and the owner of the hotel's daughter came out and she said, "Here come those old ballplayers again." You felt like vagabonds. It was all-in-all a good experience.

Do you know any of your stats?

No. Being candid, I was a better than the average fielder and adequate with the bat, but stats wasn't something that was readily available to the Negro leagues.

I was telling a friend of mine not too long ago — they had Black History Month down in North Carolina and we were down there — none of the players had a camera on the bus when I was playing. Pictures and records just weren't available. They kept some, I'm sure, but it was just for the purpose of the gates. The local paper may have had somebody to get some, but it wasn't done in the fashion that it's done today, I'll put it that way.

You don't see too many films now with black activity. They're all still pictures; no-

body had no camera back there to take any pictures of any live action, except maybe the East-West All-Star game. I did see one once of Griffith Stadium; they had some live shots there.

Does one game stand out?

No. In hindsight, I played a game that Satchel Paige came in and pitched a couple innin's. I think it was up in Lockport, New York, or Buffalo. He came in and made an appearance and pitched a couple innin's and then left. It was for us.

Speaking of Satchel, who was the best pitcher you saw?

There was a guy that played with me with the Asheville Blues. His name was Bob Bowman. He was probably the best pitcher that I saw and had any personal contact with. The Newark Eagles had a guy up there; I think his name was Radcliffe; I thought he was impressive at the time.

But I played with Bowman for a summer and people could not hit what he was throwin' up there. He was just amazing. In hindsight, you look at him like you were lookin' at Sandy Koufax or Bob Gibson. He was capable of gettin' everybody out that comes up there. He was an older guy at the time. Bob was a teetotaler; he didn't smoke or drink or do anything. He threw this ball from an underhand position and you just couldn't hit it.

Who was the best player you saw?

I played in a barnstormin' game against Jackie Robinson and Larry Doby. Junior Gilliam played in that game but he was not a major leaguer at that time. And Joe Black.

I always admired Jackie Robinson. I just can't imagine anybody other than Jackie Robinson doin' what he did, so I have all kinds of admiration for him. I just can't picture any of the other guys — maybe Monte Irvin — doin' what he did and goin' through all that. Monte Irvin may have had the temperament to do it. Robinson had the education and he was intelligent and he had all the attributes that was needed to do it. I'm sure it shortened his life by maybe 20 years. It made him a hollow man, that's all. I can never praise him enough.

How did you hurt your arm?

Strangely enough, after the season ended I was messin' around in a pickup football game, throwin' a damn wet football. Now they know about rotator cuffs, but back then I never heard the term. But I hurt the shoulder. I went to spring training in '52 and it just didn't come around.

What did you do when you left baseball?

My older brother, who was being scouted by the Giants — and I'm sure he could've made it, because Clyde could hit the ball 400 miles and that was what the black players were measured with then — had been in the military. He got his discharge and we were both playin' with Asheville at the time. We both had just got-ten married and we decided we'd better go on and get us a job so we could support our wives.

I went to barber school for about four months; that was not my niche. Then I came into the city of Greensboro, North Carolina, and started workin' for an insurance company. My wife Tiny was finishin' up school at that time; she went to nursin' school at Greensboro. She got out in '52 and we left for Washington and I got a job with the fire department here in Washington.

I worked for the Washington fire department for five years, then I bought a couple of dump trucks and went into business for myself. I did that for about ten years, then I went into delivery business and that's what I retired from.

If you were a young man, would you play baseball again?

Knowin' what I know now, most certainly. But when you're young, it's just what you do. We were travelin' around with Asheville playin', and there wasn't no guarantees. After the game we would get 35 or 40 dollars, which was a pretty good piece of change at that time. I definitely would go and play.

You mentioned earlier that you have no regrets from baseball. Is that true?

The only regret I have is I just came along too early. You know the old adage: God gave us the serenity to change things you can and accept what you can't. You can't let it consume you and I've always been that way. There's nothing I could've done about the racism back then, so you just accept it. It wasn't my time. But I look back in hindsight on my parents and it was even worse. Every generation gets better.

BATTING RECORD

Year	Team, Lg	G	AB	R	H	2B	3B	HR	RBI	BA
1950	Chicago, NAL									
1951										

Bob Motley

Negro American League Umpire 1947-1958

BORN MARCH 11, 1923, DAYTON, OH

Bob Motley wanted to be a pitcher, but the talent wasn't there. But he loved baseball and wanted to be a part of it, so he decided to be an umpire. Armed with a rule book and a strong desire, he persevered until he got on as a third base umpire for the Kansas City Monarchs' home games. Eventually he was hired by the league and became a traveling umpire. In time he rose to be chief umpire for the Negro American League. As the league died, he attended umpiring school and landed a job in the Pacific Coast League, the top minor league at that time.

MOTLEY: I was the first black umpire to go to the Al Sommers Umpire School down in Daytona Beach, Florida.

That was after you umpired in the Negro league. Did you have any training before that?

I had no training. All I had was a rule book.

How did you get started?

I went to several games watching the teams play and I went and talked to the owner [of the Kansas City Monarchs], Tom Baird, and asked could I be an umpire when they were in Kansas City. At that time, he told me all his umpire positions was taken but to go out to the stadium and talk to his head umpire, Frank Duncan. He was the umpire for the Monarchs' home games.

So I went out and talked to him to see if I could umpire. He refused me two or three times. Every time I'd go out and talk with him, he'd say, "Kid, you don't know nothin' 'bout umpiring. Why don't you play?" Every home game I'd meet him at the

dressing room and talk to him. I always took my home plate umpire gear with me when I went.

He had bad knees — he was a catcher — and finally he told me I could umpire third base. So I umpired third base for a couple of seasons every time they came in. From there, he moved me over to first base because the other guy got sick, so I umpired first base for a while.

The next home game I went out there and talked to him and he said, "You go and umpire behind home plate." That was all I wanted to do, so I called balls and strikes behind home plate.

Then I went back and talked to Tom Baird and he told me to call J. B. Martin, the president of the league, down in Memphis, Tennessee. So I called him with the recommendation from Tom Baird to start umpiring in the league. That's how I got started.

I traveled with several teams. I traveled with the Monarchs, I traveled with the Memphis Red Sox, Indianapolis Clowns.

Bob Motley (in air) (Photograph courtesy of Bob Motley.)

Then I worked my way up to be the chief umpire in the Negro American League, assigning umpires all over the United States.

What did you prefer, home plate or the bases?

Oh, I loved behind home plate, calling balls and strikes. I was a ball and strike specialist; that was my love.

Did you have many arguments?

Oh, yeah. I had several arguments. I went by the rule book; if you dispute or argue on balls and strikes, I ejected you from the game. That's what I did. That's what the rules state.

When I umpired first base and third base, I didn't have that many arguments because I used to put a little dramatics into it. By the time they'd look up I was all over, hollering "Safe" or "Out" or whatever. Everybody in the stands could hear whatever I called.

Do you remember Emmett Ashford?

I umpired in the Pacific Coast League with Emmett Ashford.

After the [Negro American] league folded up, I went to the umpire school in 1957. I came out as the top student of the class on the field and in the books, but they couldn't place me in 1957. Al Sommers told me, "You go on home and I will do my best to get you placed in some league."

In 1957 he didn't place me, so I called him up at the end of the season and asked him could I come back and take the advanced course in 1958. He said, "Yes, come on back," but naturally he'd say come on back because I had to pay.

So I went back and again I was the top student in the class. At that time, we had about 76 students. He told me the same story: "Bob, I've been trying my best to place you, but none of the league presidents would take you right now. Go on home and I guarantee you'll hear from me."

About a month later the telephone rang. It was from the Pacific Coast League to come and umpire there. My first game was with Emmett Ashford. He was a colorful umpire and he was real good. He had the plate that night.

He set his face mask down. At that time, we wore the balloon-type breast protector. He set that down and he took off running to center field. I didn't know what was going on. I didn't know if somebody was going to chase us or what. But he went out there and did a flip, hit the wall, did a flip, came back home, and slid into home plate. The fans almost went crazy. I umpired quite a few games with Emmett Ashford. I was there eight years.

I was only making $900 a month and I had a family back here. I was employed by General Motors Corporation and I talked to the president of General Motors in Detroit, and he knew what I was trying to do, so he gave me a leave of absence every year to go umpire. When I went back to the plant I'd pick up a job, whatever they had for me. I did that for eight years. I retired from General Motors with 37 years of service.

What were you paid in the Negro league?

He started me off at five dollars per game before I started traveling. Then when I started traveling in the league I was paid $300. It was good money, but I had to feed myself. I had a family and I had to send money back to her.

Did you get a meal allowance?

Oh, no. Didn't know what a meal allowance was. [Laughs] I never heard of that 'til I got to the Coast League. They gave me one there, gave me a bonus and everything. They was real nice.

Who was the best pitcher you saw?

Satchel Paige was no doubt the best pitcher I ever umpired. I umpired when Don Newcombe pitched. Dan Bankhead. All of those guys were good pitchers. Also Connie Johnson was a good pitcher. Hilton Smith used to come in and relieve Satchel Paige. He was about the best all-around 'cause he could pitch and also hit the ball. Satchel only pitched about three innings, then he'd come in and pitch the rest of the game. His ball used to really break.

Who was the best player you saw?

Willard Brown was the best hitter I think I ever saw. He went to the St. Louis Browns. If they didn't like your attitude, you weren't going to go nowhere. But he was the best hitter.

You had a better view of the catcher than anyone. Who was the best catcher?

Earl Taborn was one of the best. Campanella was good, too, I never did see Josh Gibson.

How many umpires worked a Negro league game?

When we traveled in small towns, just two. But on Sunday, I'd pick up two home umpires and we'd have four. I could call the association and get two local umpires to work third base and second base.

We traveled with each team; we rode on the same bus. I'd ride one bus, like the Memphis Red Sox, and my co-worker would ride on the other one, like the Birmingham Black Barons.

When J. B. Martin signed me to be the chief umpire, I did all the assigning. I umpired the East-West game played in Chicago. It was so exciting I'll never forget it. I worked two of those.

If you were a young man today, would you be an umpire again?

[Laughs] There's no doubt in my mind. I feel like I could umpire right now.

The umpiring today seems to be inconsistent.

You have to call what comes over that plate. I don't question the umpires, because the rule book says if the ball is from the knees up to underneath your armpits and if it's over the plate, it will be called a strike. If it don't come over, it will be called a ball. It's just that simple.

As far as I know, I'm the last living [Negro league] umpire. I've tried to contact some of the guys but I've never made contact.

Who was the best umpire, other than yourself?

We had a lot of good umpires. A fellow by the name of Frank Barnes, he was good.

Any regrets from your umpiring days?

Only thing I regret is that I didn't start out when I was four or five years old. Other than that, I don't have no regrets.

No records available

I was 21 when I started. That's what Frank Duncan would always say; he'd say, "Oh, kid, you don't know nothin' 'bout umpiring." But I did. I had a rule book.

Charley Pride
Memphis Red Sox 1953, 1955-1958
Birmingham Black Barons 1954

BORN MARCH 18, 1938 (OR SO), SLEDD, MS
HT. 6'1" WT. 185 BATTED AND THREW LEFT

One of the questions usually asked in these interviews is, "What did you do when you left baseball?" In the case of Charley Pride, the question wasn't necessary. Even if you aren't a country music fan, you've heard of Charley Pride.

To briefly recap his singing career: 36 number one hits, 25 million albums sold (including 31 Gold, 4 Platinum, and 1 quadruple Platinum), Country Music Hall of Fame, and numerous other awards and sales records. He is one of the top 15 best-selling recording artists of all time.

How did you start playing baseball?

PRIDE: By watching my brother. He was about 14 years old and he was catching and playing with the men. I was real skinny back then; I probably didn't weigh but 90 or 100 pounds. They'd say, "What are you gonna be, boy? You're too damn skinny." So I got that kind of rag all the time, so I kind of went into it with a dare, just to show 'em I could do it. That's how I got into baseball, playing in the sandlots and in the fields and in the pastures, using cow pancakes for a base.

How did you join Memphis?

I was born only 54 miles from there and I went up there to try out with the Red Sox. I didn't make it the first time. This guy — his name was Jim Ford — took a bunch of us that didn't make it and we went up to the Iowa State League. We didn't win nothing. Some of the guys that was in that league was Roger Craig and Albie Pearson, that played center field for the Angels. Little small fella, ended up being a preacher later on.

We was getting ready to starve 'cause we was playing percentage. It was beautiful all day, then when night came, man it would rain, so playing on percentage you ain't getting no money. I went and pulled up weeds and ate the roots. Finally, the old man — a popcorn king named Fisher, I think it was — took the team over and at least we started to eat. [Laughs]

I was about 16, 17 years old. My mother was getting ready to have the twins that were born that year. That was '52, I believe. We didn't have no phone. We were all writing back home and there was this lady in the rooming house where we stayed and she was probably thinking we were sending back some money.

Guys weren't getting nothing and I guarantee my mother would've wrote me back. I told the lady you might have misplaced my letters. When I grew up, and if you tried to put one over, my old man could tell when you're trying to tell a hoopy-do. I could see it in her eyes. There's no way I

Charley Pride (Photograph courtesy of Charley Pride.)

could prove it, but I think she was looking in them letters and getting them. It wasn't just me; it was all of us not hearing from home.

This guy, Jim Ford, went back and raided the Red Sox. He took Ollie Brantley and Marshall Bridges — he played with Cincinnati. Brantley ended up being a sheriff in Arkansas. He's a fine fellow. When he raided them I got a job when I got back.

Do you know your record with Memphis?

The last year I think I was about 14-and-2, 14-and-3, or something like that. I cracked my elbow that year, too.

How long were you with the Red Sox?

Including going in the Army, from '53 to '58. I was in the Army two years — '56 and '57. I was in actually 14 months but I got credit for two years.

Did you play ball in the service?

Yeah. We won the all-Army champi-

onship in 1957. I was stationed at Fort Carson, Colorado, and we won it at Fort Knox, Kentucky.

Does one game stand out?

All the Negro players in the majors used to come down and play us. The Jackie Robinson All-Stars, and when he quit playing it was Willie Mays. In all those years that Jackie was there up until 1956, the Negro league players had never won a game. I was in left field; I remember Al Smith hit a pop-up and I missed it, but we got 'em out. I came in in relief and pitched four shutout innings. Ollie Brantley pitched the first five. We beat 'em, 4-to-2, over Sad Sam Jones.

He put one in my ear. We didn't have no helmets then. We were up in Greenville, Mississippi, and I dug in up to my knees and he waited just patiently. When I got dug in, he stuck one between my cap bill and my head. That year — 1956 — he pitched a no-hitter against the Pittsburgh Pirates. And he threw me a curveball and I swung at it. It nipped my pants leg at the knee, it broke so much. He had one heck of a curve.

Who was the best pitcher you saw?

There's been a whole bunch of good ones. The guy that I think was best was with the Birmingham Black Barons. His name was Kelly Searcy. He was a lefthander. I was always a good hitter so I was going to rip this guy. He was throwing bb's; he blew me out every time that I came up. I mean, I've seen some pretty good fastballs, but, man, he had one.

I faced Warren Spahn and got two hits off of him when he was pretty near in his prime. I got a single off of him and he picks me off first. I got a double off of him and he picks me off second. [Laughs] Some memories I like, and some of 'em I don't like.

I remember getting a hit off of Connie Johnson and Don Newcombe on that tour. That made me feel good.

Who was the best ballplayer?

I'd have to say Mays. I played against him and watched him. Overall, he was just awesome. I didn't see everybody; I'm talking about the ones I saw.

By the way, on that tour the night I beat 'em — pitched that four innings of shutout ball — Mays didn't play. He was hurt, but he had hit me everywhere but on the bottom of my feet on that tour. But Aaron didn't get a hit off of me.

I had 'em, 1-to-nothing, in Albany, Georgia, prior to this game. This was in Victoria, Texas, when we beat 'em. But I had 'em, 1-to-nothing, going in the ninth inning and my catcher called for a pitchout. They had a double steal between Aaron and I think George Crowe, used to play for the Braves. Crowe was the second catcher; Elston Howard was the first catcher for the all-stars. They beat me, 2-to-1. I cried like a baby.

I had a great knuckleball. When I cracked my elbow I went to a knuckleball. I could make mine do what I wanted. I could control mine.

When my arm started getting back a little stronger, Al Smith said, "You got a fastball now?" He was baiting me, see. [Laughs] And I threw him a fastball and he rattled them boards on that wall out there.

One day he says, "I'll give you five dollars if you throw me a fastball." I said, "Why do you want me to throw you a fastball and I'm making two dollars a day eating money and a hundred a month and you want me to make you look good?"

That was my salary: two dollars a day eating money and a hundred a month. It wasn't much but it's better than picking cotton.

Charley Pride (r) with Negro leagues historian Larry Lester. (Photograph courtesy of Larry Lester.)

Why did you leave baseball when you did?

It's called a-g-e. When I was playing, if you wasn't in the majors at least by the time you were 25, they'd just mark you off. They wanted you like 18 or so.

When did you turn to singing?

I always sang, but as far as professionally, I started in '60 up in Montana.

Somebody told me you'd sometimes sing to them on the bus.

[Laughs] Well, I didn't do much of that. Some of the guys, now that I've made it, say that.

Talk about the bus travel.

What I remember most about how hard the two dollars a day eating money and a hundred a month was. We were playing in New Orleans, Louisiana, on a Friday night with a doubleheader in Baltimore, Maryland, on a Sunday. We actually left New Orleans a little after midnight. I rode shotgun. We had the water keg there sitting by the driver. We called him "Greaseball"; his name was Sam. Every 55, 60 miles he stopped to fix a valve or something on that old bus. [Laughs]

I rode shotgun 'til Saturday morning

when the sun come up. Then somebody else took over to keep him awake and I went back and went to sleep. It was an old humpback bus. We rode all Saturday night and early Sunday morning — about 8:45, nine o'clock — the sun's coming up and we stopped at a place that would be the equivalent of a 7-11 and bought some baloney and saltine crackers and a Pepsi. That was breakfast.

I pitched the first game and beat the Indianapolis Clowns, 3-to-2. I played left field in the second game. We played a nine-inning and a seven-inning. In the fifth inning I came up to bat with two on. They had us, 7-to-5, and I hit a three-run shot and we went out in front, 8-to-7.

I went back out in the outfield and our pitcher got in trouble and they brought me in in relief. I warmed up the best I could.

To make a long story short, they beat me, 9-to-8, in the bottom of the seventh. So I won one by one run and lost one by one run. The way I look at it, I messed myself up. I was a victim of my own self.

That's what I remember about riding busses and looking at that $7,500 minimum up in the majors that I was trying to get. I said, "What would I do if I could eat me a steak every now and then? Who would ever get me out or beat me?"

Were you a better hitter or a better pitcher?
Both. No brag, just fact.

If you were a young man today, would you play baseball?
I probably wouldn't get 252 million, but I'd be way up in there. But I don't look back; the Lord has blessed me well.

PITCHING RECORD

Year	Team, Lg	G	IP	W	L	PCT	HO	BB	SO	ERA
1953	Memphis, NAL									
1954	Birmingham, NAL									
1955	Memphis, NAL									
1956										
1957										
1958				14	3	.824				

Mack Pride

Memphis Red Sox 1955
Kansas City Monarchs 1956

BORN MAY 27, 1932, SLEDGE, MS
HT. 5'10½" WT. 190 BATTED AND THREW RIGHT

The Pride family of Sledge, Mississippi, were a hard-working group; sharecroppers had to be. The 15 children in the family developed strength in the fields, and two of them used this strength to play professional baseball. Charley's career is covered in another chapter; this one is devoted to his big brother, Mack. Like Charley, Mack was a pitcher, and also like Charley, Mack is a singer, having sung in nightclubs.

PRIDE: We was born and raised on a farm and I watched the Dodgers for a few years when we finally got a television. I was a catcher. They thought I was gonna be a Campanella, but I never could throw to the bases without the ball curving, so they made me a pitcher. I was 17.

When did you turn professional?

Back in '50 or '51, I think it was, but I didn't keep it up. I was still a minor and my father said no. When I got 18 I moved to Clarksdale, Mississippi, and I started pitching for the Clarksdale Brown Bombers, semipro. I pitched there, and then I went to Memphis. I forget the team I played for there.

Charley, he was playing with the Louisville Clippers. Goose Curry was there with the [Memphis] Red Sox for a while, but they got another team and he went to the Louisville Clippers in Louisville, Kentucky. I went to spring training with the Red Sox.

Ted Rasberry was the owner of the Kansas City Monarchs then. We got to Birmingham and I got a contract. We had

a little problem with Goose Curry, 'cause he thought I was gonna play with him. Jelly Taylor was the manager of the Kansas City Monarchs. I pitched for them in '56. I didn't play too long there 'cause the Dodgers was scouting me and the Cleveland Indians and the Chicago White Sox.

Bobby Boyd came out to where I was pitching. He was living there in Memphis then. He asked me, had I thought about playing with the White Sox. Minnie Minoso was there. I pitched a few games and won a few games and they was looking at me, but I wasn't too much interested in it then.

I went to Columbus, Mississippi, and pitched one night. That's when a guy started watching me. I forget his name. He asked me, had I thought about pitching in the Negro American League. I said my brother had been trying to get me to go and I just wasn't interested then. I just didn't have no desire to travel.

So in '56 I listened to him and I pitched a game against them in Columbus, Mississippi, and I called a white umpire a

G-D liar. They said, "What's wrong with you, man?" So the white umpire said, "Boy, I ain't never seen nobody with that kind of control. Those pitches you put over there, they was strikes."

My father didn't like the idea of us playing hardball, so he made us learn. He would hang three tires up on the barn — letter-high, waist-high, and knee-high — and we had to throw through all three of those tires.

We finished high school at Sledge, Mississippi, and I just moved to Memphis and was just gonna play semipro or sandlot, whatever you want to call it. That's when they started watching me.

I was drinking that white lightning, had plenty of girlfriends. I was in a mode and didn't want to get out of it, 'specially when you've been in the country all your life.

In '51 they had a guy pitching for the Brown Bombers called Black Jesse Garr. That man would call all of his outfielders in and you didn't go across first base for nine innings sometimes. They told Jackie Robinson about him after he broke the color barrier and he came to see him. He [Garr] was illiterate and he was kind of ashamed, you know. Jackie came to talk to him and he never could get him away.

The year I started playing in high school I was a catcher. That's when I went to Clarksdale, and he was pitching that Sunday. They gave he and I three innings, and I beat him out. He came up to me and shook my hand. He's a big, tall guy and he says, "Pride, man, you throw that ball so hard. It was hummin' like mine. How old are you?"

I said, "Eighteen."

I won ten games that year and he didn't win but five. He was getting old. I forget how many he lost. They called him the ace righthander, but when I beat him they called me the ace righthander. He was 6'3", about 205 or -10 pounds and he could bring it. He could throw a snuff bottle in the air and bust it when he was younger. You could hear that mitt all over the park.

We went to Greenwood, Mississippi, and they had a guy down there that pitched like Luis Tiant. He'd turn his back on you. They called him "Ata Beana Cal." We got hung up there one Sunday. He was the best pitcher down that way, farther south, and I was the best up this way. He told me, "Son, I see where you done won six games in a little time and this is your first year. I'm gonna see can you lose one."

I beat him that Sunday and he said, "We'll meet again." And I beat him both times. That's when they *really* started looking at me.

The scout for the Chicago White Sox came to Clarksdale, Mississippi, one night and I had a bad night. I won the game but I hit this guy on the wrist and shattered his wrist.

He said, "Damn! Little fella, where did you come from?"

I said, "Sledge, Mississippi."

He said, "Yeah. That's beans, cornbread, fatback, and turnip greens and sweet potatoes."

I said, "Yeah, that's what we was raised on." There was 15 of us. Them white plantation owners down there, they didn't want you with five kids and they got a hundred and some thousand acres.

They named the Clarksdale Brown Bombers after Joe Louis, the Brown Bomber. The Dark Destroyer.

This guy — the scout — came from Tupelo, Mississippi, and they wanted to pitch me against a kid. We never did get to do it. He said, "Boy, if I had you and him together on one team..."

The manager for the team in Greenwood said, "Two good pitchers on the same team, they wouldn't be no competition out there."

He had to go in the Army. He could bring it, but he didn't have no control. There's a lot of young pitchers right now in the farm systems can throw that ball a hundred miles an hour but they don't have no control. You can't throw a fastball for nine innings if you don't have some junk with it. They're gonna catch up with that fastball sooner or later.

We had a lot of fun. Back in those days you *played* baseball. It was fun. Now it's nothing but money and politics. Everybody wants millions, but soon as they get the millions they don't perform. With the Kansas City Monarchs back in those days, we was making $350 a month. That was big money. We didn't have no signing bonus and the Negro American League players played for years without a raise. You'd get three dollars a day eating money and some of those guys was pretty big. Down South you could take a dollar and eat a *whole* lot of food.

And a lot of those people, they would take you home with 'em. Sometimes you couldn't get no hotel room and some of the people would put up some of the guys.

The travel was sometimes good and sometimes pretty hard. That old flexible bus we was riding in, it was *old* and it needed mechanical work on it all the time. The guy that owned it, he was the mechanic. He kept it running.

We had a hard time traveling. Sometimes we'd travel with cars, busses. We went to North Carolina a lot of times and it would rain there 16 days, 14 days. The black league didn't have no big money and Ted was trying to run his businesses and stuff and keep the club going. It was pretty hard.

Then we'd get fined. [Laughs] I said, "Yeah, they're gonna do us like that 'cause they need the money."

Dr. W. S. Martin, he owned the Red Sox. He had a big hospital there. The stadium was on Crump Boulevard. He messed up a lot of good players. Isiah Thomas, Buddy Woods, Casey Jones — a lot of teams wanted them after Jackie Robinson broke the color barrier, but they waited too long and they got too old.

Mack Pride (**Photograph courtesy of Mack Pride.**)

Does one game stand out in your memory?

We were playing in Briggs Stadium. A. J. Jackson was supposed to pitch that night and he came up with a sore arm, so they put me in. I'd pitch like tonight and I'd be in the bullpen tomorrow night. I never had a sore arm. It was the Kansas City Monarchs and the Birmingham Black Barons. I got 13 strikeouts. I had that curveball that looked like it was gonna hit you in the back of the head on a righthand batter and as soon as it gets down there it's right over the inside corner and you're jumping back.

Satchel Paige, he came down one year when Buck O'Neil was managing. He took it over after Jelly Taylor. Satchel said, "Boy, I ain't never seen anybody *that* little throw a ball that hard."

I could throw a fastball by you, but I was a control pitcher. I hit the corners on you and come back with that heat. You can't get that 36-ounce around. Them big guys was using 36 ounce [bats].

Who was the best player you saw?

I'd go with Jackie Robinson. The next one would be Willie Mays. He wasn't nothing but a big kid; he still is at 68 years old.

We went to play the Buffalo Bisons in Buffalo, New York, and this guy gave me the nickname "The Lumberjack." I'd come sidearm, three-quarter, straight over — curveball and all. Then I'd come sidearm with a four-seamer and it handcuffed a righthand hitter.

I was throwing the ball hard. I hit this Cuban in Welch, West Virginia, one night. The helmets then wasn't as good as the ones now. It broke half in two. The umpire said, "Take your base," and I come running down there and I said, "Chico, sorry, man." The ball sailed and he couldn't get out of the way. The old people used to say, "The ball charmed you." He said, "I'm gonna have Excedrin headache no. 1,000." [Laughs]

He played like Minnie Minoso but he could hit like Roberto Clemente. You had to be on your game when he come to the bat. I forget his name.

Some of the guys I played against was Pedro Sierra and Ray Miller and Tony Lloyd. The last time I pitched against Pedro, he beat me *bad*. His stuff was working like a *champ*. He couldn't do nothing wrong. He's a big dude now.

If you were a young man, would you play baseball?

Oh, yes. All this money they're paying now. We had fun. Everything was good. You didn't have all that picking at each other. We were out there to play and have fun. These guys today go out there and mess up.

PITCHING RECORD

Year	Team, Lg	G	IP	W	L	PCT	H	BB	SO	ERA
1955	Memphis, NAL									
1956	Kansas City, NAL									

Bill "Sonny" Randall
Homestead Grays 1943

BORN AUGUST 5, 1915, HAMPTON, VA
HT. 5'10" WT. 185 BATTED LEFT, THREW RIGHT

Sonny Randall was a hard-hitting outfielder who could have played in the Negro leagues more than he did, but he had a good job and chose to stay in the semipro ranks. But he played against many of the teams and saw the stars through more than 20 years of play. He used to work out with the Homestead Grays, and on a few occasions, when they were in the Washington, D.C., area and needed a player, he would fill in.

His long career was not unnoticed. He was awarded four Certificates of Recognition at the opening of the new Black Sox ballpark in Prince George's County, Maryland, on September 21, 1996.

RANDALL: I played with the Great Lakes Negro team [in World War II]. Here's a clipping: "Negro varsity wins, 5-2, for 12th straight. Bill Randall 4-for-5." I was in the service from 1943 to 1946. I played baseball up there with Larry Doby. In fact, Larry was the captain of the team. Johnny Wright was one of our pitchers. The clipping says, "Johnny Wright allows three hits."

I played sandlot and semipro baseball from the 1930s to the 1950s on Washington, D.C., teams. I played for teams like the Indians, Georgetown, D.C. Aztecs, and Black Sox. We played at various fields throughout the city and also traveled out of town to various towns in Virginia, New Jersey, North Carolina, and Illinois.

How much did you earn on these teams?

[Laughs] We worked on a 60-40 basis. The winners get 60 percent and the losers get 40 percent.

When I worked out with the Grays, they would give me a little more money. I only played about three or four games with them at the most. I had a job at that time —

I worked for the government — and I would play on weekends.

When Josh Gibson used to hit some of those tremendous home runs, I used to take his hat and go around the stands and the fans would give money. He was one of the best I've seen. I saw some good pitchers, too. I played with Satchel one time when he was barnstorming with Dizzy Dean.

Did you bat against Dean?

Yes. I hit a long fly ball. I didn't get a hit.

I batted against Leon Day. He was one of the great pitchers. We caught him when he was coming in and we played him in Richmond. I didn't do so good against him. [Laughs] We were just working out and he had been playing. The way he was zipping the ball, we weren't ready for it.

I played against a fellow named [Laymon] Yokeley; he was playing for Baltimore. He was quite a pitcher at one time, but he was on his way out. I was lucky; I hit a couple of home runs off him that day. He told me I hit a couple of good pitches. They

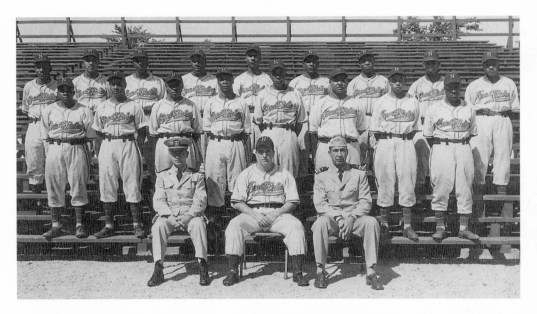

Great Lakes Naval Station baseball team with Bill Randall and Larry Doby. (Photograph courtesy of William Randall.)

looked good to me. In his heyday, he was something, I understand.

Is there a game that really stands out?

I hit a four-run homer. I was in a slump. I was batting four and Larry was batting three. I went to the manager and told him that I should be moved to another position in the batting order. He thought about it and said, "Okay, we'll move you down to seventh." Larry, being the captain of the team, said, "No. Move him down one."

So that day it paid off. I hit a four-run home run. I was lucky that day. We won the game.

Was there an opportunity to stay in the Negro leagues?

To tell you the truth, we played in Cleveland one time against the Cleveland Buckeyes and they wanted me. I had a good day that day. I had hit a ball out there to the 470 mark.

I played right field that day and Larry Doby and I had a thing going. If a man's on base and he rounds third, instead of throw-

ing ahead of him I'd just throw at the base and we'd catch him trying to get back.

I had a good day that particular day and the Cleveland Buckeyes' scout asked me to see them when I got out of the Navy, but I never did because I had a job. I knew of the hard times that the black ballplayers had trying to make it riding up and down the road in those busses.

I went to work for the Navy in 1941 as a laborer and I was inducted into the service in 1943. I went back to the same job when I got out in 1946. I worked for the Navy Department and when NASA was formed I transferred there. I worked for the government for 31½ years. I had the pleasure of meeting the seven original astronauts.

After I retired from NASA in 1973, I was recommended to be the chauffeur for the late Senator Young from North Dakota. I worked with him five years and when he retired I went to Senator Ted Stevens of Alaska. I worked for him seven years as a driver.

I came home to retire and I wasn't home two weeks when I got a call from the Mc-

Nair law firm. I worked with them around four years. I came home to retire again and in two or three weeks I was called to work for Senator Baker and his law firm. I retired from there on December 31, 2001. I had been working for about 70 years.

How was the travel when you played baseball?

Teams were segregated and so were the towns — restaurants, bathrooms, and hotels. The players couldn't eat in any of the restaurants because they were for whites only. The players could order food but would have to take it out.

There were no black hotels for the Negro teams and the players often had to change into their uniforms in the bus or even in the woods. Where they had to stay overnight, we would crowd into different people's houses — friends, relatives, etc.

The busses would often break down and the team would be late to a game.

The players had to deal with a lot of racial hatred and discrimination, both on and off the field. During the Navy years we played a team in Waukegan, Illinois. A player from the all-white team called one of the Negro players the "n" word and the two teams almost got into a fight. After that incident, the coach of the Navy team, who was white, talked to both sides. When we went back to play that team a couple of months later, the problem had been resolved and there was no incident.

Another time, in Michigan, one of the fans in the stand called the black pitcher "Sunshine." It's different now.

Bill "Sonny" Randall (l) and Outowry Butler. (Photograph courtesy of William Randall.)

You played for more than 20 years. Why did you quit when you did?

I got married and my wife had traveled around with us and she got tired of it. We met in 1953 and married in '57.

Any regrets from baseball?

No, not really. I think if the time was right I could've made the majors. I do believe that.

How many times did you see Josh Gibson play?

Oh, I saw him *many* times. I saw him and Buck Leonard. I used to deliver things to the hotel where they stayed when I was a young kid. That's why they allowed me to come out there and work out with them.

Buck Leonard was quite a ballplayer. I played against Buck over in Virginia. We played a night game and that night he hit two over my head out of the park. And he was a gentleman.

Was there a pitcher who was tough on you?

There was one with the Newark Eagles. I can't remember his name. They had been in training and we were just beginning. He was a big lefthander and he could throw pretty hard and had a good curveball. He made the ball look funny to me. [Laughs]

If you were a young man today, would you play baseball?

Yes, because I like the game. They've improved on it with the conditions.

BATTING RECORD

Year	Team, Lg	G	AB	R	H	2B	3B	HR	RBI	BA
1943	Homestead, NNL									

Henry Saverson
Detroit Stars 1954-1956

BORN DECEMBER 14, 1929, WEST POINT, MS
HT. 5'11½" WT. 185 BATTED AND THREW RIGHT

It's safe to say that most college students have a summer job to help with expenses. Henry Saverson was no different, but his summer job was. He played second base for the Detroit Stars and was also the team's traveling secretary. The team belonged to his cousin, Ted Rasberry, who can safely be called a sports entrepreneur; he owned, through the years, both baseball and basketball teams.

Saverson's goal was an education; he realized that, as a .260-.270 hitter, the major leagues were not going to try for him, so he concentrated on school. He earned both his bachelor's and master's degrees.

SAVERSON: I played in high school and I played two years in college. The second two years I was not playing college ball. Those last two years I played in the Negro league.

How were you signed?

I had played with the Grand Rapids Black Sox here and when Ted Rasberry bought the Detroit Stars I had a tryout and went to spring training and stuck with the team for the next three years.

Who were some of your teammates?

Buddy Ivory was the shortstop. [Ralph] Rosado — I can't remember his first name — was a catcher. Willie Harris, a pitcher. A guy by the name of Hubbard played right field. Good right fielder. John Winston, a pitcher. [Laughs] He was sort of erratic, behavior-wise. Juan Soler; I think he was signed [by a major league team] but I think somebody killed him in Puerto Rico. Heck of a ballplayer.

Does a game stand out?

One that stands out in my mind was when we were traveling with the Memphis Red Sox. We went into Mississippi, into West Point, Mississippi, where I was born. I had a lot of relatives who had come to the game that night. I was not really a home run hitter but I hit a homerun that night with a man on base we beat Memphis. That's the most memorable game for me.

Do you know your batting average?

I never kept that, but I was around .260-.270. I was not a .300 hitter.

I was also the traveling secretary. The owner here — Ted Rasberry was my first cousin — entrusted that part and handling the books and all that sort of stuff to me.

Did you book lodgings?

Yes. I had to take care of meals, hand out meal money, pay the players off because oftentimes we were on the road. In order to keep them happy we always made sure that the payroll was there. Mr. Rasberry would wire it to me wherever we were going to be on a particular day.

What were you paid?

It seems to me it was something like two-fifty a month.

How much was meal money?

I think that was about two-fifty or three dollars. I remember going into places like Birmingham or Memphis, you could get a breakfast for a dollar and you would get sausage, eggs, grits, toast — a lot of things for a dollar.

You saw the travel from a different perspective as the secretary.

We had to know who to contact. Back then you could only stay at black establishments and in most places they had black rooming houses and travel lodges. That's where we would stay. They were reasonable; they were decent places. No hotels.

How much was a room typically?

I can't recall, but it wasn't that much. Maybe three-fifty or four dollars or something like that.

Who was the best player you saw?

[George] Altman. He was good. He finally went to the Cubs. He played with Kansas City.

And then there was a pitcher named [Kelly] Searcy. And John Kennedy, he went to the Phillies. Herm Green was signed by the Yankees. He went up to class A; he played first base. There was a fellow named [Ezell] King; he was a big first baseman. He was signed by one of the professional teams. Rangy fellow.

Was there a pitcher who gave you a hard time?

I think the one that was hardest on me was a Cuban named [Enrique] Maroto. He was a good pitcher for his size and everything. You wouldn't think that he could throw the ball; it seemed like a hundred miles an hour. He was probably one of the most outstanding pitchers that I saw.

Some older pitchers had been around for some time. Birmingham Black Barons and Memphis Red Sox had some real good pitchers that had been around for a while. They were sort of intimidating for us young ballplayers. [Laughs]

Why did you stop playing ball?

I stopped when I finished college. I knew that I wouldn't get any major league signing, so I concentrated on a career at that point. I was married and had a child, so I just decided that that would be the end of it.

What did you do when you left baseball?

I worked for Kent County here in juvenile court. I was a probation officer. Then I moved up from probation officer to assistant director of court services. Then I left and went to the state as a child welfare licensing consultant. And from there I became a regional manager for child welfare licensing for the state of Michigan. I worked in that job for the state for 21 years and with the county 12 or 13 years.

I retired in '92. I've been blessed with good health and I do a lot of volunteer work, both with the community as well as the church. I've been really busy and I'm very happy and satisfied.

If you were a young man again, would you play baseball?

Yes. I think that's a great experience.

The travel and meeting people were the things that impressed me most. I'd never been exposed to different types of people with different backgrounds, different values. Back then, there was segregation and I had a chance to see what blacks were able to do with an education. That was a motivating factor for me to go on and get my degree.

In Michigan the racial situation was so different from the South.

I knew what it was and I respected it. I knew I couldn't expect to have the privileges and the experiences in the South that I had here unless it was confined to the black community. They didn't venture beyond

that, although we had some contact with some white promoters
and white businessmen. We were
treated very respectfully by those
men.

*What percentage of the attendance
at games was white?*

It depended on where we
were. A lot of times we played in
black communities and the attendance was almost entirely black.
In Pulaski, Tennessee, however, it
was more or less all white, 90-95
percent. Up through Minnesota
and some of those places — Wis-
consin, Iowa, Kansas — those were
white crowds. Memphis and
Birmingham and those places I
guess it was 90 percent black.

There was not much money
there at all. You had to love it to
play under those conditions.

**Henry Saverson (Photograph cour-
tesy of Henry Saverson.)**

BATTING RECORD

Year	Team, Lg	G	AB	R	H	2B	3B	HR	RBI	BA
1954	Detroit, NAL									
1955										
1956										

Eugene Scruggs
Detroit Stars 1956-1958
Kansas City Monarchs 1958

BORN MAY 17, 1938, HUNTSVILLE, AL
HT. 6' WT. 155 BATTED AND THREW RIGHT

Eugene Scruggs appeared in a previous book, but he had more to say and his story is interesting, so this is an encore.

SCRUGGS: As I reflect back to a time when the South was segregated, my wish then was to see all children playing together as a team. Now you can see in these pictures the different races of children are getting ready for opening day ceremonies for the Little League games. I wonder now how things would have been for me if I had as many opportunities in my life as these children of today, such as little leagues, high school baseball, college baseball, etc. After all these years, the memories that I have seem like it just happened yesterday. The years have gone by; however, my memories will live on forever.

At the tender age of nine, I remembered when Jackie Robinson became the first Negro to play in the major leagues. I said to myself, "One day I'm going to be like him."

In downtown Huntsville, on the corner of Church Street and Holmes Avenue where all the city's business addresses for the African-Americans during segregation, was the Sweet Shop, Sugar Bowl Café, beauty salons, movie theater, and Welch and Harris Funeral Home, where the owner and operator was Mr. R. E. Nelms, the man who

came into my life after the death of my mother. He became a father figure to me and offered me sound advice. Mr. Nelms was the booking agent who organized the Negro leagues games to come to Huntsville. I loved to play baseball with my friends and family members who were much older than myself. We played sandlot games on Saturday evening and Sunday afternoon.

Mr. Nelms told me about the Negro league teams: the Birmingham Black Barons, the Kansas City Monarchs, the Detroit Stars. He asked me would I be interested in playing for one of these teams. My answer to him was "*Yes!*" so he made a telephone call to Mr. Ted Rasberry, the owner of the Detroit Stars and the Kansas City Monarchs, and Mr. Ed Steele, the manager of the Detroit Stars, gave me a tryout. I made the team with a salary of $250 a month at the tender age of 17.

Those were the good old days and now I can reflect back and remember when I was in a hotel in downtown Memphis, Tennessee, with the windows open in the spring of 1956. I was a 17 year old on an adventure of a lifetime some 200 miles from home, when I was awakened by the sounds of

trucks rumbling and growling, brakes hissing and screeching to a stop. They had trucks to come over from Arkansas into town to pick up day workers to chop cotton. They stopped on the corner and yelled, "WE'RE PAYING TWO-FIFTY A DAY." I thought I was back home in Alabama when I realized I was in Memphis getting ready to play in my first Negro league game against the Memphis Red Sox on May 17, 1956, my eighteenth birthday, a day I will never forget. I only pitched five innings because Mr. Steele did not want me to pitch more until I got in shape. I knew I had the speed it would take and my curveball was one of the best in the league.

The biggest problem we had was getting something to eat and hotel accommodations, but through it all everything worked out for us. At the end of the season I returned home and I started working with my mentor, Mr. Nelms, in the funeral home.

In the spring of my third season, I did not report for spring training. During this

Top: Huntsville, Alabama, Little League. (Photograph courtesy of *Huntsville Times.*)

Bottom: Eugene Scruggs (Photograph courtesy of Eugene Scruggs.)

Top: Eugene Scruggs (l) and Carl Holden. (Photograph courtesy of *Huntsville Times.*)
     Bottom: Mr. and Mrs. Eugene Scruggs with Mrs. Jackie (Rachel) Robinson. (Photograph courtesy of Eugene Scruggs.)

era, the civil rights movement had begun and one night when I was on my way home from the funeral home, I was stopped by a state trooper, who asked me where I was going. I told him I was going home; I had just left work. He called me a liar and hit me upside my head and told me I was one of the Negroes with Dr. King. Dr. Martin Luther King, Jr., was in town at the local First Baptist church. The only reason the trooper stopped is because someone in the car with him told him to stop because I was okay. It was unsettling during this time period because of the civil rights movement and segregation.

I made the hardest decision in my life when I decided not to return to the team because of all that was going on in this time period for African-Americans riding on busses in the South. By this time I was married and my wife had just given birth to our first child. Mr. Ted Rasberry and Mr. Satchel Paige came to my home to talk me into returning with the team. When they came by to pick me up, I left home, because I knew I would go if I stayed there and I

needed to be home to take care of my family.

Now as I look back over my life and see where I have come from, I know I have been blessed with six children, 15 grandchildren, and three great-grandchildren. I was able to see five of my grandchildren — all girls — graduate from college in the year of 2001.

Now, over 40 years later, I have had the opportunity to be reunited with many of my old friends who played with me in the Negro league. Some of the players only live 100 miles away from me and we have rekindled our friendship like we have never been apart after all these years. During the 75th anniversary of the Negro leagues held in Kansas City at the museum, I saw all of my old friends. It was a wonderful reunion. I had the opportunity to meet Jackie Robinson's wife, Mrs. Rachel Robinson, during the 50th year celebration of his entering the major leagues. Now all these years later I can remember at the age of nine sitting, listening to the radio with my brothers about the first black man who entered into the major leagues.

PITCHING RECORD

Year	Team, Lg	G	IP	W	L	PCT	H	BB	SO	ERA
1956	Grand Rapids, ind.			5	0	1.000				
	Detroit, NAL			8	4	.667				
1957	Detroit, NAL			8	5	.615				
1958	KC-Det, NAL			7	4	.636				

Willie Sheelor

Chicago American Giants 1952
Memphis Red Sox 1953-1955

BORN FEBRUARY 23, 1928, KANNAPOLIS, NC
HT. 5'9" WT. 165 BATTED AND THREW RIGHT

Willie Sheelor was a middle infielder who was adept at turning the double play. He was, at different times, both a regular shortstop and a regular second baseman. In his first season with Chicago, he was a fill-in infielder, but with the Memphis Red Sox he was in the lineup every day. A broken leg in 1954 slowed him and he played only one more year after that.

SHEELOR: I played here on the local team in Kannapolis [North Carolina] called the Kannapolis Blues. I don't know how this guy got my name, but Winfield Welch come by and got me to go with the Chicago American Giants. They had somethin' like scouts go around to watch these little sandlot teams and that's what the Blues was.

So I went to play with them for a year and then I got with Memphis, Tennessee, the next year. I was with Memphis about three years. I played four years.

Did you have trouble adjusting to the higher level of baseball with the American Giants?
Yeah. It's a lot different than sandlot. They called that the major league back in those days. I had a lot to adjust to. They had somebody to work with me.

How were the overall conditions?
They had their own bus with "Memphis Red Sox" wrote on the side. It was a big ol' transit bus and they had a bus driver. Also, they had a secretary. They was well organized.

A doctor owned the ballclub in Mem-

phis. We had our own stadium there on East Crump Boulevard. We had rooms in the stadium and when we were in town that's where we stayed. That was the only ballpark like that.

We stopped several places to buy gas and we couldn't use the restrooms. Most of the time we had to pull over to the side of the road and go down in the woods. And we couldn't live in the motels. We stayed at something like a rooming house; the blacks had rooming houses in about every town we went in.

The pay was good compared to jobs we could've had, but I can't remember what it was I was paid. That's been a long time.

We played about every day and we had to travel all night to get to the next town. All the games were memorable for me because I loved the game, but no particular one is in my mind.

Why did you retire from baseball?
I broke my leg and I came back home and I met my wife. I played one more year and I give it up after that. I worked in the

158

Willie Sheelor (Photograph courtesy of Willie Sheelor.)

mill, a place they call Cannon Mill. I worked there for 27 years and I retired from there.

Who was the best ballplayer you saw?

I played against Hank Aaron. Hank Aaron was the best ballplayer I've seen. He

could hit the ball out of the park. He was a small, skinny guy, but he had a lot of wrist action. A really amazin' ballplayer.

Who was the best pitcher?

Satchel Paige barnstormed in that league. He was something, I'll tell you. He would take a piece of chewing gum paper; that's how he'd warm up. He'd put the chewing gum paper down and throw strikes over it when he warmed up.

Did you bat against him?

Yes. I popped up. [Laughs] You had to start swinging right when he'd go through his motions to catch up with him. He was something.

Who was the best pitcher on the Red Sox?

I can't remember really. Charlie Davis was good. He's a lot of fun.

Charley Pride was a good ballplayer. Charley had it in his head, whatever he decided to do he was gonna do it. He'd pitch and he'd play outfield. Anywhere you put him he'd try to play it. One thing about him, if you beat him today he'd be wantin' to pitch the next day. That's the kind of fella he was. He was a go-getter.

Sometimes riding on the bus — sometimes we'd ride all day and maybe all night — he'd start singing. He made a remark I remember that one day he was gonna be somebody. You know, there were about nine of them in his family there in Sledge, Mississippi. I heard that the street uptown there wasn't even paved. He's a great fella.

Would you play baseball again if you were a young man?

Yes, I sure would. I love the game. It was something I really loved.

BATTING RECORD

Year	Team, Lg	G	AB	R	H	2B	3B	HR	RBI	BA
1952	Chicago, NAL									
1953	Memphis, NAL									
1954										
1955										

Sam Taylor
Kansas City Monarchs 1952-1954
Indianapolis Clowns 1954

BORN JANUARY 27, 1929, CHARLESTON, MS
HT. 5'6" WT. 195 BATTED AND THREW RIGHT

Sam Taylor was proof that good things come in small packages. Also powerful things. He was a strong 195 pounds, compressed into a 5'6" frame. He was impressive enough to be scouted by major league teams, but the contract never came.

TAYLOR: I started playin' in Mississippi when I was a small kid in school. When I was playin' ball in Sumner, Mississippi, I was the superstar at my school. I never would have to bring my lunch; all I had to do was wait until someone would choose a team. When they would choose me to play on their team, whoever had the best lunch, that is the one I would play with. That's the way I would eat lunch every day, because if I was on any of their teams they knew I was a winner.

My contract was lunch. I was doing all right until my sister, Titus, told my mom about it. Some of the boys didn't have good lunches; all they had was buttered biscuits. So my mother told me that I had to play on the other boys' team no matter what they had. Have you ever tried to eat a cold buttered biscuit? It was not good at all. I would get my orders before I left home from my mother: "Play with the other boys today that had the buttered biscuits and the good lunch later." And that was that; I had to carry out the orders.

Then I moved to St. Louis and I played with the East St. Louis White Sox, which

was managed by Marlon Starling. I played with him about two seasons. Then we got up a neighborhood team of our own called the Sixth Street Stars. We kept that goin' I'd say a couple of years.

Then I moved on to the big teams. The big team at that was the East St. Louis Giants. I played them a couple of seasons, then I went on to a bigger team, the East St. Louis Colts. They was nationally known 'cause quite a few made the major leagues from that team. I played with them for years.

Then I left them and went to another team called the East St. Louis Midgets. We took over the championship in East St. Louis. One boy left the Midgets and went to the majors: Ted Savage. We played on the Midgets together. He went to the major leagues and I went to the Negro league.

I played with the Monarchs in part of '52, part of '53, and part of '54. I played with the Indianapolis Clowns the first part of '54 and then I went back to the Kansas City Monarchs 'cause I didn't like their setup.

I played with the Monarchs that whole

season of '54 before I hung it up, because it just seemed like they kept givin' me the run-around. The Milwaukee Braves was supposed to sign me; they gave me the run-around. The Pittsburgh Pirates gave me the run-around and the St. Louis Cardinals gave me the run-around. I just got disgusted and gave it up.

I played for a good decade. When I quit, I went back to my old job. I worked at a chemical plant.

Who were some of the other players you played with?

I played on the team Ernie Banks played on for a little while. Doc Conners, he was on there; he come up to the White Sox farm club for a little while. I played with Francisco Herrera; he was a Cuban. I played with Juan Armenteros and I played with Hank Mason on the Monarchs. Jeff Williams, I played with him; he got sold down to Puerto Rico and I never did see him anymore.

Do you know any of your stats?

When we was with the Monarchs we really didn't have nobody keepin' battin' averages. I guess I was a pretty fair hitter. I could hit in the teens in home runs and I could drive in runs.

Who was the best player you saw?

Herrera was one of 'em. He played first base for the Monarchs. The next guy was Jeff Williams. Our third baseman was named Hank Bayliss. They was good ball-players. Sherwood Brewer was a good ballplayer.

I played with Toni Stone, too. I'm not considerin' her no good ballplayer. She was there just for publicity, to draw a crowd. We had a couple of Cubans on there. We had one named Nunez. I think it was Delberto Nunez. He was small but he could hit that ball a *long* way.

Who was the best pitcher you saw?

I'd have to again go to a couple of 'em.

Sam Taylor (**Photograph courtesy of Sam Taylor.**)

Hank Mason was one of 'em and the other one was a Cuban named Enrique Maroto.

How was the travel?

Oh, it was kinda tough. We'd have to ride the bus all night; sometimes we'd get there with just time enough to dress. We'd have to ride all night; I remember one time we rode all night and all day and got to New York just in time to get out and get on our clothes and get to the ballfield. We didn't have time to eat or nothin'.

Sometimes the bus would break down and Buck O'Neil was the manager and he's have to hire cars. The bus would break down and he'd have to rent cars to go on with the trip.

In Clinton, Iowa, I had an experience I never will forget. I ran over a snake that was about six foot long and I'd say he was about eight or ten inches in diameter. That was one of the biggest snakes I ever seen, but he didn't bite.

Buck called the security guard to get out and look for him. They killed that one and they said to come out and I said, "No.

Sam Taylor (Photograph courtesy of Sam Taylor.)

I want the whole field searched. If that one's out there, there might be another one." They got over in right field and there was another one just like him. [Laughs] They said they had *never* seen a snake on that diamond before.

When I ran over him I fell. I thought it was a baseball bat or somethin' out there. I called time and come back lookin' for it and this big snake was rollin' there. I just took off and ran into the dugout. When I got to the dugout, I thought if there's one on the diamond there might be another one in the dugout. They said, "What's the matter with you?" I said, "Man, there's a snake out there!"

Everybody cleared the dugout then. We went out to the middle of the diamond where there wasn't no grass 'til they got that field searched. People in the stands even came out. I *never* will forget that.

Does a game stand out?

That would be one that stood out. The other one would be, I guess, the day in Cincinnati ol' Hank Mason pitched a no-

hitter. That was the onliest game I'd ever been in that was a no-hitter. It was against the Indianapolis Clowns. I think I came in and caught the last couple of innin's.

What were you paid?

[Laughs] It was almost a song and a dance. We played because we loved the game. I was gettin' two hundred and fifty dollars a month. Your meals had to come out of that. They didn't give extra money for your meals. They gave us money, but it was taken out of the check when you got paid. That knocked you down to maybe $175. That was tough. I had a wife and two kids so I had to give it up and come home.

The Milwaukee Braves had told me, "If you stay on here 'til the end of the season, we're gonna take you to spring trainin' with us." So I tried to get them to give me a little bonus or somethin'. They told me, "We ain't started givin' coloreds a bonus yet." I tried to show 'em there wasn't no better time to start than with me. I never heard anythin' else from 'em.

The scout had managed the Dodgers, Charlie Dressen. He went to the Milwaukee Braves as a scout. That's who I was talkin' with. That's what he explained to me. He said, "When Hank Aaron signed, he didn't sign for no bonus contract. He was just playin' for a payday." That's when him and O'Neil got into it and I never did hear no more from him after that.

If you were a young man today, would you play baseball?

Oh, yeah. I tried my best to get my grandsons to play; they love football. I can't get none of 'em to play baseball. I had one I thought was gonna play baseball. Ted Savage works for the Cardinals and I got him to talk to the head scout over there. We got a chance for the oldest grandson to go to the minor league. He didn't show no interest and they sent him back. That hurt me. I wish they'd have loved baseball like me. Fishin', huntin', and baseball — that was me.

BATTING RECORD

Year	Team, Lg	G	AB	R	H	2B	3B	HR	RBI	BA
1952	KC, NAL									
1953										
1954	Indianapolis, NAL									
	KC, NAL									

Ron Teasley
New York Cubans 1948

Born January 26, 1927, Detroit, MI
Ht. 5'11" Wt. 175 Batted and Threw Right

Most people never become inducted into a hall of fame. Ron Teasley is in *five:* Afro-American Hall of Fame, Wayne State University (where he batted .500) Hall of Fame, Northwestern High School Hall of Fame, Michigan High School Coaches Baseball Hall of Fame, and Meals on Wheels Hall of Fame.

He coached 15 high school championship teams and is a senior Olympic award winner. And he was an all-star both years he played in the ManDak league.

TEASLEY: I was born in '27. When I was about 12 years old I started going up to the field where former Negro league players were playing and practicing. I started hanging around. A couple of guys had played with the Homestead Grays, Philadelphia Stars, and Pittsburgh Crawfords.

Soon they had me serving as a little gofer, and before long I was shagging fly balls. They went on trips and would take me along if not enough players showed up. Then they started putting me in the game on a regular basis, usually in right field.

I also had a neighbor, Julius Lanier, who was a pitcher. He would ask me to catch for him. This helped to develop my hitting skills. He worked for Kelsey-Hayes Wheel Company, Local 174. The union team asked me to play with them and I agreed. These men were 10-20 years older than me; however, I held my own despite the age difference. Basically that's how I got started. That was 1939.

Detroit had black semipro teams called the Detroit Wolves and the Motor City Giants. They traveled around Michigan and adjoining states. We played in Traverse City and Grand Rapids. They had a Cherry Festival in Traverse City. We also played House of David in South Bend, Indiana.

Toledo had a team called the Toledo Cubs and they also played under the name of Toledo Crawfords. The team was owned by Hank Rigney.

There was also another team in Detroit owned by a gentleman by the name of Dee Jennings, and we did a lot of traveling with him. His team had various names. We were sometimes the Detroit Black Sox, sometimes the Detroit Red Sox — different names. We'd travel around Michigan and into Ohio quite a bit. That was around '42, '43.

Hank Rigney was quite a prominent businessman. I was contacted by him and soon I started going down there and playing with them. That was interesting, because Mr. Rigney also booked Jesse Owens a lot to travel with the team. He would run against racehorses and against players.

I ran against Jesse Owens in a couple of places. It was pretty interesting. The first time we raced he gave me a ten-yard head start. The starter said, "On your mark, get set ..." and Jesse would take off a little early. [Laughs] Naturally he beat me, but the second time, I said, "I've got to be smart. I've got to take off early, too." And I tied him — with the ten-yard head start.

Jesse put on a marvelous show. He had a very dramatic presentation. He talked about his experiences in Germany and he also would use German terms to highlight some of the things that happened to him.

I played with the Toledo team a lot. I enjoyed playing with them because we usually made more money. The money would not be given to me, however; it was given to my father to make it appear that I was not getting paid. I was still in high school. It would be around $15. We played on PC — percentage. I wasn't married; I was playing baseball and traveling. I really enjoyed it. Money wasn't a big thing to me; it was always given to my dad.

Another place I always liked to play was Louisville, Kentucky. Louisville was a great baseball city. We'd have tremendous crowds and we'd come away with $45-50. It was good money in those days and it was also mailed to my dad,

The United States Baseball League was formed when Jackie Robinson was with the Brooklyn Brown Dodgers. In 1947, I was playing with the Motor City Giants and we were on our way to Brooklyn to play against the Brooklyn Brown Dodgers. We made a stop in Warren, Ohio, and the manager made a call and when he came back to the bus, he said, "We're not going to Brooklyn because the league's been disbanded. The Dodgers signed Jackie Robinson."

I went into the service in 1945; I was only in for 13 months. I also played baseball in the service, in the Navy. There were many semipro and pro players. Mel Queen was one of the players I played against. It was a good brand of baseball. Most of the players had jobs in recreation.

I was called a Specialist A — athletic specialist. I ran the recreation program on

Ron Teasley (**Photograph courtesy of Ron Teasley.**)

Saipan while I was there —about six or seven months. And I played baseball. Gene Woodling was our manager. He didn't play with us. He managed, but he wouldn't play. Mel Queen was an outstanding pitcher. He had a vicious curveball. I also participated in several boxing matches while in the service.

The level of baseball with the Toledo team was quite good. Cecil Kaiser was one of our better players from this area and we all looked up to him. I've always admired him because he loved to play baseball. He was really an outstanding pitcher.

Ron Teasley (Photograph courtesy of Ron Teasley.)

He would come home and play on the sandlots with us. He just loved to play. He would stay home for a couple of days and then he would leave, going down to South America or somewhere else to play. He had quite a long career. He did a lot for me because he considered me *his* first baseman. Whenever he came home and we had road trips — we took little trips — he would always say, "I want Teasley to play first base." He really liked the idea of me playing first base when he pitched. He had enough influence that they would listen to him. He got what he wanted.

The Toledo situation was quite good because we played at Swayne Field. It was on Detroit Avenue and it was a nice ballpark. I think the Toledo Mud Hens played in that park.

I played at Wayne State University. I played at Northwestern High School, which had quite a reputation because such players

as Willie Horton and John Mayberry and Alex Johnson and Hobie Landrith, all played at the school after I graduated. It was well known for its baseball program.

After that I went to Wayne State and in the summers I would play with the other teams. I batted .500 in my freshman year and set a school record that still stands. I also played basketball. I was versatile enough to play right field instead of first base, my regular position.

In 1947, I worked out for a Detroit Tigers super scout at Manz Field. He said he was impressed and would keep in touch. We didn't hear from him.

Then in 1948, I was signed by the Dodgers. That was interesting because Will Robinson, who at that time was an outstanding high school coach and a reporter for one of the local black weekly newspapers. Later, he became an outstanding basketball coach. He was one of the first African-Americans to coach a major college team. He was quite instrumental in getting me signed by the Dodgers. He had a good friend by the name of Wendell Smith, who worked at a Chicago paper. He's in the Hall of Fame as a journalist. Through their collaboration, Sammy Gee and I were signed by the Dodgers. We were the eighth and ninth African-Americans signed by a major league baseball team.

We were contacted; we got telegrams telling us when to report. We were told to report to Vero Beach. They gave us train tickets. When we got on the train in Detroit everything was fine until we crossed the Mason-Dixon line. Then they wanted us to move to the front of the train because of the segregation laws. It was dirtier there because of all the smoke and soot coming in from the engine.

We finally got to Vero Beach. Actually, we went down for a tryout, more or less, and we were both signed. We were assigned to play in the Class D PONY League at Olean, New York.

Ron Teasley (r) with Sammy Gee. (Photograph courtesy of Ron Teasley.)

The stay in Florida at Vero Beach was interesting, something we weren't accustomed to. We went to the city to the movies; we had to go in the back door and sit up in the balcony. That was kind of strange for us. It was a big adjustment from a city like Detroit.

That was another thing about playing in those [Negro] leagues. It was scary. I remember one time we were playing a team called the Chicago Brown Bombers and we were in Fort Smith, Arkansas. The fellows had told me, "Look. When you're down there and if you're stopped by the police and they ask you a question, just shake your head or nod." They were afraid that I was not going to say "Sir."

I found out what they meant by this incident in Fort Smith, Arkansas. The Chicago Brown Bombers traveled in limousines and one of the players did not say "Sir" to an officer and I actually saw them beating these guys up.

Once around '44 we were traveling with Jesse Owens and they [police] wanted to know how we were able to travel with gas being rationed. But when they found we were traveling with Jesse Owens they let us go.

We played against Satchel Paige at Dequinder Park at Six-Mile and Dequinder. This was early in my career, and my first time at bat, I got a triple off of him. There was only one problem; I was playing under another name. But I have the clipping. At that time think I was Ronald Donald. [Laughs] And I used the name Blazer Johnson a couple of times. Johnson was my mother's maiden name.

We also played against the Grays. I remember a game when Cecil was pitching against the Grays in St. Louis. I remember the game so well because we were leading, 2-to-1, in the last inning with the count 2-and-2 against Buck Leonard. Cecil threw what looked like a beautiful, perfect pitch and Buck took it and the ump called it a ball. Then the next pitch Buck hit a home run in the upper deck in left field in Sportsman's Park.

I also remember playing against Josh Gibson and I remember long home runs.

One of the players said, "When we go to this ballpark"—we were playing somewhere in southern Illinois—"we're going to find the oldest fan that we can find and ask him who hit the longest ball." We did this in several cities. In each city, the fan would say, "The longest ball was by Josh Gibson. You see that light pole out yonder." This happened in three or four cities.

Who was the best player you saw?

I guess Buck. I always did like him. I guess I was a first baseman and I admired him because he was just so confident. We played them several times here in Detroit. Buck Leonard was my favorite. He was an outstanding defensive player as well as a steady hitter.

After we were released by the Dodgers, we were signed by the New York Cubans and I remember we were playing the Grays in Washington. Buck heard about us being released and he sat down and talked to us for an hour, just telling us how these things happen and we must learn to overcome them, don't let it get us down.

Why were you released? You weren't doing badly.

Team officials came to us one day and said, "We have some players who are coming down from a higher classification and we have to make room for them." And that was it.

I was batting .270, but leading the league in home runs. I only had three or four, but still I was leading the league. The other player [Gee] was batting .320, however he was not playing regularly as I was.

The manager at that time was George Scherger. I think he's still with Cincinnati. He was a playing manager.

When I signed with the Dodgers I wasn't sure I wanted to sign or not because I wanted a bonus. It seemed that all of the players who got bonuses were being retained longer, so I wanted a bonus—$100 or something. They said that they couldn't give me

a bonus, so I hesitated and said, "I'd like to call my college coach or my father or somebody and talk to them about it." They told me they didn't have time; they wanted me to sign right away; the offer was only good for so long. Several of the players they kept received bonuses and had much less playing time than Sam and I.

When I left the city [Detroit], there was a big headline in the local African-American paper: "Teasley and Gee have been ordered to camp by the Dodgers." I've still got that clipping somewhere. The release by the Dodgers was a major shock at the time.

I don't think I played my best with the Cubans. You know, it was such a disappointment being released. We were just so downhearted.

I'd been playing first base with the Dodgers and I had played some right field at Wayne. We played a game at the Polo Grounds and of all places, they put me in center field. [Laughs] When they asked me if I could play center field I said yeah, naturally. It was a chance to break into the lineup.

When I was out there a guy hit a line drive in the first inning. That's a tough play anyhow. The ball is rising and I started in and then I had to retreat *all* the way to deep center field to get the ball.

I had some interesting experiences with the Cubans. I never really got to know many of my teammates. After all, I was there to take their jobs.

Minnie Minosa was on the team; so was Rafael Noble, the big catcher the Giants signed. I saw him almost get into a fight with another player over who was going to hang their clothes at a certain spot. [Laughs] These guys had their superstitions. Even riding on the bus, you had to ride in certain spots. The rookies had to sit in the back over the motor where it was real hot or you had to sit over the wheel where it was a bumpy ride.

I stayed with the Cubans a few months. Sam stayed longer. Then I came in 1949, I played in Canada in the ManDak League. It was really good baseball and I really enjoyed it. I enjoyed more success up there; I made the all-star team the two years I played there.

One of our best pitchers was Gentry Jessup; he played with the Chicago American Giants. "Lefty" Cobb — Dillard Cobb — was from Detroit, a friend of mine, was our other outstanding pitcher. We also had a pitcher from Detroit named John Wingo; he pitched for Wayne State University. Willie Wells was up there, a Hall of Famer; and Leon Day, a Hall of Famer, was there as well.

After the couple of years up there, I found employment in a plant. I only needed a few hours to complete my degree work, so I returned to the university.

I majored in health and physical education. I got into coaching finally at Northwestern High School, my alma mater. I coached basketball, baseball, and golf. My coaching record: JV basketball, three years, 26 wins, 4 losses; varsity basketball, two years, 26 wins, 4 losses; baseball, 20 years, 224 wins, 125 losses.

I was very fortunate throughout my coaching career. I had some very good young men and good ballplayers. We had a pretty good record. Quite a few of my players went to college. Fifteen were drafted but none of them made it all the way to the top.

Would you go back and be a baseball player again?

Oh, yes. Definitely. I loved it. I loved baseball. I enjoyed it.

You don't have much control over what happens to you. When I was at Vero Beach, there seemed to be one man that decided whether or not you made it and if this one man gave you thumbs up, everybody else gave you thumbs up. They all just seemed to agree with him. The idea was to try to impress that one guy.

Ron Teasley (**Photograph courtesy of Ron Teasley.**)

I loved the Negro leagues. When I was growing up I wasn't as interested in playing in the major leagues as I was in playing in the Negro leagues. Those guys were my heroes. My father was a baseball fan; he grew up with Candy Jim Taylor. He talked baseball a lot; he loved baseball.

Another person I came in contact with was Turkey Stearnes. We played together briefly and he must have been in his 50s. We played together in Toledo. In one of the games in the mid-'40s, he scored from first base on a single. My father worshipped him. He took greater interest in my playing when he found out that Turkey Stearnes and I were on the same team. On a southern trip, Turkey and I were roomies.

In conclusion, I would say that I enjoyed my baseball career. I think baseball is a great game. It requires so much physical and mental talent to play the game. The segregation era deprived so many of the op-portunity to see the best baseball players, both black and white.

BATTING RECORD

Year	Team, Lg	G	AB	R	H	2B	3B	HR	RBI	BA
1948	Olean, PONY							3	15	.267
	NY Cubans, NAL									

James Way
Lexington Hustlers

BORN AUGUST 1, 1923, CYNTHIANA, KY
HT. 6'1"? WT. 180 BATTED BOTH, THREW RIGHT

The Lexington, Kentucky, Hustlers were not affiliated with any league, but they played teams from both the Negro National and American leagues. The team was officially classified as semipro.

When a South Atlantic League team was granted to Lexington there was some sentiment to name it the Hustlers, but instead Legends was chosen. But in a way that honors the Hustlers; they are all legends today.

The Hustlers was originally a black team, but in 1946 it became the first integrated team in the South when Bobby Flynn began playing. Later a city councilman and the father of major leaguer Doug Flynn, Bobby and the Hustlers made history that year.

James Way caught for the Hustlers in their final years. He was a defensive specialist who went to college on a basketball scholarship. Baseball was learned the hard way, on the sandlots. His high school did not have a team and he did not play in college, but he learned the game well enough to play for what was probably the best team in the state of Kentucky, the Hustlers.

WAY: I played all over central Kentucky. I was a pretty fair catcher so I played for the all black teams in Cynthiana. That's where the Hustlers saw me. I played for Cynthiana, I played for Mount Sterling, I played for Paris, and I also played for Millersburg. This was at different times. If they had a good team coming in and they wanted a good catcher, they would call on me.

In our school in Cynthiana we didn't even have a high school baseball team. The only baseball we got was out in the sandlots. I guess I was about 12 or 13 years old when I started playing with the Negro team there in Cynthiana. When I came along everybody had a team. There was a black team and a white team in just about every little town.

I remember when I was real young my dad played baseball. He was a third baseman and he used to take me to the games. I enjoyed carrying his spikes. [Laughs] I remember on Sunday morning he would sit down on the cistern we had out in the backyard of our house and he'd take a file and sharpen those things. [Laughs] They were vicious with those things. They would try to cut people up with 'em.

When you played with the Hustlers, where was the ballpark?

It was out on Newtown Pike. There used to be a grandstand; I'm not sure what happened to it. It was on Newtown Pike just before you got into Lexington. It was called Blue Grass Athletic Park.

The Homestead Grays came through Lexington in those days.

We played Homestead Grays and we

played the New York Black Yankees and we played the Indianapolis Clowns — just about any of those teams that were barnstorming and came through town.

How did the Hustlers fare?

Pretty good. I think we might have beaten the Clowns once. When we did get beat, it was one run or 2-to-nothing or 1-to-nothing.

The team was classified as semipro, but you got something. What?

Not much. [Laughs] Maybe a glass of beer after practice. Sometimes three or four dollars here or there. I'm not sure what happened to the money. We didn't get paid. Most of the guys that played on that team just loved to play baseball. That was pretty much the type of team that we had.

Did any members of the team go on to play professionally?

[Lou] Slick Johnson played with the Brooklyn Dodgers. He was a young fella at that time, played outfield for us. He went with the Brooklyn Dodgers and I think he's still involved in the administration some way or other.

Was there much of an opportunity for you or your teammates to turn professional?

Not at that time. They weren't taking blacks into the professional leagues. It was just the beginning. Johnson was much younger than most of us. I think he was probably just in college or just beginning college when he played with us, and it was after that when the Dodgers looked at him and became interested in him.

Do any games stand out?

I was mostly a line drive hitter. I can't remember any games that because of my hits we won. I think I might've got two home runs in my whole career. I hit mostly doubles and singles.

Where were you in the batting order?

It depends on who we were playing, but most of the time I was down near the end of the batting order, maybe one or two up from the pitcher.

Who were some of your pitchers?

I can't even think of their names, it's been so long. I know one boy that I brought with me who pitched against the Homestead Grays. His name was Preacher Florence from Cynthiana. He was pretty good. They beat us, 2-to-nothing, and I think both those runs were unearned. They made a statement that evening that he was one of the best pitchers they had faced in all the games. He was righthanded. He was a white boy. We were integrated.

How far did the Hustlers travel?

We went as far as Ohio. We played a couple of games up in Cincinnati. Most of the travel was around central Kentucky, like Danville and Winchester. I'm not sure if we played in Louisville.

What was the best part of your game, offense or defense?

Defense.

Who were some of the players you saw?

Josh Gibson, he was one of the best catchers I think that I've ever seen. He never did make it to the big leagues. Oh, he could knock the ball. I remember when we played 'em. In that particular game I caught, he had two strikes on him and I called for a changeup and he swung at it twice really. [Laughs] He was way out ahead of it and he drew his bat back and he really hit the ball with a grunt. It went over the left field fence. It was all with the wrists, I guess, because he was way out on his front leg. Some way he drew the bat back a second time and out it went.

We played the team that Willie Mays played with. Birmingham Black Barons I believe was the name of it, but I don't remember Willie Mays as such. But I knew there was a young guy that played center field. I learned later it was Mays.

Who was the best player you saw?

Gibson was the best that I can recall — all around. Because he played my position, that's one reason I noticed him more than the others.

Who was the best pitcher you came up against?

Satchel Paige. It seems to me like we played a Negro league team that he pitched for. He was something else.

Do you remember what you did when you faced him?

Yeah. I didn't hit him. [Laughs]

If you were a young man again, would you play baseball?

Oh, yes. I loved it. That was my second sport, I guess. I went to college on a basketball scholarship. I went to Central State in Ohio, near Xenia. At that time it was called Wilberforce. That's where I graduated from. I didn't play baseball, though; that's the peculiar thing.

I played center at that time. They called me "Tree" 'cause I was the tallest thing that they had. Six-one and a half, weighed about 180 pounds.

I played against Bevo Francis. I guess he was the biggest guy I ever came up against. Close to seven feet. He was the only guy I couldn't out-rebound that I ever came up against. Nobody was as big as he was at that time.

[Bevo Francis attended Rio Grande College in Illinois. He was a legend in his time, setting college scoring records every year, but Rio Grande was later classified as a junior college and all of his records were disallowed.]

What did you do outside baseball?

When I came back to Cynthiana in '47, I came back as a schoolteacher. I spent 20 years coaching football, basketball in Harrison County, then I left there and came to Eastern Kentucky University here in Richmond in 1967. I retired in '83.

Do you have any regrets from your baseball days?

Oh, no. I started playing baseball when I was a teenager. We started out playing stickball. I became a catcher because I guess I was the only one crazy enough to get behind the bat without any protection. We started out with rubber balls and tennis balls. I had pretty good reflexes and, of course, I never did get hit in the face or anything like that.

I caught for a while with the Hustlers without a breast protector — I had the shin guards — because I couldn't throw well in that. Back in those days I was kinda slender and the breast protector evidently was made for somebody that weighed about 400 pounds. [Laughs] I never could get it tight enough on me and I couldn't throw with the thing, so I said, "Heck, I'll never get hit in the stomach area anyway 'cause of my reflexes." So I just didn't even use a breast protector the latter part of my career up there.

I never got hit. Some way my reflexes always came through, even on foul balls. I'd get hit in the face or around the knees but I never got hit in my midsection.

I started out catching in the alleys playing stickball with a finger glove. At that time we didn't have any protection so I started out catching rubber balls and tennis balls. We finally found an old hard ball and taped it up and I started catching that. [Laughs] I became pretty good.

I think I could've caught without a mask because my reflexes were that good. When I got a little older and got a little more sense I wore one.

One thing I always regretted was not having a photo. When the Hustlers took one team picture, it was before I joined 'em. Then when they took another one, I was hurt and wasn't in it. I never could show anybody. I could tell 'em I played with the Hustlers and they'd say, "What? I've never seen you on any of the pictures."

Of course, not many guys are still living that I know played with 'em. There's
Scoop [Brown], Bunny Davis, Bobby Flynn;
they could verify that I played. Most of
those other guys are dead now.

When I was playing with the Hustlers
they never did spell my name right. It was
always "Wade" in most of the papers. The
guys called me "Wade." The papers had my
name in there as "James Wade," but most
people knew who it was, the player from
Cynthiana.

NO RECORDS AVAILABLE

Sam Williams
Birmingham Black Barons 1947-1952

BORN OCTOBER 12, 1922, BIRMINGHAM, AL
HT. 5'11" WT. 170 BATTED AND THREW RIGHT

The West Texas-New Mexico League was a hitter's league. The light desert air was a factor, but an awful lot of balls that didn't go out fell in for base hits. In 1953, there were five .400 hitters and 17 regulars who batted .350 or higher. This made for some high ERAs; only one pitcher was below 3.00 and just three were under 4.00 for the season.

But there were some big win totals put up by those hurlers who could withstand the offensive onslaught. There were two who won more than 25 games and six who won 20 or more. Sam Williams was one of the winningest; he racked up 25 victories for Pampa that year. This earned him the league's Rookie of the Year award. The next season with Pampa, 1954, he pitched a double header on July 4 at Abilene, winning both games by scores of 7-3 and 9-0.

On two other occasions he won 15 games in the minor leagues and in 1950, with Birmingham in the Negro American League, he won 13. In his career, both in the Negro league and the minor leagues, he won 105 games and lost 90. He would have won more, but a suspension, along with his wife's desire for him to stay home, led to his retirement.

WILLIAMS: I have always liked baseball. When I was a kid we used to play in the fields with little neighborhood teams. Then when I went in the service I played there. In World War II I played.

When I came out, Birmingham had a lot of companies there that sponsored baseball and they had a pretty good city league. At one time, you could go to Birmingham and pick up any kind of a good ballplayer that you'd want to, but the thing about it, the fellas didn't want to leave. They was workin' for those plants and they didn't wanna leave.

I played for the Clow Pipe Shop, a pipe-makin' company, and we won the city championship in '46. In the winter, the city formed the all-star team to play against the Barons — the Birmingham Black Barons —

and I was chosen to pitch that game because I had a good record that year. The Barons were so elated over me. I happened to know Artie Wilson, so they came out to my home the next day and talked me into pitchin' for the Barons. It was '47 when I joined 'em. I played '47 to '50.

When the Negro league started breakin' up in 1950, in '51 and '52 I went to Mexico. A lot of the fellas that was in that [Negro] league was in Mexico playin'. A fella by the name of Quincy Trouppe, a catcher, he was at Guadalajara, and Bill Greason and I went there to play. Bill didn't go back in '52 because he signed with Oklahoma City.

I've been told that the conditions in Mexico were much better for the players than they were in the United States.

Oh, yes, this is true. Down there, a baseball player was a god at that time. You were a big-time celebrity in Mexico. We were treated real well.

The pay was more. The owners in the Negro league didn't have the funds. Mainly, we were playin' baseball because we liked it. We wasn't makin' no money. This is why I chose to go to Mexico, because we could make more money down there.

Down there we didn't play every day; you only played three times a week. I was there when Preston Gomez was managin' Mexico City. In fact, Preston was gonna try to get me. I was at Poza Rica at the time and he was gonna try to get me for the Mexico City Reds, but the club found out about it and they didn't wanna turn me loose.

I ended up getting suspended. [Laughs] Ol' [George] Trautman, the minor league commissioner, suspended me. I wanted to get with Preston and the Mexico City Reds, so when the contract time come up I asked for more money. They tried to get me to report and they would talk about the money after I reported. I didn't wanna do it. I told 'em no, get it all settled before I come down there. And they wouldn't do it, so they wrote to the minor league commissioner and told him that I refused to report for spring trainin'.

Trautman and I was corresponding and he demanded that I go down and go to spring trainin' and I told him I wasn't goin' down; when I signed a contract I would go. We wrote back and forth about it and he gave me a deadline. I told him I didn't care nothin' about his deadline, I still had to have a contract. [Laughs] So he suspended me for a year. That was somewhere 'long about '59.

Everywhere I ever played I was a winner. I played up in Oregon with the Eugene Emeralds and we won the championship. I was one of the best pitchers that they had on that team.

The highlight of my pitchin' career was there. Remember Max Patkin? I was a pitcher that always had good control and he was up in Eugene to put on his performance. He was gonna hang upside down against the netting back there in the backstop and hit the ball, but he wanted somebody with good control; he didn't want nobody to kill him. [Laughs]

He asked the manager — our manager was Cliff Dapper at that time — who was the best control pitcher that he had and he told him, "Sam Williams. He's the best control pitcher we got."

He and I went out and worked out one day before his performance and he liked it. I was just what he wanted. He told me, "I should hire you. You make me look good." [Laughs] I got a kick out of it. He used to put on a good show.

When I was with Birmingham, they had a pretty good ballclub when I went to 'em in '47. They had room for one more pitcher; I think they were carryin' six or seven pitchers. Since they wanted me, I was on the staff but I wasn't gonna be a starter because they already had their rotation. You might know some of those fellas: [Bill] Powell, [Nat] Pollard, [Jimmy] Newberry.

Alonzo Perry and I went to the Barons the same year. In fact, we was the two youngest fellas on the team when we went there in '47.

The regular league games they didn't let no rookies pitch; that was for the starters. I would pitch all through the week; the only time that I'd pitch on a Sunday was when one of the other pitchers'd get knocked out. I knew that when I went there, 'cause they explained it to me. It was all right with me. That was good experience for me.

The travel, if it was today it would be terrible. We traveled by bus — we had our own bus driver — and we traveled for a solid week without sleepin' in a bed. We would play here tonight and we'd be on the road goin' to the next town to play. I remember once we came from Birmingham to New

York and from New York back to Birmingham and then to Kansas City. [Laughs]

One thing that I liked about it, we were a very close group of fellas. There was no animosity or nothin'. We were just like a bunch of brothers. I always tell people that was the best team that I ever played on, as far as personnel. We all got along just like brothers. We were a close-knit group and that meant a lot to me. Under the conditions that we were travelin'—busses and changin' clothes in busses at the ballpark—everybody pitched in, nobody grumbled. All we wanted to do was play ball. That was the highlight of my career, them bus rides.

The last couple of years I was there, I would help out the bus driver drivin' the bus. When I was in the service I drove heavy equipment and the driver'd get tired and I'd relieve him and give him some rest.

We look back on it and we say that was real tough, but, you know, we got to where we was enjoyin' it. We would look forward to it because we knew we had to play and pack our bags and get on the bus and ride to the next city. That became a routine.

We all loved the game. We weren't playin' for the money, because we wasn't makin' no money. I was paid 300 a month. It wasn't bad but we didn't get more because they didn't have the money and we knew that.

Who was the best ballplayer you saw?

The best ballplayer I saw was Piper Davis. He was the best all-around ballplayer. He really did help me. He was a very nice man and he could play any position. I think his last game out here in the Coast League in Oakland he played all nine positions. He was a really good ballplayer. He stands out in my mind.

Now Artie Wilson was another good ballplayer. He was a real nice fella, too.

Who was the best pitcher?

The best pitcher I saw was Chet Brewer, and Pat Scantlebury was good, too. Those two fellas always stood out in my mind as real good pitchers. In fact, Chet Brewer would always give me good advice whenever we would play them. Piper told me to talk with Chet and he really did help me on my control when I first went to the Barons. I could throw hard, but I was wild, and Chet Brewer really told me how to get my control. I never forgot that. It really helped my career. He was a good man, a very good man, and those two fellas stand out in my mind.

Does one game stand out?

Yes, and it wasn't a league game. We used to play those city teams back East. New Haven, Connecticut, had a team called the New Haven Sailors. They had a good ballclub; there was some ex-major leaguers on that team. I got those kind of games. I pitched against them and shut 'em out, and the owner came to me and told me that was the first time that team had ever been shut out. It was real close; it was one run or two runs. It was a good game.

Then the next year we went back and we played 'em again. The owner asked was I still on the team, and Piper told him, "Yeah. You're probably gonna see him again." And I pitched against 'em again and I beat 'em 2-to-1. The owner told me, "If you shut us out again tonight, I'm gonna buy you a brand new suit of clothes." [Laughs] I remember that score because that suit of clothes was in it. He was a colorful-lookin' guy, kind of a short fella. That game sticks out in my mind.

I didn't give up too many hits. This is something Chet Brewer would always tell me. He said, "You watch your base on balls and your hits. Strikeouts is not too important, but they're good. Watch those three things when you pitch a game."

Why did you leave baseball when you did.

I had a wife and two children and my last game I played out here in California. But I also played in Panama, in Colon. After

Sam Williams (Photograph courtesy of Sam Williams.)

I got suspended and my children were gettin' to be pretty good sized — I had a son and daughter — and my wife figured she had had 'em all those years and she wanted me to stay home and be some help. I thought about it. That was the hardest thing I ever done in my life.

It's a funny thing how things happen to you in your life. She had wanted me to quit anyway and when I got suspended by Trautman that helped me to make the decision. I often think about that. Oftentimes things happen to us and we think it's so bad but a lot of times it's for the betterment. I'm glad I did.

A lot of funny things happened to me. I was pitchin' against the New York Cubans one Sunday in New York in the Polo Grounds. [Sandy] Amoros, you know the fella that made the catch in the World Series, was young and I was young and we were talkin' to one another. I never did believe in knockin' hitters down, but I told Sandy, "If you play today, I'm gonna knock you down."

He said, "If you pitch today, I'm gonna hit a home run off you."

I'm gonna tell you the truth. The game was goin' along good and I was pitchin real well. He came up and I could throw pretty hard. I threw close to that man's head. I remember the look on his face and his eyes got so big. It shook me up. The next pitch I threw him was a high fastball. You remember how the Polo Grounds was made, when Mays made that catch? They had three decks down there in right field. He hit that ball in that second tier. [Laughs] I have never again knocked no hitter down. [Laughs] I never will forget that.

He and I talked about it after the game. We laughed. That really shook me up; that was so frightenin'. I could have hurt him. We was just jokin' around, but that's serious stuff. I never knocked another hitter down in my whole pitchin' career. I've seen a lotta guys get hit. Sandy was a pretty good hitter.

Would you go back and be a ballplayer again?

Oh, yes. That's the best job I ever had in my life. I wouldn't take nothin' for the experience. You meet a lot of nice people, you get a chance to see the world and some of the country, and the value that you get from meetin' people you can't put no price on. It's an education.

What did you do when you left baseball?

When I retired from baseball, do you believe I drove a bus for the city of San Jose? I said, "I'll do this for three months and then I'll get me another job." But I liked it because of the people. The people were friendly and nice to me and I'm a fella that likes to laugh and talk and I just got a kick out of it. I ended up 25 years later retirin' from that. [Laughs]

PITCHING RECORD

Year	Team, Lg	G	IP	W	L	PCT	HO	BB	SO	ERA
1947	Birm., NAL									
1948		12	84	6	3	.667	84	13	51	3.21
1949		21	146	8	6	.571	150	36	60	3.21
1950		22	151	13	7	.650	161	44	60	3.81
1951	Jalisco, Mex			5	10	,333				3.97
1952	Birm, NAL									
	Wisc. Rapids, WiscSt			0	0	.000				0.00
1953	Pampa, WT-NM			25	12	.676				5.13
1954	Ok City, Tx			0	3	.000				—
	Pampa, WT-NM			15	10	.600				4.54
1955	Superior, Nor			0	1	.000				—
	Eugene, NW			9	7	.563				3.42
1956	San Jose, Cal			15	9	.625				3.10
1957	Veracruz, Mex			8	8	.500				4.63
	Dubuque, MW			2	1	.667				—
1958	Poza Rica, Mex			9	11	.450				5.21

Walter "Buddy" Williams
Newark Eagles 1937-1940

BORN APRIL 26, 1914, NORTH CAROLINA
HT. 6' WT. 170 BATTED AND THREW RIGHT

Walter Williams began his baseball career as a freelance pitcher. When a team from around his area of North Carolina needed a victory, it would send for Williams. His fame spread into Virginia and the same thing happened there; he was hired to pitch important games for various teams.

This kept happening, and eventually he saw the entire country and finally ended up with the Newark Eagles in 1937. He remained an Eagle until he was drafted into the Army in 1941. When he was discharged in 1945, he did not return to baseball, but instead stayed home to help his wife raise their six children, of whom he is very proud. Three completed college and two have completed postgraduate work. One has a Ph.D. All of his children are leaders in civic and community activities and have received local, regional, and national recognition for these accomplishments.

WILLIAMS: I got started in baseball in North Carolina. Around that time, every little ol' country team around there would see me pitch and they would get me to come and pitch a game for them. I got my start right there in North Carolina, a little ol' place there called Roanoke Rapids, Littleton, Oxford, Rocky Mount, and Kinston, around there.

Those people out of Virginia, like out of Norfolk, began to see me pitch and they come and get me to pitch a game for them. 'Long then, I was pitchin' about twice a week for a dollar-and-a-half a game. [Laughs] Didn't nobody have no money then. 'Long then, as they began to see me pitch around there in North Carolina, the longshoremen in Norfolk, Virginia, saw me pitch on all those country teams at Seaboard and Jackson and all the places. Johnny Bright was workin' for 'em; he was from Wallburg, North Carolina. He got me to

come down and pitch a game for the longshoremen in Norfolk, Virginia. They paid me five dollars a game. Quite naturally I was goin' down there.

But I couldn't pitch on Sunday. My mother and father thought I wasn't pitchin' on Sunday. 'Long then, you didn't play no ball in North Carolina on no Sunday. You went to church. So what I had to do — Johnny would come and get me on Friday evenin' and my mother and father thought I was pitchin' on Saturday, but he was savin' me over for Sunday. I'd pitch my game on Sunday; they'd give me my little five dollars and bring me on back home. They never found out. [Laughs]

From then on, we'd run into Tom McLain and Bertie Johnson in Norfolk. They had come out of New York; they'd do all the teams all over the United States. Then they got up a team called the Tarboro Tigers in Norfolk. From then on, I began to spread all over North Carolina, all the way to Alabama on through Atlanta — the Atlanta Black Crackers and the Alabama Blackbirds. Tommy Sampson — I thought he was the greatest second baseman I ever seen in my life.

From then — all over the country. Back to Chicago, the Chicago American Giants. That boy Cool Papa Bell they had playin' there — he could hit that ball. But you know, I didn't fear none of 'em — Josh Gibson or none of 'em.

I pitched a game in New York. The Newark Eagles was playin' the Homestead Grays and they called me in to relieve. We were playin' one big game there and Leon Day was pitchin' and in the ninth innin' Leon Day had the Homestead Grays, 2-to-1. Pop Wilson come up with a man on and hit a line drive that hit Leon Day on the knee. The great Buck Leonard was comin' up, so I told [manager] Dick Lundy, "Why don't you bring [Freddie] Hopgood in to pitch against Buck Leonard and I'll come in and pitch against Josh Gibson. Tell him to walk Buck," 'cause Buck could hit that ball. [Hopgood was also known as Hobgood.]

So Dick brought Hopgood in to pitch to him 'cause he was lefthanded and then I come in to pitch. I guess they had about 30- or 50,000 fans in the grandstand hollerin' for Josh Gibson to hit a home run. I would've loved to see myself when I walked over the third base line; I couldn't hear 'cause everybody's hollerin' for Josh. The whole stadium stood up.

I come in there with two straight curveballs and the umpire called 'em strikes on him and he was so scared. They had told me, don't throw him no fastballs, and I throw him another curveball. He had to lunge over to hit it 'cause he was scared to let it go by, 'cause I had a good one. I *knew* I had a good one, see, and I loved myself. He hit a little soft line drive to Willie Wells at shortstop and we threw him out.

The great Count Basie that night was

Walter Williams (Photograph courtesy of Walter Williams.)

playin' up in Harlem and do you know the fans told me I better not come up there to that dance that night? [Laughs] They took me back home to Newark, New Jersey; they wouldn't let me go up there. They were so mad at me because I got out Josh Gibson.

The way that I come to join 'em [the Eagles], I didn't know I was as great as I was, and from Alabama all over Atlanta all over Chicago everybody talked so much about me. Mr. Abe Manley — you know, he was halfway rich — had heard so much about me, *he* wanted me. Quite naturally, you know, I was goin' where the money were at that time and that's the way I went to work with Mr. Manley.

We had this boy, big Mule Suttles, played first base. We had so many nicknames for everybody, I can't even think of some of them players' names. [Laughs] Thousands of people always called me Buddy Williams. They didn't know my name was Walter. They called me Buddy and when I got in trouble on the mound, you know what they'd say? "Okay, Buddy. All right, Buddy." They didn't call me Williams or Walter; they didn't say, "Williams, you've gone far enough."

If I come up there and I was pitchin' to Josh or Buck or some of 'em and threw 'em two straight balls, you know what they'd tell me? "Okay, Buddy, you've gone far enough." [Laughs]

This little boy played with the [Ethiopian] Clowns. He didn't weigh 35 pounds. [Dave] Skinny Barnhill. He didn't look like he weighed 35 pounds to me. [Laughs] Him and I, we were pitchin' down in Tarboro — the Tarboro Tigers, that's where we started. Went on to the Durham Black Sox and the House of David; we would play them. They was passin' me 'round like I was a drink of water. [Laughs] Every team would see me pitch.

I didn't drink, didn't smoke. If we were playin' in a place and there was a dance that night, you can bet your life, if I had to pitch the next day, the team that I was pitchin' for wouldn't let me go to the dance. I couldn't go to the dance. I used to love to hold them girls in my arms. I knew I could dance. You talk 'bout havin' a good time with all them players.

This great boy come out of Canada, Mayo. That boy could pitch, too. I forget the team that him and I was on together. You hear talk of the Belvoir Grays, out of Portsmouth. I'm gonna tell you the truth; that ol' boy could throw that ball. He really could throw that ball. Another great pitcher I saw comin' up was Peaches Peel; he was from Norfolk. He played with the Norfolk Tars, and also that boy Pie Watson. All of 'em.

After they drafted me in 1941 and I had to go in the Army, when I come back out I was scouted the same night as Campanella, Joe Black, and Junior Gilliam. I wouldn't go; I say, "I'm gonna stay home. I'm gonna help my wife raise these children." At that time, we had five children.

You know when Campanella and Joe Black and Junior Gilliam went up with the Brooklyn Dodgers farm team they weren't payin' but $7,000. So I came back out of the Army and I got this little ol' job makin' $39 a week. I stayed home and helped my wife raise these children. My wife and I, we had six children and I ask anybody in the world to meet 'em. All of them are well educated and are leaders in the church and community. My lovely children.

I look now at Jackie Robinson, Campanella, Junior Gilliam, and all that bunch now they done gone away from here. I stayed home and helped my wife raise these children and we are *proud* of these six children we got, and grandchildren.

I found out in life at my age, when you get a certain age you gotta let that world alone. I tease my children; I say, "All me girlfriends is dead I used to go with 'fore I married your mother." They say, "Who?" I say, "Ella Fitzgerald, Billie Holiday, Sarah Vaughan." [Laughs] I found out when you get a certain age that night life will kill you dead. [Laughs]

You have named some great players. Who was the best?

The best player I think I saw, besides Tommy Sampson, was this young boy come up with the Cuban All-Stars This boy was Russell Awkard. Russell, for a country boy out of Sandy Spring, Maryland, could hit and play that outfield.

Like I tell everybody, and I've said it thousands of people, it's hard to go into a team or the church or the street or anywhere and get in that little clique. There's a little circle in everything. Am I right or not? And you just can't break right into it.

The first game I pitched against Leon Day — Leon Day is from Alexandria, Virginia — the Richmond Elks had seen me pitch and they were playin' this team out of Alexandria down there in Richmond one Saturday. So the Elks had seen me pitch all around in North Carolina there. They come down and got me to pitch against Leon Day. That's when I first met Leon Day, back in the early '30s, right there in Richmond. We played right in Richmond. After Leon Day went up in New York and Newark before I did, he got in that circle.

But my dad always told me, "Never envy no man. Do what you can and just go on and be peaceful." That's the reason why I guess I get along so good with everybody in the world.

What was your best game?

The best game I had was against the Belvoir Grays right in Portsmouth. I was with the Norfolk Tars against Bishop H. C. Plummer's team. He was well known all over the United States 'cause he was the youngest bishop in the Oddfellows at that time. So the Norfolk Tars was playin' the Belvoir Grays and Bishop H. C. Plummer told our manager—his name was Joe Lewis—told Tom McLain and Bertie Johnson, said, "If Williams beat my team, I'm gonna buy him." At that time, the Belvoir Grays wouldn't play nobody but the Homestead Grays and also the Elites and the Philadelphia Stars.

Joe Lewis said, "Williams can beat the Belvoir Grays." I goes over there and they let us play in that big white park there in Portsmouth. You couldn't get in there for people; all of the people knew him. I walked up on that hill and shut them there Belvoir Grays out, 2-to-nothin'. Do you know Bishop H. C. Plummer carried me on back to Portsmouth?

The second real great game that I pitched was in Atlanta, Georgia. I was pitchin' for the Tarboro Tigers. They didn't want to give Mr. Joe Higgs a game, because he say the Tarboro Tigers would ruin his crowd, see? They didn't figure we could beat 'em.

We goes down to Atlanta and you couldn't get in that park. I walks up on that

hill and that's when I met that shortstop "Mexico," a boy we used to call "Mexico." I never knew his right name; he always used to go to Mexico in the wintertime. And they had a great center fielder named Boy Thomas. They had a great team now and I walked up on that hill and shut 'em out. They couldn't understand it.

That's when I met that Tommy Sampson. Tommy Sampson was down there in a group from Alabama that day. They saw me beat the Atlanta Black Crackers and then *they* wanted me. That's the way I got spreaded all over from one good game to another. And I eventually got to the Newark Eagles.

When the great Monte Irvin and Larry Doby first come up, they didn't play the whole year with us. They just played the last two or three games we played to see could they play. Abe Manley and Dick Lundy could see they was great ballplayers. When one or two old players went out, they brought them in. That's the way Monte Irvin and Larry Doby got with the Newark Eagles.

Do you know your record with the Eagles?

I think I was something like about 9-and-3, or somethin' like that, the first year and all together I think I won about 60 or 70 games with them. I was with the Eagles from '37 on up 'til 1941, when I went in the service.

We played the Kansas City Monarchs and this boy Jackie Robinson just come out of UCLA. He was a great boy but he just come out of college and you couldn't tell him nothin'. [Laughs] Satchel Paige was down there. That was another game I pitched back in the early '30s against Satchel Paige in Norfolk, Virginia. Satchel Paige beat me, 2-nothin'. That's when I met that boy playin' first base, Buck O'Neil.

People used to say, "He ain't no rubber. You can't stretch him; he can't play with all the teams." From one team to another, I got all over the United States.

Went out there in Seattle, Washington. Played that team in Seattle. What really tickled me so bad, they sent *nine* lefthand batters in there on me. I'm a righthand pitcher. I lost that game out there. They took me out in the sixth innin' and they was leadin' us 5- or 6-to-nothin'.

We played in Oakland, San Francisco, and Los Angeles. I come back the fourth day to play Seattle there in Fort Lewis as we come back to the East. I pitched against them again; I couldn't believe they could beat me like that.

They had never seen too many underhand curveballs. Them lefthand batters come in there and I started breakin' my curveball 'round the corner and huggin' 'em with my fastball and I shut *them* out. And they wanted to keep me on the West Coast and I say, "I'm goin' back home to my momma and daddy."

I had a great time in baseball all over the United States, and there ain't no place I ever been I can't go back again. [Laughs] I had a good time. It was a wonderful life.

Would you do it again?

Oh, yes, sir! I tell my wife all the time, "I sure wish I was young again."

I never went too wild like all the other players would do. Some of 'em would go to the nightclubs and have drinks. See, when they drink and smoke, you can't do all that and live. It'll catch up. I told my mother when I was nine years old I'd never drink or smoke. And I never did.

I used to love to buy liquor to get on with women. If their dress was down to the ankle, when they take a drink, that ol' liquor would tell them to pull their dress up. [Laughs]

When I first met Campanella, everybody said, "Man, you can't get Campanella out." I said, "I can." He was playin' with the Elites. I said, "I can get him out 'cause I ain't gonna throw that ball by him. I'm gonna try to keep him off balance." That's what I done pitchin' to all those great batters.

I loved it.

PITCHING RECORD

Year	Team, Lg	G	IP	W	L	PCT	HO	BB	SO	ERA
1937	Newark, NAL			9	3	.750				
1939										
1939										
1940										

Willie Young
Birmingham Black Barons 1945

BORN JULY 12, 1912, BIRMINGHAM, AL; DIED 2002, BIRMINGHAM, AL
HT. 5'10" WT. 170 BATTED AND THREW LEFT

The stories of Pete Gray and Jim Abbott — one-handed players who made it to the major leagues — are well known. Not so well known, indeed not known at all but by a very few, is the story of Willie Young.

Young was born with only a left hand, yet it didn't stop him from reaching the only major leagues available to a black man in the 1940s. In 1945, at the age of 33, he pitched for the Birmingham Black Barons.

Over the years, Young has been widely recognized and honored by several groups and was named Senior Citizen of the Year in 1996. He has coached the girls' softball state champions and received the Outstanding African-American Award for his service to the local Little League.

When did you start playing baseball?

YOUNG: I played Little League baseball when I was seven years old. I've been with baseball all my life.

Before the Black Barons, I played for the Birmingham Foxes. We traveled all through Florida, Georgia, Mississippi — all around the South. That was back when I was about 19 years old.

I was with the Black Barons in '45. I knew all the ballplayers. They lived in Stockham and I worked at Stockham. I played ball with Stockham. I left the Barons because I didn't like the way you had to do everything. I came back to work.

Batting must have been difficult.

I could hit the ball and I could run. I could put the glove on my hand and throw the ball, and before the ball would get to the batter I could have the glove on, catch the ball, lay the ball down, and change the glove for the ball before he'd get to first base. I was quick.

Who was your manager?

[Winfield] Welch.

How much were you paid?

I had a contract for $300 a month.

Does one game stand out?

Sure, when I pitched in Chicago against the American Giants. A guy came up named [Clyde] Nelson, and my catcher wanted me to throw Nelson a fastball. I didn't do it; I could throw my curveball. He said, "Nelson can hit a curveball." I said, "He can't hit my curveball." I had a six-foot drop and I struck Nelson out. Nelson asked me where'd I get that curveball and I told him, "God give it to me."

How did you travel?

We traveled in busses. We enjoyed it. We played ball because we loved the game. We had fun playin' ball on the road.

Who was the best player you saw?

In my time? Herman Bell was the best catcher. He never missed a fly ball. And

 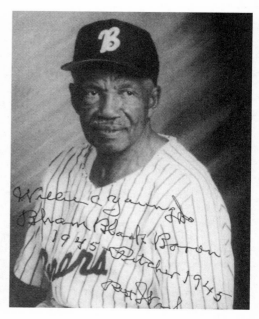

Left and right: Willie Young (Photographs courtesy of Willie Young.)

Artie Wilson was the shortstop. He was a good one.

Who was the best pitcher you saw?

Marcus. He pitched for the Birmingham Black Barons. He played in '45.

Would you play baseball again if you were a young man?

Sure. I wouldn't play nothin' but baseball.

What did you do when you left baseball?

I went to Stockham and I retired from there.

You coached kids' ball.

Yeah, I coached Little League baseball and girls' softball. The Little League teams were named after Negro leagues teams. I had the Birmingham Black Barons and there was the Kansas City Monarchs, the Memphis Red Sox, and the New York Black Yankees. We had the real uniforms.

PITCHING RECORD

Year	Team, Lg	G	IP	W	L	PCT	H	BB	SO	ERA
1945	Birm., NAL									

Bibliography

Clark, Dick, and Larry Lester, eds. *The Negro Leagues Book*. Cleveland: The Society for American Baseball Research, 1994.

Kelley, Brent. *Voices from the Negro Leagues*. Jefferson, NC: McFarland, 1998.

_____. *The Negro Leagues Revisited*. Jefferson, NC: McFarland, 2000.

Riley, James A. *The Biographical Encyclopedia of the Negro Baseball Leagues*. New York: Carroll and Graf, 1984.

Index

Numbers in *italics* represent photographs.

189